G000243511

JACK THE RIPPER

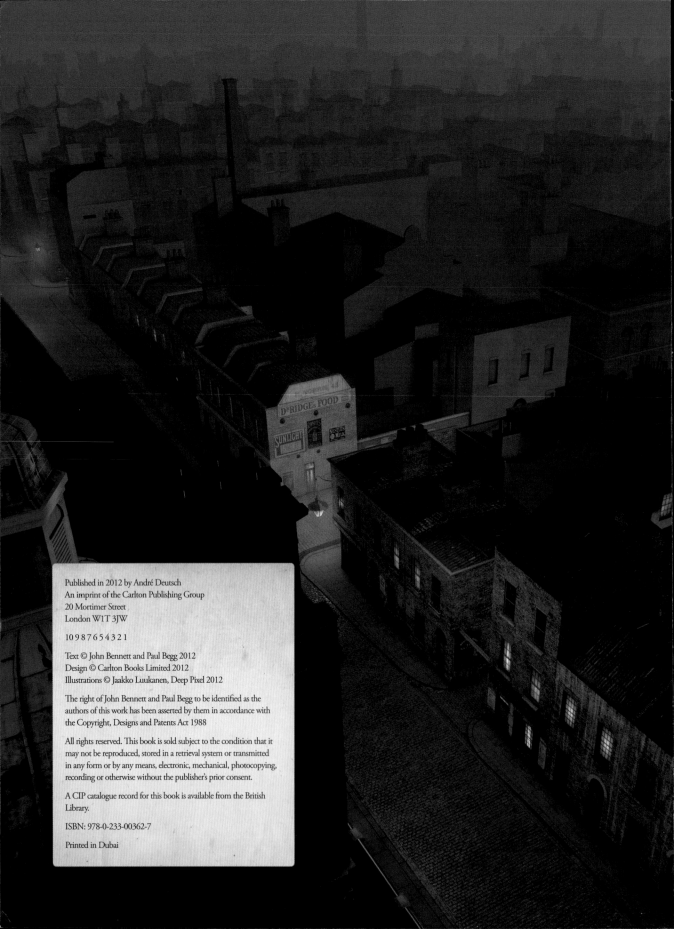

Published in 2012 by André Deutsch
An imprint of the Carlton Publishing Group
20 Mortimer Street
London W1T 3JW

10 9 8 7 6 5 4 3 2 1

Text © John Bennett and Paul Begg 2012
Design © Carlton Books Limited 2012
Illustrations © Jaakko Luukanen, Deep Pixel 2012

The right of John Bennett and Paul Begg to be identified as the
authors of this work has been asserted by them in accordance with
the Copyright, Designs and Patents Act 1988

All rights reserved. This book is sold subject to the condition that it
may not be reproduced, stored in a retrieval system or transmitted
in any form or by any means, electronic, mechanical, photocopying,
recording or otherwise without the publisher's prior consent.

A CIP catalogue record for this book is available from the British
Library.

ISBN: 978-0-233-00362-7

Printed in Dubai

JACK THE RIPPER
CSI: WHITECHAPEL

PAUL BEGG AND **JOHN BENNETT**

ILLUSTRATED BY JAAKKO LUUKANEN

ANDRE
DEUTSCH

Contents

ONE WEDNESDAY IN APRIL 1905 A GROUP OF gentlemen gathered to take a tour of the East End, specifically the sites where 17 years earlier several woman had been murdered by an unknown killer nicknamed Jack the Ripper. The most famous member of the group was Arthur Conan Doyle, the creator of Sherlock Holmes. Their guide was Dr Frederick Gordon Browne, who had actually examined the corpse of one of the victims within an hour of the murder. They visited the famous Petticoat Lane, toured a doss house, a Jewish fowl-slaughtering house and, of course, the places where Jack the Ripper set to work. It was a ghoulish adventure, not only because they were visiting the places where gory murders had

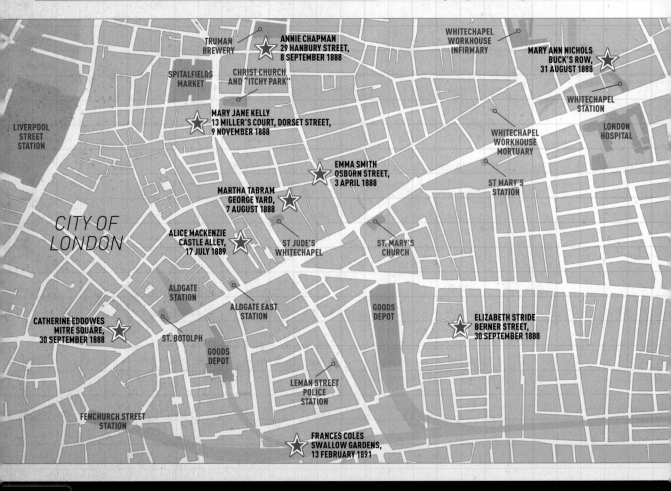

been committed, but because they were gazing upon the East Enders as if they were in a zoo.

One of the most memorable and often repeated stories about the East End is that told by the American author Jack London in the first chapter of his book *People of the Abyss* (1903). It was the summer of 1902, just three years before Doyle and his friends walked the East End pavements you can still tread today, and Jack London decided to find out what life was really like in the East End. He famously claims to have visited the offices of Thomas Cook in Ludgate Circus, where, to his amazement, he discovered that the company which boasted that it could organize a trip to "Darkest Africa or innermost Tibet" could not send him into the East End of London. The East End was a distant land, an alien planet, a world apart. Over 120 years later, it is visited by more than one million people every year. Now gentrified and arty, an extension of London's commercial heartland, in the pages of this book you can travel back in time and see the scenes of the crimes just as Doyle saw them. Just as they were seen by Jack the Ripper himself.

Fascination with Jack the Ripper's London has been a constant since those fateful nights in 1888 and with each new outrage the newspapers tried to convey the sense of place by printing illustrations of the crime scenes, sometimes accompanied by plans and maps to give readers a clearer sense of the unfolding events. Inquest hearings were furnished with more accurate plans of the locations, along with information relating to the position of the body, the placement of evidence and, in some cases, the position of witnesses. Unfortunately, not many of these documents survive.

Over the last century practically every aspect of the Jack the Ripper case has been dissected, analyzed, assessed and reexamined. The victims, witnesses and officials have become fleshed out through biographical research, the politics surrounding the age and the ramifications of the murders upon it have been given academic scrutiny, and the social milieu of the East End has become irrevocably entwined with the events of 1888 and

beyond. It is with this latter field that a continuing and rapidly developing fascination with the "scene of crime" has developed.

Despite much of the old East End having fallen to redevelopment, research continues to make new photographic and illustrative discoveries of the Ripper murder sites and those places which played a part on the periphery – mortuaries, doss houses, police stations, pubs – giving us an increasingly accurate picture of the district as it existed at the time. For those wishing to carry out their own "crime scene investigation" (and there appear to be many) such information is crucial, for only with a good understanding of the local geography can we plot the the routes victims took in the last hours of their lives, assess the position of witnesses and the police beats and get a detailed understanding of the crime.

We have attempted to bring together much of this information in order to build a picture of what happened on those dreadful nights, helped by wonderfully evocative – and accurate – artist's reconstructions. These illustrations give the viewer a chance to see Jack the Ripper's London in a way they would never be able to, essentially bringing the streets of Jack the Ripper's London back to life. Maps show what happened on the nights in question and the positions of many places of importance can be seen in context, building up an overall picture of the events surrounding each murder.

We have also chosen to include all of what are considered to be "Whitechapel Murders", from Emma Smith in April 1888 to Frances Coles in February 1891. Whether the miscreant popularly called "Jack the Ripper" is responsible for all of these crimes is the subject of continuous debate, for in the massive scope of Ripper research, the exact nature of the authorship of these murders has been pulled apart and reconstructed many times. By presenting an overall picture, it is felt that the reader may best be served by deciding for themselves.

Paul Begg and John Bennett, 2012

LEFT: Map showing the positions of the murder sites for victims of Jack the Ripper discussed in this book.

 Murder Site

THE EAST END

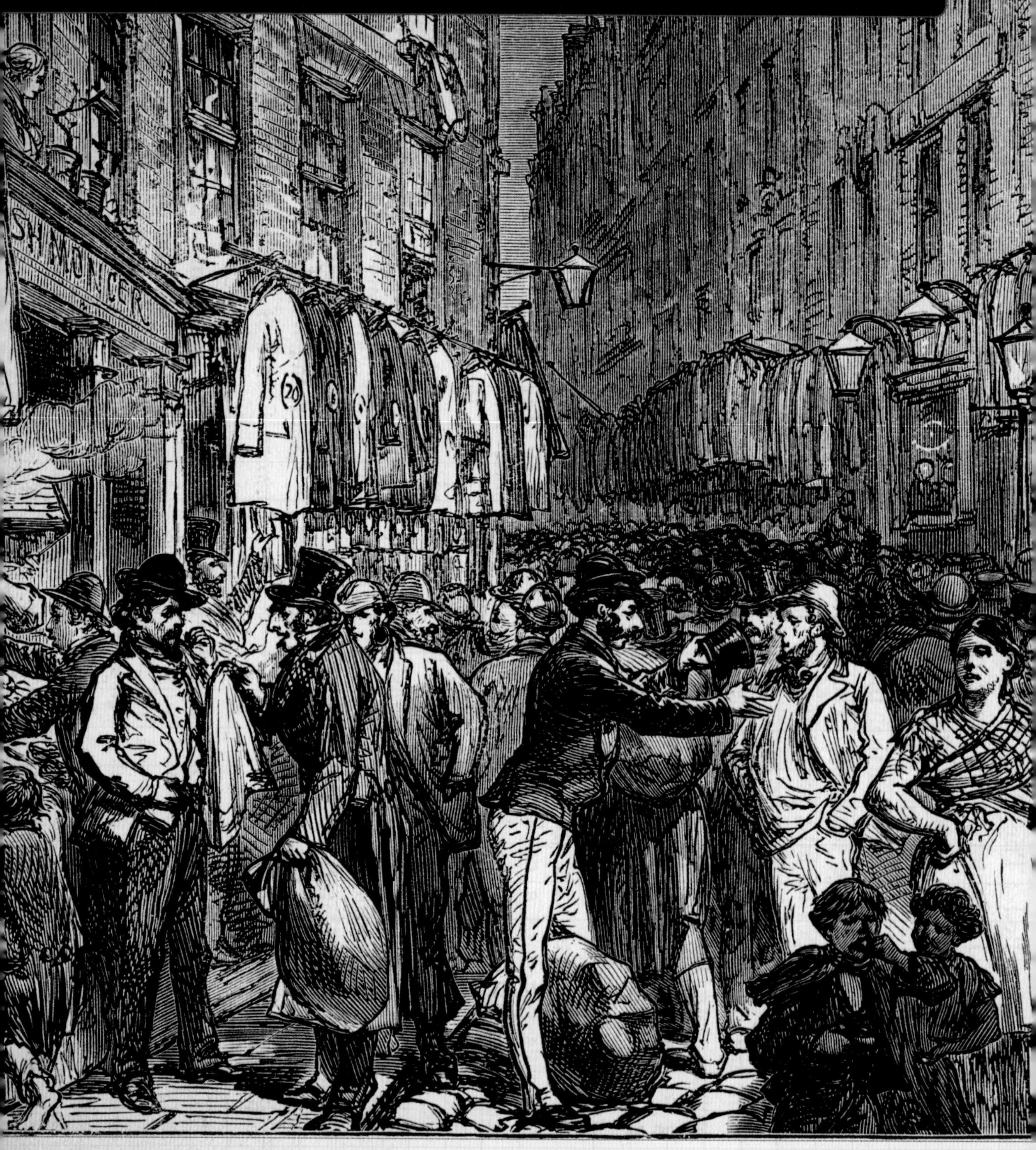

Briefing

At the time of the Jack the Ripper murders, towards the end of the nineteenth century, London was, to coin a rather hackneyed phrase, the heart of the greatest empire that the world had ever known, and, consequently, was colossally wealthy and powerful. The East End was the beating heart of that great metropolis, full of factories, warehouses, markets, abattoirs, breweries and the ever-present London docks, all servicing the city, providing the necessities of life, the means of survival, the fuel on which the great commercial heart depended. It was also overcrowded and poverty-riven, its grimy side streets flanked by often poorly constructed and decaying buildings. Many of these were converted into doss-houses which, for a few pence, provided a bed and warmth to an otherwise homeless, transient population.

LEFT: Middlesex Street in the 1800s. Marking the boundary between the City and the East End and known famously as "Petticoat Lane", it was one of many thriving markets in the area.

BELOW: Eviction, often at short notice, was a common occurrence in the slum tenements of the East End.

HERE, LIFE WAS LIVED – IF LIVING ISN'T A misnomer for what was in truth no more than survival – in all its stark reality, and it provided a banquet of inspiration for an ever-growing army of writers, artists, philanthropists and politicians who were shocked and humbled by the awful conditions suffered by the East End's inhabitants. These same people were just a little fearful of what would happen if these East Enders spilled out and infected the relatively ordered middle-class society that sat next to them cheek by jowl.

The name "East End" was coined in the press in the 1880s, at around the same time as

"unemployment" and "unemployed" entered the language, and over time it has come to represent many things. It was a dreadful other-world of crime and immorality, a fearful place where danger lurked in every shadow and waited round every corner, a place diseased in mind and spirit. In the 1880s, many poor and desperate Jews flooded the East End in a flight from the vile brutality of the pogroms in many Eastern European villages. To many people, the area became an unknown and unwelcome "foreign" land, full of people speaking alien languages, who had strange faces and an eager willingness to work harder and for longer hours for less money than anyone else would. It was also a place full of hard-working people, a true community, with the corner pub always open for a sing-song, pie and mash and jellied eels, mugs of black tea and the offer of a helping hand in a shared adversity. Rough and ready, coarse and crude, ducking and diving, and sometimes sailing good naturedly beyond the boundaries of the law, the East Ender was the loveable, no-nonsense rogue, the backbone of England, the collective fist that would later be shaken at Adolf Hitler as the bombs dropped during the Second World War.

But where exactly is the East End? Undoubtedly, it is defined by the boundaries of the ancient City of London on the west and the River Thames on the south; arguably, the River Lea marks its furthest extent eastwards, with Hoxton and Shoreditch jostling for the mantle of its most northerly reaches. At its heart lie the parishes of Whitechapel and Spitalfields which, owing to their proximity to the City, were to develop and become among London's first true suburbs. Whitechapel came first and since its main thoroughfare (today still marked by the continuing line of Aldgate and Whitechapel High Streets and Whitechapel Road) was the main route out of the City to Essex, its urbanization was inevitable.

Whitechapel takes its name from the former church of St Mary Matfelon (the derivation of the name Matfelon is still uncertain) which stood at the confluence of the High Street and Whitechapel Road. The church was built as a chapel of

ABOVE: Gustave Doré's engraving of Wentworth Street from his 1872 book *London: A Pilgrimage*.

ease to accommodate worshippers in the district when nearby St Dunstan's, in what was then the small hamlet of Stepney, could no longer cope with increased demand. It was painted with white limewash, thus creating the appearance which gave a name that is still in use today. Whitechapel, situated outside of the City walls and therefore beyond City control, quickly became a less than salubrious place. Many small industrial concerns that were unwelcome within the City owing to their pollutant nature settled here: tanneries, breweries and slaughterhouses. One

BELOW: A Bethnal Green slum neighbourhood circa 1902.

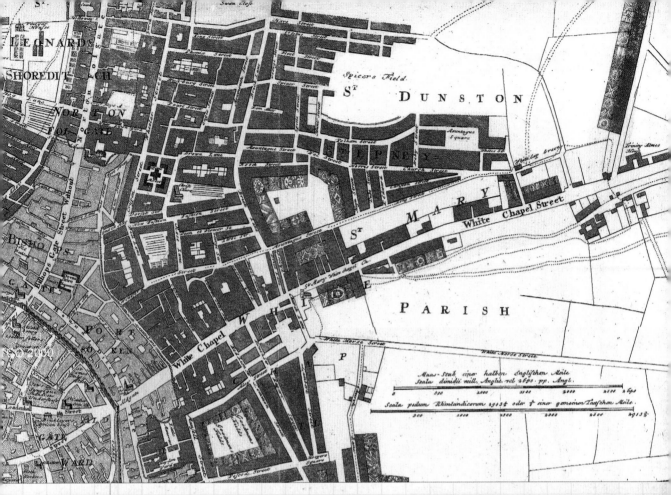

Spicer's Field

ST DUNSTON

STEPNEY

ST MARY

White Chapel Street

PARISH

White Chapel

St Mary Whitechapel Ch.

ST LEONARD'S
SHOREDITCH
NORTON
FOLGATE
BISHOPS
GATE
PORT
SOKEN
GATE
WARD

ABOVE: Whitechapel and Spitalfields from an engraved map of 1736. The encroaching urbanization to the west is in stark contrast to the rural neighbourhoods on the right which had yet to be developed.

of them, the Whitechapel Bell Foundry, still operates today.

It was these industries that attracted people from the outlying rural neighbourhoods. The arrival of these migrants, largely poor, resulted in a steady growth in population and the development of Whitechapel as a "second half" of London itself. As for the White Chapel, there were several replacements over the centuries; the final church was built in 1878, but was badly damaged during the Second World War and was finally demolished in the early 1950s. A small park, originally known as St Mary's Gardens and now called Altab Ali Park after a young Bangladeshi tailor who was murdered nearby in 1978, is all that remains.

The development of Spitalfields began in earnest much later, significantly in the late seventeenth and early eighteenth centuries, and it was immigration, one of the most persistent characteristics of the East End's varied existence, that put this previously pleasant district on the London map. Originally the site of a Roman burial ground which was later covered by the "New Hospital of St Mary Without Bishopgate", founded in 1197 by Walter Brune and his wife Roisia, the name Spitalfields is a contraction of "hospital fields". The earliest developments in the western area of the district date from this time, but the land to the east was predominantly rural, including the large Lolesworth Field. The famous Spitalfields Market was granted its charter by Charles II in 1682.

Building proceeded slowly until the mid-seventeenth century and only stretched as far east as Brick Lane. Considerable development ensued, however, after the arrival of French Huguenot silk weavers following the revocation of the Edict of Nantes in the latter part of that century. From 1598, this decree had granted basic rights to Protestant Huguenots in essentially Catholic France; with this protection now gone, French Protestants settled in the area outside of the London walls as their supposedly "noxious" trade was not permitted within the City bounds. The Huguenots prospered, and they laid out many streets, as well as gardens and orchards,

followed by the construction of handsome houses in the 1700s. Spitalfields was originally part of Stepney and did not have a nucleus of its own until 1729, following the completion of Nicholas Hawksmoor's Christ Church. This handsome church was itself built in an attempt to overcome the rising tide of non-conformism which had become evident with so many non-Anglicans in the area.

The lifting of duty on imported silks and the industrial revolution, effectively put paid to Spitalfields' prosperity since the expensive handmade Spitalfield silks were now cheaper for others to make. As the now-struggling Huguenots left the area, the district fell into a gradual decline. The once-handsome houses were sublet and property developers seized the opportunity to build more homes on the former gardens, resulting in cramped tenements, often accessed by dark passageways. A similar thing was happening in Whitechapel as its own population increased. Thanks to the arrival of the nearby docks at the beginning of the nineteenth century, there were

even more reasons for those poorer classes seeking work opportunities to settle here. By the 1850s, both areas had become seriously overcrowded.

The construction of the London Docks and, soon after, the coming of the railways, geographically compounded the problems of inner-city life in this part of the East End. Warehouse walls towered over once-open streets, casting a foreboding gloom in alleyways and small lanes, while railway lines, perched on seemingly endless arches, cut their way through already tightly packed neighbourhoods. To the north on the Spitalfields–Shoreditch borders and to the south through the parish of St George-in-the-East, the railway lines ploughed through dense communities, effectively isolating many from main thoroughfares as a result. Access was often only gained via dark and narrow entrances, so the criminal minded and those with a reason to lie low gravitated to these dens. Known as "rookeries", these were the dangerous lairs of fictional characters like Fagin, Bill Sykes and the Artful Dodger, who at this time were being brought to

ABOVE: Whitechapel High Street circa1905. In the distance stands the final version of St Mary's church, which was demolished in 1952 after receiving severe damage during the air raids of Second World War.

To read contemporary reports of the conditions apparent in certain parts of the East End would lead many an observer to believe that it was little more than a giant slum, filthy, dangerous, racked by vice and crime and offering no redemption to visitor or inhabitant alike. This is a popular myth that survives in historical accounts to this day and though there were areas of shocking deprivation, this perception is largely the result of the writings of philanthropists, social commentators and the burgeoning radical press who homed in on the worst of Whitechapel and Spitalfields in an attempt to make the authorities of the day see what could unfortunately exist within the powerful, wealthy city that was the heart of Queen Victoria's illustrious empire.

There were plenty who were comfortably off – the shopkeepers, publicans, the businessmen and of course, the property owners. Many who were poor did not feel it necessary to resort to criminal activity and lived lives of frugal honesty. The main thoroughfares of Whitechapel were wide, spacious and well-populated at any time of the day. Yet, attention was often drawn towards the conditions that hid behind the everyday facade

of simple East End life. The image we have had passed on to us is the London of Charles Dickens and Arthur Conan Doyle's Sherlock Holmes, resounding with the clatter of horses' hooves, piano music drifting out of public houses, the dim glow of gaslight and an almost permanent smog. Smog (a mixture of fog and the smoke generated by innumerable factory and domestic chimneys) was a problem for an area of such density. It coated the district in grime, which only added to its undesirability. It is no surprise that the main causes of death in Whitechapel where bronchial diseases. This statistic comes to us from the 1887 Bill of Mortality and it is interesting to note that "homicides" that year numbered zero, a surprising figure for such a supposedly dangerous area. Murder probably did occur, but it is possible to speculate that such incidents may have been classified in other ways, such as accident or even manslaughter.

The real problems of Whitechapel and Spitalfields lay in the dark recesses behind the main roads, mainly yards and courts with limited access, which provided cover and created small, self-perpetrating microcosms of vice.

ABOVE: A classic scene of poor East End domestic life. It would not be unusual for a family of this size to live solely in the one room, which often doubled up as a workspace if the parents, and frequently children, worked from home.

LEFT: This photograph of the corner of Whitechurch Lane and Whitechapel High Street in the 1900s shows the church of St Mary in the background adorned with Hebrew text, such was the influence of the huge Eastern European Jewish population at that time.

life in *Oliver Twist* by the pen of Charles Dickens. It is fair to say that these popular anti-heroes had their roots firmly planted in the real East End. For many, its reputation was sealed.

Housing became an issue for the predominantly poor, working class and ever-transient demographic of Whitechapel and Spitalfields. Many families were unable to afford furnished rooms at the often punitive rents demanded by the landlords. Those that could, crammed their entire (often extended) families into dwelling spaces no more than 3–4 square metres (10–12 square feet) in size; contemporary reports of eight or nine people sharing one tiny room were not uncommon. Sanitation was rudimentary at best and the risk of disease hung over the heads of those forced to live in such squalor – the infant mortality rate in these worst areas was appalling, with as many as 55 per cent of children dying by the age of five.

A considerable number of common lodging houses were scattered around this part of the East End. These offered a bed and use of a communal kitchen at a relatively affordable price. The charge was generally 4d (approximately 81p in today's

money) for a single bed, 8d (approximately £1.61 today) for a double, but with so many "doss-houses" in the neighbourhood, the quality of accommodation varied. Some allowed single women only; some were for men only; others allowed mixed couples and it was believed that these latter doss-houses were little more than unlicensed brothels. Several lodging-house keepers, perhaps resigned to their lot and unable to be too selective about who stayed in their premises, turned a blind eye to the nefarious activities which regularly took place behind their own front door.

Frederick Charrington, heir to the Charrington brewing dynasty, was one who tried to make a difference in this respect. As a young man, he had watched in horror as a drunken husband beat his wife and child as they begged him for food outside a pub. The pub bore his own name and feeling shocked and culpable, Charrington renounced his fortune and set upon a tireless philanthropic journey that would affect the poor, the wanton and, notably, those disposed to using the doss-houses for immoral purposes. He was instrumental in having local brothels closed down and after raiding one doss-house where it was

OPPOSITE: Seen from Brushfield Street, the majestic frontage of Hawksmoor's Christ Church has cast its shadow over Spitalfields for nearly three centuries.

Common Lodging Houses

From 1851 it was a legal requirement for common lodging houses to be inspected and registered; documentation listed the owners' names and addresses, the number of rooms and how many lodgers could be held in each of those rooms. Despite the bureaucracy in evidence, many of these establishments would cram in more people than they were supposed to, in order to increase the profits available to the owners.

In 1875 it was estimated that the registered common lodging houses in the Flower and Dean Street area of Spitalfields nightly accommodated 757 people in 123 rooms, revealing an alarming density of poor and transient people. The owners of the properties rarely lived there, instead employing deputies to run them. The least-salubrious lodging houses were often filled with old and decrepit furniture, some of it bought second-hand from hospitals, complete with infections. The beds in many cases were little more than coffins with thin straw mattresses that a lack of cleaning turned into a perfect home for lice and bugs. Life for the lodgers centred round the communal kitchens. Although the buildings were not always pleasant and were occasionally dangerous, they were preferable to workhouses. Many gravitated towards doss-houses for the warm hearth of the kitchen and the camaraderie of others in the same position as themselves.

ABOVE: The Flower and Dean Street neighbourhood in 1888. The mass of shaded properties are Common Lodging Houses. Before the arrival of the model dwellings (for example, Rothschild, Lolesworth and Wentworth Dwellings), there would have been dozens more.

suspected that a young girl was being held against her will, he noted that a picture of him hung on the wall. It was there to alert the housekeeper as to the identity of the man who was going to close them down!

But it was not just Frederick Charrington who chose to explore and expose the dark heart of East London. Journalists, treading carefully through the slums, often accompanied by a protective police officer, related their experiences in newspapers, while authors such as Margaret Harkness and Andrew Mearns deliberated over protracted studies of what would later become known as "outcast London" and "The Abyss". Henrietta Barnett, wife of Samuel Augustus Barnett, the vicar of St Jude's Church in Commercial Street wrote in her book, *Canon Barnett: His Life, Work and Friends* (1919):

None of these courts had roads. In some the houses were three storeys high and hardly six feet apart, the sanitary accommodation being pits in the cellars; in other courts the houses were lower, wooden and dilapidated, a stand pipe at the end providing the only water. Each chamber was the home of a family who sometimes owned their indescribable furniture, but in most cases the rooms were let out furnished for 8d a night. In many instances, broken windows had been repaired with paper and rags, the banisters had been used for firewood, and the paper hung from the walls which were the residence of countless vermin...

Eventually, it would seem enough was enough. In 1875, the Artisans' and Labourers' Improvement Dwellings Act (the "Cross Act") was passed, allowing local authorities to buy up land for redevelopment. Previous attempts to clear the slums of Whitechapel and Spitalfields had partly failed, significantly the creation of Commercial Street between 1845 and 1858. Not only was this new thoroughfare intended to create a link from Commercial Road to the northern trade routes, thus facilitating further commercial travel from the docks, but it would cut through and clear some of the worst slums in the district. As the demolition crews carved their way through the fetid dwellings and pungent cellars, those who had once called the path of this new road home were unceremoniously displaced. With nowhere to go and perhaps with links and loyalties to a neighbourhood that offered them little in the way of comfort, these banished masses merely settled into the adjacent streets, already overcrowded and presenting a life that maintained, for them at least, the status quo.

The problems of the Spitalfields rookeries had been exacerbated, not relieved, and so the Cross Act would serve to do what previous attempts had failed to do: remove the slums and create something in their place that would provide housing for the benefit of all. Targeted were the blighted areas around Flower and Dean Street, Goulston Street and George Yard, but progress was slow. Flower and Dean Street and Thrawl Street were only half cleared and five years passed before the land was employed as intended, allowing some of the slums to live on as the empty plots became the home of itinerants and the truly destitute. By the time rebuilding started, however, a new element of change was happening in earnest, one

which would hold a considerable influence over the lives of those in Whitechapel and Spitalfields, creating a frisson, generating real unrest and ultimately becoming a more positive legacy that lasted well into the twentieth century.

During the 1880s, a great displacement of Jewish citizens from Eastern Europe, especially from Poland and Russia, but also from Germany and Hungary, descended upon the East End. Many were fleeing awful poverty and, later, the persecution which followed the assassination of Tsar Alexander II in 1881, which was dubiously blamed on Jewish instigators. The result of this terrorist act was a pogrom, or organized massacre, of the Jewish community. Many of these escaping immigrants intended to settle in America, "the new land", but thousands only got as far as the River Thames and its disembarkation

RIGHT: An illustration from 1893 showing the sort of eighteenth century dilapidated properties that were still being used as homes by many in Spitalfields.

point near the then partially-built Tower Bridge. Conveniently, both nearby Whitechapel and Spitalfields had ancient associations with the Jewish community and a number of synagogues were extant from earlier times, such as the Great Synagogue at Duke's Place near Aldgate, Bevis Marks close by and Sandy's Row in Spitalfields. By the late 1880s, approximately 40,000 Jews had made their home in the East End.

Such a huge influx of "aliens" came at a price, certainly from the standpoint of the indigenous East Enders, Whole districts appeared to be taken over, where the air resounded to the sound of foreign languages, particularly Yiddish. One area south of Whitechapel High Street became known as "Little Odessa", such was the dominance of the Jewish "greener" or newcomer. Whole streets became part of "the ghetto" – Wentworth Street, Old Montague Street, and others which branched off Brick Lane and Commercial Road. Many of these newcomers found work in the tailoring and cabinet- and cigarette-making

trades and the bosses of these concerns could see the financial advantages of employing these new workers desperate to eke out a living in their new home. The Jewish immigrant workforce attracted accusations of undercutting other potential employees in terms of wages and their employers were fast being represented as greedy and unfairly opportunistic. Allied with wage reductions at the docks – already a huge source of work for men in the area – and an ongoing economic depression which had started in 1873, the problem of unemployment was soon becoming an added ingredient to the melting-pot of misery faced by the poorest East Ender. In essence, there were not enough jobs for the number of people who desperately needed them.

These hard times resulted in a political thrust towards the left. Socialism, if not just fair play, was a concept fast becoming attractive to the poor of London, seemingly faced with brazen displays of wealth in spite of their own hardship. The discontent often erupted into violence and

ABOVE: Tower Bridge under construction in 1888. It was near this point that many of the Jewish settlers first set foot in London.

OPPOSITE: East London's commercial heart, the London Docks, photographed circa 1890.

ABOVE: A typical scene inside the communal kitchen of a Dorset Street doss-house. Despite the often poor conditions in some of these dwellings, they could offer the homeless a sense of camaraderie.

the East End was seen by some as the breeding ground of that anger. A number of serious disturbances had taken place in 1886 when gangs of unemployed men descended upon the West End, smashing shop windows and looting the stores of Bond and Oxford Streets. This trend towards civil unrest culminated in what became known as "Bloody Sunday" when on 13 November 1887, Trafalgar Square became a warzone after a march originally organized to protest against the situation in Ireland, was bolstered by Socialist demonstrators. Sir Charles Warren, newly appointed Chief Commissioner of the Metropolitan Police, countered the threat of unrest with a strong police and military presence and the ensuing clash resulted in many injuries. It was a major incident from which Warren's reputation, vital to his integrity as he attempted to coordinate unprecedented events the following year, would never recover. The year 1888 would prove to be a pivotal moment for him, East London and beyond.

For many, the problems of the East End were considered to be the spark for such problems. Some were quick to notice that the Jewish immigrants, struggling to survive as much as anybody else, embraced Socialism and Anarchism and brought those political ideals with them from abroad, forming organized clubs and societies from which political education, discussion and action could be mobilized. But disenchantment was already beginning to show itself outside of the "alien" mindset. Unionization was fast becoming popular with the common workforce; small outbreaks of industrial action had begun as workers put their heads above the parapet to force

LEFT: The Jewish inhabitants of Spitalfields may be all but gone, but traces of their settlement can still be seen, such as the mezuzah on the door jamb of this house in Princelet Street.

The Match Girls' Strike

In 1850 two Quaker businessmen, Francis May and William Bryant, started importing matches made in Sweden, and by 1853 they were selling over 8 million boxes a year. In 1861 they began making their own matches at a factory in Bow in London's East End, producing both safety matches and the traditional "Lucifer Matches" made with white phosphorous, which was both dangerous and seriously damaging to workers' health. The health risks, coupled with harsh working conditions, long hours and poor pay, led to a great deal of discontent. Unrest ignited when a worker was sacked in July 1888 because she, along with others, refused to sign a document contradicting serious criticisms of Bryant and May, which had been published in a halfpenny weekly paper called *The Link*. The sacking led to an immediate strike of about 1,400 staff, mostly women and girls, which was virtually unique in labour history. A strike fund was set up, assorted organizations backed the strike, which was by now for improved pay and conditions, and although the management stood firm for a time, it eventually capitulated. Although the match girls gained minor improvements, the health dangers in the production of Lucifer white-phosphorous matches had not been addressed and working conditions and pay had otherwise only marginally improved. But the reputation of Bryant and May was almost irreparably damaged and suffered further over the next five years or so as newspapers such as *The Star* revealed further cases of "phossy jaw", one of the bone disfiguring diseases white phosphorous caused, and accused the company of paying hush money to prevent workers talking about it. The Government fined Bryant and May a paltry £25 (approximately £1,207 today), the maximum that could be imposed at that time, but the bad name the accusations gave were far worse and in 1901

Bryant and May announced that it had abandoned the use of white phosphorus in match production altogether. The irony is that William Bryant and Francis May had originally wanted to produce only safety matches, but the higher cost and accordingly lower sales had forced them to produce Lucifers. Even as late as the 1950s and 1960s, when Bryant and May produced its most famous and iconic match brand England's Glory, the company name was still popularly tainted. Although the Match Girls' Strike achieved little, it demonstrated for the first time that workers had muscle and could bring about change. It was an important precursor to the far more influential Great Dock Strike of August 1889, which established that unionization was possible and could be effective.

ABOVE: Workers from the Bryant and May factory photographed during the ground-breaking 1888 matchgirls' strike.

ABOVE: A contemporary – and highly sensational – press illustration of the Bloody Sunday riot in Trafalgar Square, from *The Graphic*, 19 November 1887.

the issues of inadequate wages and poor working conditions. The Match Girls' Strike of 1888 was not the only example of such activism, but it was certainly the most famous and, historically at least, the most important up to that time.

By 1888, all that was deemed wrong with the East End was coming to a head. For those in the comfortable townhouses of the West End and the leafy suburbs of the expanding metropolis, the area had become something to be feared and, alarmingly, it seemed to break its boundaries with increasing regularity. It was therefore no accident that Charles Booth, about to commence his great survey of London poverty, chose the East End as his first study.

Booth, brought up in Cheshire, was the son of a ship-builder and corn merchant and joined the family business at the age of 16. His later interest in politics led him to stand, unsuccessfully, as a Liberal parliamentary candidate in 1865 and after this failure, his political enthusiasm waned. He felt that he could have more influence by educating the populace, rather than being a representative in Parliament. Booth was critical of the statistical data on poverty available at the time and thus embarked on his *Life and Labour of the People* which was eventually published in 1889, employing numerous researchers who, accompanied by local officials or police officers with good local knowledge, inspected the streets, businesses and homes of the East End. The results came in the form of extensive notebooks, interviews and more famously, detailed maps where the residents' standard of living was colour coded. Booth's first survey proved to be revealing.

Now, observers could see where the true poverty lay: great chunks of Whitechapel and Spitalfields were coloured light blue, denoting poor families, interspersed with dark blue, the sign of chronic want. Main thoroughfares, home to businessmen and shopkeepers, were marked in red, revealing a middle-class in uneasy co-existence with the poor, but beyond these oases of respectability there were regions coloured black, which denoted "vicious, semi-criminal". Some of these black areas were unsurprising – Flower and Dean Street, Thrawl Street and Dorset Street had reputations that preceded Booth's explorations. However, other vice-ridden neighbourhoods abutted directly onto more wealthy parts, such as the courts and alleyways that led from Old Montague Street to Whitechapel Road, the warren of slums that made up the area around Great Pearl Street and, not surprisingly, a number of streets that sat in the shadow of the railway lines. It was these black areas that inspired the consternation of those brave enough to peer into their dark recesses. Booth's calculations declared that 35 per cent of the inhabitants of the East End were living on or below the poverty line and an alarming 13 per cent, undoubtedly the residents of those black warrens, faced starvation on a daily basis.

It was these "black holes" that generated the true dangers of the East End. They were the homes of thieves and other petty criminals, desperation having forced them to work outside of the law in a last-ditch attempt to survive. Any stranger venturing into these criminal enclaves risked personal injury and certainly loss of money or belongings and the felon in any case could equally be male, female or – unnervingly – a child. Criminality bred criminality. For those with no hovel or doss-house to go to, there were, of course, the streets themselves – open spaces such as Victoria Park in nearby Hackney and the gardens

of Christ Church Spitalfields made convenient resting places for the homeless. It is no wonder that so many despaired of the problems faced by the East End – it was fast becoming a predicament insoluble on its own terms.

For the poorest and most dispossessed women, there was a final option – prostitution. A Metropolitan Police figure of the time estimated there were as many as 1,200 "unfortunates" or "fallen women" operating in Whitechapel alone. This could never be an accurate statistic as it was often the case that a woman, desperate at a particular time, would sell herself on the streets just to make up for an occasional financial shortfall. In other words, the number of women prepared to solicit for money would no doubt be higher than the police had assumed. Many of the die-hard prostitutes would have been users of common lodging houses and the average price for a client to go with these women was a mere 4d, the same as for a bed in a doss-house, the act itself often taking place in a secluded court, alley or side turning. Through experience, these women would get to know the ideal places to conduct their furtive business: lonely, poorly lit spots, irregularly patrolled by police – in any case, the beats of these officers would soon become familiar and thus timing would be of the essence. As with the activities of today's sex workers, the job was a dangerous one. Any client could turn out to be violent or prepared to steal from them, added to

---

KEY EVIDENCE Annie Millwood (?–31 March 1888)

A good example of the violence inflicted on the vulnerable women of the East End can be seen in the case of Annie Millwood, who on 25 February 1888 was admitted to the Whitechapel Workhouse infirmary suffering from "stabs". Millwood was a 38 year-old widow and possibly a prostitute, who had been living at Spitalfields Chambers, a common lodging house at 8 White's Row, a street in the heart of Spitalfields' most notorious district. While the "stabs" description is rather vague, the injuries as described by a newspaper at the time were very specific:

It appears the deceased was admitted to the Whitechapel Infirmary suffering from numerous stabs in the legs and lower part of the body. She stated that she had been attacked by a man who she did not know, and who stabbed her with a clasp knife which he took from his pocket. No one appears to have seen the attack, and as far as at present ascertained, there is only the woman's statement to bear out the allegations of an attack, though that she had been stabbed cannot be denied.

Annie Millwood survived the assault and made a complete recovery, only to die of natural causes on 31 March. Her death was not linked in any way to the attack, but the stabbing itself and the specific targeting of the lower abdomen and thighs has since been perceived as an interesting precursor to what was to follow throughout 1888.

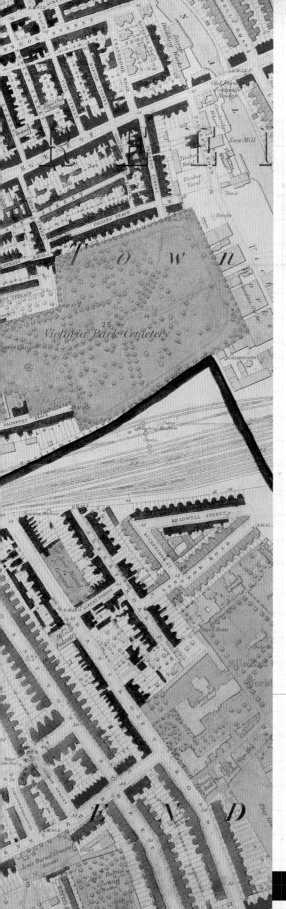

ABOVE: Sir Charles Warren, the much vilified Chief Commissioner of the Metropolitan Police at the time of the Whitechapel Murders.

which was the threat from local gangs who would see these women as vulnerable and easy prey.

Collectively, the problems offered to politicians, philanthropists and churchmen by the conditions within the East End slums appeared to depict a vision of Hell. In J H Mackays *The Anarchists* (1915), it was described as:

> *...like an enormous black, motionless, giant Kraken, the poverty of London lies there in lurking silence and encircles with its mighty tentacles the life and wealth of the City and the West End.*

Before 1888 was through, the concerns of the socially aware would become common knowledge, not just in London but throughout the world. Names like Dorset Street, Thrawl Street and Flower and Dean Street would appear on the pages of newspapers with predictable regularity, and the lives of those driven to live in "The Abyss" would come into sharp focus. For in 1888, a district that thought it had seen everything was about to be confronted by a new horror – death at the hands of an unknown assassin, whose acts shocked the civilized world; a supposedly random and motiveless series of murders, starting in Whitechapel before spreading to Spitalfields and even encroaching on the territory of the City of London. These crimes would stretch the resources of both the Metropolitan and City Police forces to the limit. The burgeoning radical press gave the stories an enormous amount of coverage, peering intrusively into the lives of those affected: the women who died, the witnesses who saw them, the authorities who struggled so manfully to put an end to it all and ultimately, some would say, the conditions in the East End, which should never have been allowed to endure for so long. The killer went by many names during his mercifully brief reign of terror, but one has survived into the present day. Whatever he is considered to be, whether a character from folklore, the nemesis of neglect, a misguided social reformer or a sexual maniac, he will always be the lurker in the shadows.

He is Jack the Ripper.

LEFT: A section of Charles Booth's colour-coded poverty map showing a large area of Bethnal Green. Note how some of the poorest districts, coloured black and dark blue, sit adjacent to the comfortably off, marked in red. Such were the contradictions of the East End.

Briefing

Emma Elizabeth Smith struggled to reach her lodgings in George Street, which ran between the notorious Flower and Dean Street and Wentworth Street in the heart of one of the worst slum districts in London. She lived at No.18, one of several common lodging houses in a depressing row of dilapidated three-story buildings. It was the early hours of Tuesday, 3 April 1888, and bitterly cold. Emma was in considerable pain, for only a few hours earlier, a mere 275 m (300 yards) from her lodgings, she had been attacked and so brutally assaulted that she would die from the injuries she sustained.

NOTHING MUCH FOR CERTAIN IS KNOWN about Emma Elizabeth Smith; she was apparently 45 years old, 1.57 m (5 ft 2 in) tall, and had light brown hair. She was almost certainly an alcoholic and could be nasty and belligerent when drunk, often sporting bruises or a black eye gained in drink-fuelled brawls. Those who knew her believed that she had been married to a soldier and that she had had two children, but how and why her life had taken a wrong turn was a mystery. Walter Dew, who would become famous as the policeman who pursued the fleeing murderer Dr Crippen across the Atlantic in 1910, was a young policeman in Whitechapel at the time of her murder and he wrote about her in his memoirs, providing information unrecorded elsewhere, perhaps suggesting that he was directly involved in the investigation. He wrote:

Her past was a closed book even to her most intimate friends. All that she had ever told anyone about herself was that she was a widow who more than ten years before had left her husband and broken away from all her early associations... There was something about Emma Smith which suggested that there had been a time when the comforts

BELOW: Walter Dew in his youth. As a young police officer at the time of the Whitechapel murders, he was party to the events of that autumn and had much to say on the subject in his memoirs, published in 1938.

of life had not been denied her. There was a touch of culture in her speech unusual in her class.

The dirty streets along which Emma Smith laboured had once been open fields and it is known that in the 1600s a Captain Conisby owned a large area of land there, including a field in which he had 17 long tenters (a framework on which material is stretched taut for drying), a place for spinning, a nursery and two gardens planted with a variety of fruit bushes. Eventually the land was acquired by two brothers, Thomas and Lewis Fossan, whose name was commemorated, albeit corrupted, in nearby Fashion Street. Another chunk of the land was bought by two bricklayers, John Flower and Gowen Deane, their names remembered in Flower and Dean Street, and so it was that streets were laid out and building began. It was the Fossans who laid out George Street and a man named Henry Thrall or Thrale built Thrawl Street to connect it with Brick Lane to the east in the mid-1600s. The district was a slum almost from the time it was built. Most of the houses were poorly constructed using inferior materials, and within a few decades many would have to be demolished. By the 1880s the area was considered to be a dangerous and crime-infested neighbourhood, a breeding place of degeneracy and a home to disease.

The slum clearance that was intended as the outcome of the construction of Commercial Street in the 1840s failed, and so in 1877 the Metropolitan Board of Works decided under the provisions provided by the Artisans' and Labourers' Dwellings Improvement Act (1875) to grasp the opportunity to demolish the crumbling old buildings and sell off the land for redevelopment. Two principal organizations acquired the land: the East End Dwellings Company, and the curiously named Four Per Cent Industrial Dwellings Company. The latter was founded in 1885 by prominent figures in the Anglo-Jewish establishment, highly successful banker Nathan Mayer Rothschild, philanthropist Frederick Mocatta and the politician Samuel Montagu. Its mission was to provide decent and healthy accommodation for the working classes and the money to undertake the work was raised by guaranteeing investors a 4 per cent return, hence the company name. The west side of George Street was demolished in 1883 and

the Charlotte De Rothschild Dwellings and Lolesworth Buildings were built four years later, leading to a westward extension of Thrawl Street, now joining Commercial Street. The doss-houses on the eastern side of George Street remained until the early 1890s when the thoroughfare was renamed Lolesworth Street. With the building of Ruth and Helena Houses between 1895 and 1897 and Keate and Spencer Houses in 1908, the slums were finally eradicated. These buildings were themselves demolished between 1973 and 1980 and the former George Street vanished altogether with the building of the Flower and Dean Estate between 1982 and 1984.

Easter Monday fell early in 1888, on 2 April, and the weather was still wintery. A dull, heavy and overcast sky had threatened rain and dampened spirits in the morning and by the afternoon, a drizzling rain and bone-chilling

BELOW: A contemporary illustration of the junction of George Street and Wentworth Street. The City of Norwich pub on the right was owned by Frederick Gehringer, also a prominent lodging house keeper in the district.

18 George Street

Emma Smith's home, 18 George Street, was first registered as a common lodging house in 1864 by George Willmott, who owned several other lodging houses in the area. Originally it was licensed to accommodate 21 lodgers housed in three rooms, one on each of its three floors. The property was later taken over by a local publican named Frederick Gehringer and he managed to subdivide the floors, packing in more than double the previous number of tenants. Gehringer was quite a figure in the neighbourhood – not only did he run the City of Norwich pub on nearby Wentworth Street, but he was also the landlord of a tight enclave of slum properties in Little Pearl Street, Spitalfields. He sold No.18 in 1886 to a man named Daniel Lewis, another prominent local lodging house keeper, who owned it at the time of the murder, selling it soon after to William Gillett, who kept it until it closed for good in May 1891.

ABOVE: A George Street doss-house from the *Illustrated Police News*, 15 September 1888.

north-westerly wind made being indoors all the more appealing. As darkness fell, the temperature dropped to just above freezing and there were short flurries of snow, but Emma Smith did not let the bad weather keep her indoors. She probably visited a few pubs – it would later be said that she had been drinking – which were busy with noisy drunks who, it was reported, made the streets that night hideous with their cries and antics.

She was seen by a friend and fellow lodger at 18 George Street, 54-year-old Margaret Hayes, who had had a bit of a rough night herself. It is testimony to the violence of the East End streets and the dangers these women risked nightly that just before Christmas 1887 she had been assaulted and so badly hurt by some men that she'd spent two weeks in the infirmary. On Easter Monday night she had been assaulted again: two men stopped her and one of them hit her in the mouth. Hayes saw Emma Smith at the corner of Burdett Road and Farrance Street in the company of a man who was dressed in a dark suit and wore some sort of white scarf, but as she was hurrying away from the area she paid the couple little

attention. Although at this time the women were a 3.2 km (2 mile) walk from Whitechapel, their presence there was not perhaps surprising – in all probability they were soliciting, taking advantage of the previous night's bank-holiday revellers and the proximity of the West India Docks and Limehouse, with their ready clientele of sailors on shore-leave.

At about 1:30 a.m. on 3 April, Emma Smith was walking along the wide thoroughfare of Whitechapel Road on her way home and had reached Whitechapel Church when she saw a group of men, one of them a youth aged about 19, coming towards her. She crossed the road to avoid them, and turned down Osborn Street, which merges after a short distance into Brick Lane. The men followed her, and near Taylor Brothers Mustard and Cocoa Mill on the corner of Brick Lane and Wentworth Street she was knocked to the ground and robbed of what little money she possessed. By the time the men had finished with her, she had been injured about the head and someone had rammed a blunt object into her vagina. Seriously injured, Emma Smith was

LEFT: Osborn Street, Whitechapel, looking north towards Brick Lane circa 1900. Emma Smith claimed she walked up this street in the direction of her lodgings, closely followed by the three men who eventually attacked her.

BELOW: The towering bulk of Charlotte DeRothschild Dwellings, opened in 1887 as part of the long running schemes to improve living conditions in the Flower and Dean and Thrawl Street neighbourhoods.

left to get home as best she could, and struggling with pain and exhaustion it took her as much as three hours to cover the 275 m (300 yards) to George Street. Nobody saw her. These streets could be busy even late at night, when drunken revellers were reported to be noisy and disruptive on the streets. A number of police officers should have been on duty in that area, patrolling their beat despite the freezing cold and snow flurries, yet Emma Smith was apparently seen by neither civilians nor police. There was nobody to help her at the time.

Very little is known about the actual attack, for Emma seemed to have been reluctant to say much about what happened, a reticence that has led some modern commentators to speculate whether her story was altogether true. There is no doubt that she sustained terrible injuries, but it is questioned whether she was the victim of a gang attack or not. It is generally accepted that serial killers do not start with a murder but with less serious crimes and, while the attack on Emma Smith was brutal and violent, it may not have been intended to be fatal. Could it therefore have been an early attack by the Whitechapel Murderer? Walter Dew certainly thought that it was, writing: "The silence, the suddenness, the complete elimination of clues, the baffling disappearance all go to support the view which I have always held that Emma Smith was the first to meet her death at the hands of Jack the Ripper." Oddly enough, Dew also wrote that Emma Smith was found lying unconscious in the street, which, if true, would certainly help to explain the time that elapsed between the assault and Emma reaching 18 George Street. Problematically, however, apart from Drew's assertion, there was no claim from anybody else that she was found in the street after the attack.

OVERLEAF AND PAGES 24–25: Artist's impression of the close-knit lodging houses near Wentworth Street. Often, the lamps outside these premises made up for the poor street lighting in the thoroughfares as a whole.

Where Did It Happen?

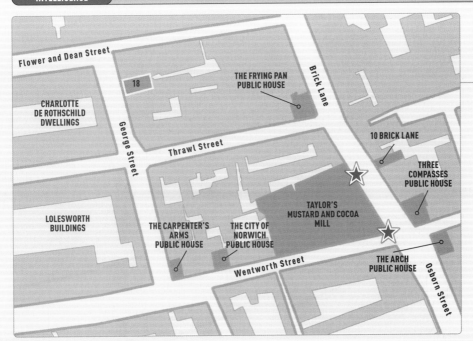

Flower and Dean Street

18

CHARLOTTE
DE ROTHSCHILD
DWELLINGS

George Street

THE FRYING PAN
PUBLIC HOUSE

Brick Lane

Thrawl Street

10 BRICK LANE

THREE
COMPASSES
PUBLIC HOUSE

LOLESWORTH
BUILDINGS

THE CARPENTER'S
ARMS
PUBLIC HOUSE

THE CITY OF
NORWICH
PUBLIC HOUSE

TAYLOR'S
MUSTARD AND COCOA
MILL

Wentworth Street

THE ARCH
PUBLIC HOUSE

Osborn Street

⭐ LEFT: Possible sites
of the attack on
Emma Smith

Owing to the vagaries of Emma Smith's account of the attack made upon her, it is not clear exactly where the incident occurred. On the way to the hospital, she pointed out to her companions the spot where the men had set upon her, essentially outside Taylor Brothers Mustard and Cocoa Mill, a large building at the corner of Wentworth Street and Brick Lane. Although a number of sources stated that it was on that corner where the outrage took place, another stated that it happened opposite 10 Brick Lane, technically still by the Cocoa Mill, but interestingly more specific nonetheless.

ABOVE: Dr George Haslip in middle age. As a young house surgeon at the London Hospital on 3 April 1888, he examined the injuries inflicted upon Emma Smith and subsequently performed her autopsy.

When she eventually made it back to the comparative safety of No.18, Margaret Hayes was already there, talking with a fellow lodger called Annie Lee and the lodging house deputy, Mary Russell. Emma's face was bleeding and her ear was torn, and she was clearly in distress, so they decided to take her to the London Hospital in Whitechapel Road, about 1 km (half a mile) away. Emma was reluctant to go there, perhaps because she was in such excruciating pain but also perhaps because she feared the hospital as many locals did. As Dr Frederick Treves, who would become famous through his association with the so-called "Elephant Man" and was a surgeon and head of the school of anatomy at London Hospital, later wrote in his book *The Elephant Man and Other Reminiscences* (1923), "The poor people hated it. They dreaded it. They looked upon it primarily as a place where people died. It was a matter of difficulty to induce a patient to enter the wards."

Nevertheless she went, and at the hospital the house surgeon, George Haslip, gave her such assistance as he could. Dr Haslip was only 24 years old and although he didn't know it, he was embarking on what would be a distinguished medical career. He had trained at the London Hospital and qualified in February the previous year. He would build up a large private practice at 8 Suffolk Place, Pall Mall, and afterwards at 23 St James's Square, and would be a medical adviser to several large insurance companies and physician to a number of the largest West End hotels. In 1916 he was elected Treasurer of the British Medical Association and would be one of the architects of the National Health Service. He married Anna, the daughter of a privy councillor to the Imperial Austrian Government, and one of their two daughters, Joan, would earn distinction

The London Hospital

ABOVE: The London Hospital on Whitechapel Road circa 1900.

The London Hospital was founded in the Feathers Tavern in Cheapside, London, in 1740 by a group of professional men, businessmen and philanthropists to treat the sick poor of "the merchant seamen and manufacturing classes". Its first patients were admitted to a house in Featherstone Street, Moorfields, where it went by the name of "The London Infirmary". A few months later, it relocated to rented accommodation in Prescott Street and it was soon apparent that a larger, purpose-built premises was needed. In 1752, a site was found on Whitechapel Road and in 1757, the new infirmary was opened. At this time, much of the surrounding area was fields and the hospital wards offered patients soothing views of the countryside down to Limehouse and the Thames. Its renowned medical college was founded in 1785 and it was here that philanthropist Thomas Barnardo began his medical career in 1866, introducing him to the poor of the East End and kick-starting his work with destitute children which continues today through the organization that bears his name.

The London Hospital is probably best known for its links with Frederick Treves and Joseph Merrick, "the Elephant Man". Merrick spent the last four years of his life at the hospital and was there during the period of the Whitechapel Murders, dying in 1890. Another patient in 1888 was Robert D'Onston Stephenson, an enigmatic character suffering from neurasthenia (a psychological disorder characterized by extreme fatigue). He was later a Ripper suspect, and in turn wrote to the police with his own theory that one Dr Morgan Davies committed the crimes. The proximity of the hospital to the murder sites of Jack the Ripper (particularly Buck's Row, a mere 137 m [150 yards] away) has indeed led some theorists to suggest that the perpetrator was someone connected with it.

Throughout the twentieth century, "The London" continued to expand and in 1990 it was given a royal charter and renamed The Royal London Hospital, the same year it acquired London's first air-ambulance service. It remains one of London's busiest hospitals.

as a biographer. He died in 1924 after a long and painful illness.

A blunt instrument had been rammed into her vagina with such force that it had ruptured the peritoneum, the membrane which lines the inside of the abdomen and internal organs, allowing bacteria to enter and cause a dangerous infection. Emma Smith would have suffered severe abdominal pain and, alas, in 1888 the prognosis would have been poor. Indeed, within 24 hours she weakened and at 9:00 a.m. on Wednesday morning she died of peritonitis. Dr Haslip performed an autopsy and confirmed the cause of death.

An inquest was held at the London Hospital before Wynne Edwin Baxter, the coroner for East Middlesex. He concluded by saying that from the medical evidence it was clear that Emma Smith had been "barbarously murdered", adding that he had never heard of such a dastardly murder and that "it was impossible to imagine a more brutal case."

ABOVE: Emma Smith's death received little press coverage at the time, but it warranted press illustrations months later when the other murders took place. This is a detail from *The Illustrated Police News*, Saturday 13 October 1888.

RIGHT: A contemporary press illustration of the flamboyant and often outspoken coroner Wynne Baxter, responsible for the inquiries into the deaths of many of the Whitechapel murder victims.

MR WYNNE E. BAXTER.
CORONER FOR EASY MIDDLESEX

MARTHA TABRAM

Brie ng

Emma Smith's attack and subsequent death were shocking to the people of the East End, warranting brief coverage in the local press and a few national newspapers. However, a four-month gap passed before an atrocity of comparable violence took place in the locale and, whereas the notion that Smith had been murdered by a gang was given credence at the time, the events surrounding the death of the next victim proved less yielding to any de nitive solution. It was a homicide that appeared to have no motive, was excessive in its brutality, was noticeably close to the location of the previous crime and, with no solid clues available to the investigating authorities, became what some deemed as an early murder by somebody who would increase their savagery in the weeks to come.

LEFT: Artist's impression of the entrance to George Yard Buildings. The faint glow of the solitary lamp within would have been extinguished at 11:00p.m.

MARTHA TABRAM LIKED A DRINK. SHE LIKED one too much. The man with whom she had lived for the last few years of her life had eventually left her for good because of her excessive drinking. He was reported in the *East London Observer* on 25 August 1888 as saying "If I gave her money she generally spent it in drink. In fact, it was always drink." A sometime landlady of Martha's was slightly more charitable, as people tend to be towards the dead, especially when they die in tragic and horrible circumstances, saying that Martha "would rather have a glass of ale than a cup of tea".

RIGHT: Martha Tabram drinking with two soldiers on the last night of her life in an illustration from *Famous Crimes Past and Present*, 1903.

Monday 6 August 1888, was another bank holiday and another cold and miserable day, although the lowering skies, dark and heavy, threatening rain throughout the morning and afternoon, held off until early evening. Bank holidays were big days in the 1880s and venues across London scheduled spectacular events to attract the hundreds of thousands of people who went out determined to enjoy themselves on their sacrosanct day off. How Martha Tabram spent much of her day isn't known, but in the evening she went out – drinking. At about 9:00 p.m. she met a friend and fellow prostitute, a husky-voiced and masculine-looking woman with a face reddened by drink. She was incongruously nicknamed Pearly Poll, but her real name appears to have been Mary Ann Connolly, and at some point they were picked up by two soldiers, a private and a corporal, who took them drinking. Where they went is not certain because Connolly, one of the few sources of information regarding that night, told different stories. She told the police that they had spent all their time in a single pub and were only together from 11:00 to 11:45 p.m., but at the inquest into Martha's death she claimed that the pair had been on a bit of a pub crawl, roaming the hostelries of the area from about 10:00 p.m. onwards. What is known is that at about 11:00 p.m. Tabram was seen by her sister-in-law, Ann Morris, entering a pub on Whitechapel High Street, which Mrs Morris believed to be the White Swan. Since she was part of Martha's family, it is unlikely she would have misidentified her, yet her statement made no mention of Connolly or the two soldiers. Connolly and Martha later left the pub with their soldier companions and made their way up Whitechapel High Street; Martha went off with one of the soldiers, going with him into a narrow passage leading into a street called George Yard. Connolly claimed that she took her man into the adjacent Angel Alley.

When Martha was next seen she was dead, stretched out on the cold concrete of a tenement stairway, having been frenziedly stabbed nearly 40 times.

Martha Tabram was born Martha White across the river in Southwark on 10 May 1849, the last of five children born to a warehouseman named Charles and his wife Elizabeth (née Dowsett). On Christmas Day in 1869, Martha married Henry Samuel Tabram. She was just 20 years old and he was a 33-year-old widower with a son who was nearly ten years old. Martha may have appeared to be a good catch and Henry, a foreman packer in a furniture warehouse in Deptford, may have offered her stability, but the marriage, seemingly much troubled by Martha's heavy drinking, did not last and in 1875 they separated for good.

Martha was not happy with this and sought redress in the courts, forcing Henry to pay her 12s a week (nearly £50 in today's money), and although he paid it regularly, Martha was not satisfied and began accosting him in the street, creating scenes and demanding more money. Henry retaliated by reducing the amount he paid, but Martha again took action in the courts and it was not until he discovered that she had started living with another man that Henry was able to refuse to pay any more. He got his life back and rarely heard or saw Martha after that.

OPPOSITE: Artist's impression of George Yard Buildings.

BELOW: George Yard Buildings, then called Charles Booth House, in 1967.

Satchell's
LODGINGS
FOR
TRAVELLERS

89

ST GEORGES RESIDENCES

BOARD AND LODGING FOR RESPECTABLE GIRLS

The White Swan

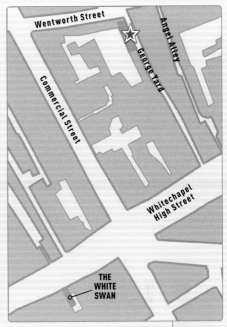

LEFT: The White Swan can be seen in this 1914 photograph, marked by the hexagonal hanging sign.

ABOVE: Map showing the proximity of the White Swan to the location of the murder.

⭐ Murder site

The White Swan is one of many East End locals to have vanished, swept away by often faceless redevelopment. It was located on the south side of Whitechapel High Street at No.20. The landlord was Frederick Davis, who came from Great Baddow, one of the largest villages in England, not far from Chelmsford in Essex. He'd followed in the footsteps of his father James to become a butcher, but changed vocation to take over the White Swan in the mid-1870s. Over time the pub became known locally as "Davis'". It seems to have been a tightly run pub, seldom featured in the newspapers other than for things that Davis couldn't control. At the end of 1887, for example, a man named Henry Bullivant broke into the pub and stole some cigars and other things, for which he was sent for trial. Towards the end of 1888, just as the Ripper scare was in full-swing, Davis and his wife Emma celebrated the marriage of their daughter Bessie to Charles Christie at the renowned church St Martin-in-the-Fields in the heart of London. Other family members also worked at the pub, notably daughter Florence Emily Davis, who in 1891 had to give evidence at the inquiry into the death of Francis Coles (who for a while the police thought may have been a victim of Jack the Ripper). Davis left the pub in the 1890s when both he and his wife were in their 60s and probably in need of a quiet and comfortable retirement.

OPPOSITE : The forbidding entrance to George Yard, showing part of the White Hart pub at No. 89 Whitechapel High Street.

Whitechapel High Street

Whitechapel High Street runs west to east as a continuation of Aldgate High Street, terminating at the junction with Osborn Street and Whitechurch Lane, after which it becomes Whitechapel Road. Once known as Algate Street, it originally formed part of the main route to Essex and was consequently built up very early – it was paved during the reign of Henry VIII, although even then it was known for its shabbiness.

Its purpose as a main thoroughfare out of London led to numerous coaching inns being built along its length, many of them serviced by narrow courts and alleys. Although many of these inns closed down following the arrival of the railways in the mid-nineteenth century, in 1888 ten pubs were still trading. Today there are only two left, of which the only original is the White Hart at No.89. The High Street was also the site of the Whitechapel haymarket which existed from 1708 until 1929, when increased traffic led to its abolition on safety grounds.

Whitechapel High Street crosses the busy junction of Commercial Road, Leman Street and Commercial Street, once marked by the prominent clock tower of Gardiner's department store. This local landmark was closed in 1965 and was demolished in 1972 soon after a fire ripped through it. Much of the north side of the High Street remains a mixture of nineteenth- and twentieth-century buildings. The world famous art gallery and former library were constructed from 1897–1899.

The south side has been effectively decimated by late-twentieth century redevelopment, particularly following the construction of the one-way system at Gardiner's Corner in the mid-1960s. The London Metropolitan University building dates from 1965. Development continues, albeit erratically and much of this is probably evidence of an eastward encroachment by the City from Aldgate.

ABOVE: Whitechapel High Street looking towards Aldgate in 1914, with the haymarket in full swing.

The last time he saw her, he wasn't surprised to see she was drunk.

Martha also harassed her sister-in-law, Ann Morris, a respectable young widow Martha thought had encouraged Henry to leave her. On one occasion Martha had turned up at her home and smashed the windows. As a result she was hauled into court and sentenced to seven days hard labour.

Some nine years before her death Martha had started to live on-and-off with William Turner. In stark contrast to Henry Tabram, who was described at the time of the murder as neatly dressed and sporting a moustache and iron-grey hair, Turner was described as short, dirty and slovenly, and unkempt in appearance. A sometime carpenter, he and Martha had hawked cheap trinkets around the streets. Their relationship was marked by frequent separations caused by Martha's drinking, with the last being shortly before her death. Turner saw her for the final time on 4 August 1888, in Leadenhall Street near Aldgate Pump, whereupon he gave her 1s 6d (about £4 today) so that she could buy trinkets to sell.

Martha moved into a common lodging house at 19 George Street and Mary Ann Connolly also lived there. It was next door to the lodging house Emma Smith had used (see chapter 2).

The cold bank holiday night of 6 August 1888 had turned into a good one for Martha Tabram and Mary Ann Connolly, who had found the two soldiers willing to entertain them and supply them with drinks, but their generosity came at a price and the debt had to be paid. Mary Ann Connolly, perhaps more concerned with her own companion, observed only that Martha had disappeared up the forbidding George Yard with hers.

George Yard was accessed from the south via a covered archway between Nos. 88 (John Telfer's pawnbroker's) and 89 Whitechapel High Street. No.89 was the White Hart pub, an old bow-windowed establishment dating back to the eighteenth century, which in 1888 was run by a Mr George Cross. Above the archway was a sign saying "St George's Residences – Board and Lodging for Respectable Girls", a reference to the accommodation offered in the newly constructed building (1886) to the rear of the White Hart. Opposite this was the George Yard Ragged School, which since 1861 had offered

BELOW: The rear of George Yard Buildings in the 1960s. The flat belonging to witness John Saunders Reeves is on the top balcony, far left. From here he could see Lolesworth Buildings in George Street from where he and his wife heard disturbances on the night of Martha Tabram's murder.

19 George Street

A three-storey building like its neighbour, No.19 benefitted from having a kitchen in the basement, thus freeing up the ground floor for more tenants. It was first registered by Patrick Sullivan in 1868, but he did not stay long and the following year, the lodging house was taken over by John Satchell, who remained until it closed down in 1891. Commonly known as Satchell's, no doubt thanks to the keeper's long ownership, it was originally licensed for 72 lodgers with room for 38 people on its second floor alone. Satchell also owned 32 Flower and Dean Street, the lodging house frequented by Elizabeth Stride (see chapter 7) up until her death.

19 George Street was also the scene of another proposed Ripper attack, albeit one that has been roundly discredited. Annie Farmer had taken a man into the house at 7:30 a.m. on 21 November 1888, but two hours later, the man fled the house with a distraught Farmer nursing a wound to the throat and shouting that she had been attacked by the Ripper. The fact that the man remarked on the incident to two passers-by and that Annie Farmer was hiding coins in her mouth has led many to believe that she had tried to cheat him out of money, receiving a knife injury for her troubles.

No.19, like all the lodging houses on this portion of the street, closed down in May 1891 prior to demolition.

RIGHT: No.19 George Street, as depicted in the *Illustrated Police News* of 1 December 1888. The crowds had assembled following the attack on Annie Farmer at the lodging house which was briefly suspected of being another Ripper crime.

education and shelter to the poorest children in the neighbourhood. Its opening had helped to improve the street's notorious reputation as a dangerous place.

Continuing north on the east side was the flat wall of a colour-and-varnishing factory known as St George's Works, followed by lodging houses running all the way up to the junction with Wentworth Street. These were owned by George Wildermuth who also ran several similar premises in neighbouring Angel Alley and were part of George Yard's less respectable past (they would be demolished a few years later). Behind these stood the Whitechapel Board of Works' dust-destructor facility, where rubbish would be collected and incinerated – the floating smoke and debris often made this end of George Yard a singularly dirty and unpleasant place to live. Its chimney loomed over the neighbourhood for many years.

On the western side of the street, north of St George's Residences, was a stable yard, known previously as Black Horse Yard (it belonged to an inn of the same name that had once stood here), with a small complex of brick buildings serving the stables and other commercial concerns. Next to these was the imposing frontage of St George's House, a large model dwelling with about 40 rooms, constructed around 1880 following the demolition of a number of slum courts a few years before.

And finally, almost at the extreme north-west corner with Wentworth Street stood George Yard Buildings, built around 1875 on the site of an old timber yard under the instruction of a well-known local gentleman by the name of Mr Crowther. It was a purely philanthropic venture; in its 47 rooms lived, as one contemporary commentator described, "the poorest of the poor, but very honest".

The layout of the building's interior is difficult to ascertain exactly, but entrance from George Yard was through a pointed archway, leading to staircases which served the upper three floors of the building. Each flight of stairs had a landing and although they were lit after dark, it is believed that these lights were turned off after 11:00 p.m. These landings may also have had communal latrines, a feature common to this type of dwelling and certainly present in St

OVERLEAF: George Yard, looking north from the rear of the White Hart pub.

George's House next door. Each floor of George Yard Buildings had a long external concrete balcony, reached via the stairwells and allowing access to rear rooms. Thus there were three in total, overlooking Toynbee Hall, which had been completed in 1884. Although George Yard Buildings' arched entrance also passed through the building and out the other side, there was no access to Toynbee Hall, a wall having been erected to define the boundary and in doing so, creating a small courtyard. In 1890, the buildings were taken over by Toynbee Hall and renamed "Balliol House", as accommodation and administrative offices for their neighbour. Balliol House was later rechristened Charles Booth House and after a long period of debate about its usefulness and the integrity of its structure, it was demolished in 1973 and replaced by the current Sunley House. George Yard itself was renamed Gunthorpe Street in 1912 after John Gunthorpe, a rector of St Mary's Church in the fifteenth century.

Among the residents of George Yard Buildings during the August of 1888 were a young couple, Joseph and Elizabeth Mahoney. Joseph had a job as a carman (a delivery driver) and Elizabeth worked in a match factory at Stratford. Her work hours were grinding, from 9 a.m. until 7 p.m. but, although dangerous and for little money, at least it was respectable, paying work. While it was never referred to by name in the newspaper at the time, the factory where she worked would have been Bryant and May in Fairfield Road (see page 19).

Joseph and Elizabeth had been out enjoying the bank holiday with friends all day and it was at about 1:40 a.m. that they returned to George Yard Buildings. With the lights in the building having been extinguished hours before, they wearily climbed the wide stairway to their room in darkness. Almost immediately, Elizabeth returned down the stairs to buy some supper from a shop in nearby Thrawl Street, returning with the food about five minutes later. She saw nothing, although a body could have been lying hidden by the darkness on the broad stairway without her seeing it. However, it was at about this time that 31-year-old Police Constable Thomas Barrett, 226H, was in Wentworth Street and saw a Grenadier guardsman near the entrance to George Yard. He asked why he was

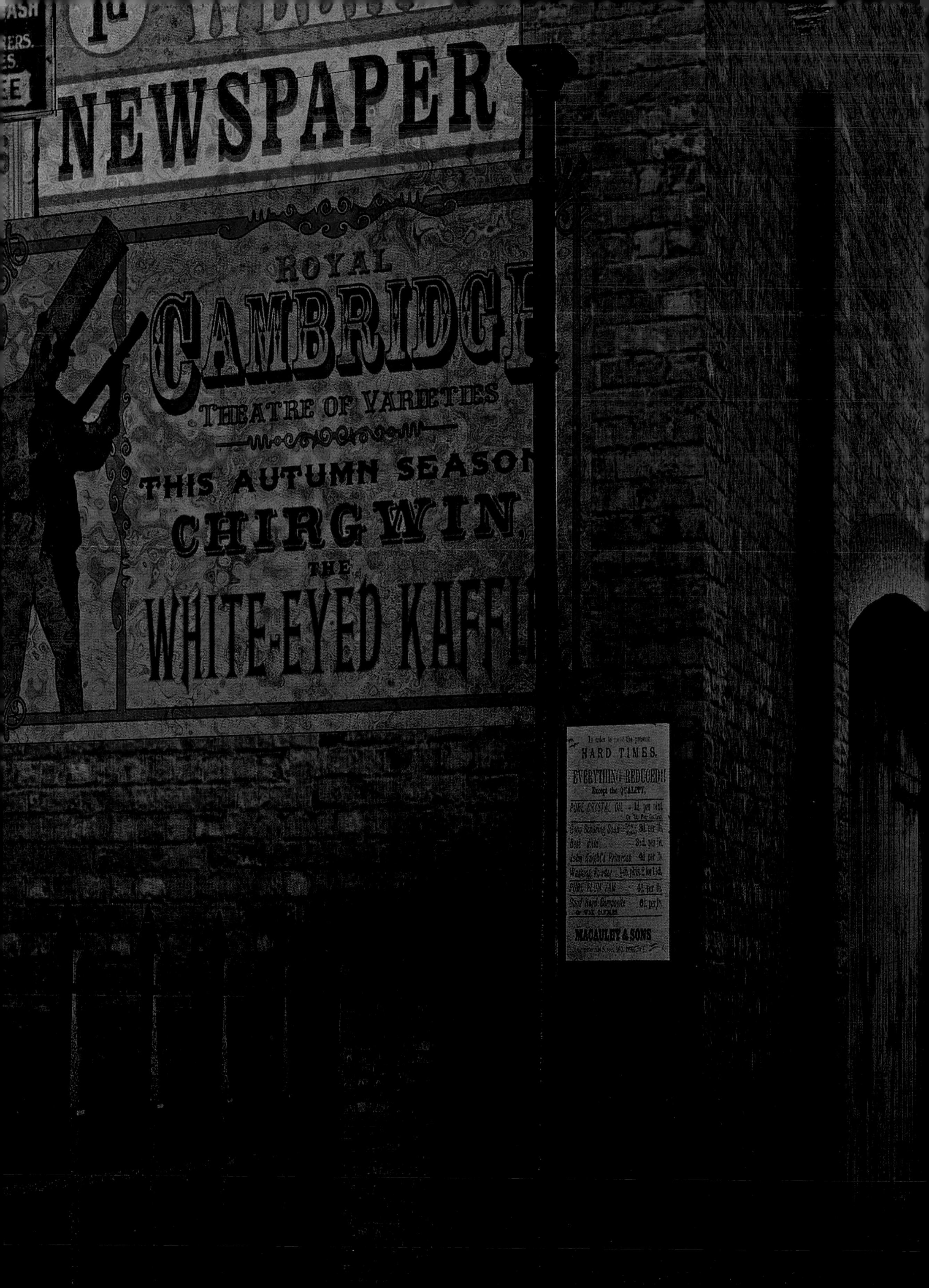

NEWSPAPER

ROYAL
CAMBRIDGE
THEATRE OF VARIETIES

THIS AUTUMN SEASON
CHIRGWIN
THE
WHITE-EYED KAFFIR

HARD TIMES.
EVERYTHING REDUCED!!
Except the QUALITY.

MACAULEY & SONS

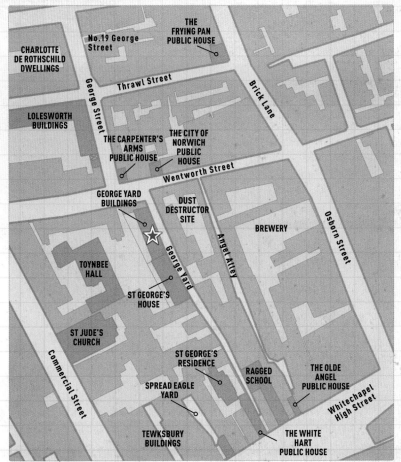

ABOVE: Map showing
the murder site and its
surrounding area.

☆ Murder site

OPPOSITE: George Yard
Buildings as seen from
Wentworth Street. It
was at the corner of the
two streets where
PC Thomas Barrett,
encountered a soldier at
approximately 2:00 a.m.

a body, undoubtedly that of Martha Tabram, on the first floor landing, but paid it no attention because it was not uncommon to find people asleep there. On two separate occasions that night, John Reeves, a waterside labourer, and his wife Louisa, residents of No.37, had heard animated disturbances in the area, loud enough for them to venture onto their balcony on the top floor of George Yard Buildings to investigate. It was apparent that the noise was not coming from within the tenement itself, but rather from Lolesworth Buildings, a recently built block of flats on the corner of Thrawl and George Streets. Being able to see where the sounds were coming from and satisfied that they were of no immediate concern, they went back to bed. At 4:45 a.m., John Reeves, heading out early in the hope of finding a day's work, discovered the body of Martha Tabram on the first-floor landing and raised the alarm.

Too scared to touch the body, he ran for a policeman and returned with PC Barrett, who immediately set in process what, by modern standards, was a rudimentary police investigation. Barrett sent Reeves to fetch Dr Timothy Robert Killeen from his home at 68 Brick Lane and after a cursory examination – which was intended to do little more than determine that life was extinct – Martha Tabram was placed on what was essentially a handcart but was dignified by being called an ambulance, and was taken to the mortuary.

While the injury to Emma Smith had been appalling and brutal, it failed to attract much media attention. The attack on Martha Tabram was different: in the East End and beyond there was horror at the frenzy of the stabbing. The police, though, faced an almost insurmountable task: their only clues were Mary Ann Connolly's story about the soldiers and the possibility that at least one of Martha's injuries had been inflicted with a bayonet.

loitering there, and was told that the guardsman was waiting for a mate who had gone with a girl. Given that PC Barrett saw a soldier waiting for a companion who had apparently gone into George Yard with a female friend, just as a soldier had gone up there with Tabram, it is tempting to suppose that the man seen by Barrett was Mary Ann Connolly's companion. It was now two hours after Connolly and Martha had paired off, however, and assuming that Connolly's timings were even remotely correct, on the face of it, it seems unlikely that this Grenadier had anything to do with the murder. Nevertheless, the police investigated this lead thoroughly.

At 3:30 a.m. Alfred Crow, who was aged about 21-years and was employed as a cab driver, returned home to George Yard Buildings, where he lived at No.35 with his parents and two younger brothers, and climbed the same staircase as had Elizabeth Mahoney. He noticed

POLICE · BUDGET · EDITION   EDITED BY HAROLD FURNISS

Famous CRIMES

PAST AND PRESENT   ONE · PENNY

THE DISCOVERY OF "JACK THE RIPPER'S" FIRST MURDER.

The injuries inflicted upon Martha were extensive, brutal and by all appearances, motiveless. She had received 39 stab wounds to the body. Dr Killeen, who arrived at the scene at approximately 5:30 a.m., believed she had been dead some three hours. Killeen's inquest testimony was reported in *The Times* on 10 August 1888:

The left lung was penetrated in five places, and the right lung was penetrated in two places. The heart, which was rather fatty, was penetrated in one place, and that would be sufficient to cause death. The liver was healthy, but was penetrated in five places, the spleen was penetrated in two places, and the stomach, which was perfectly healthy, was penetrated in six places. The witness did not think all the wounds were inflicted with the same instrument. The wounds generally might have been inflicted by a knife, but such an instrument could not have inflicted one of the wounds, which went through the chest-bone. His opinion was that one of the wounds was inflicted by some kind of dagger, and that all of them were caused during life.

Further testimony revealed Dr Killeen's opinion as to the type of weapon used, instrumental in bringing suspicion against Martha's unidentified soldier companion: "An ordinary penknife could have made most of the wounds, but the puncture in the chest must have been made with a sword bayonet or a dagger."

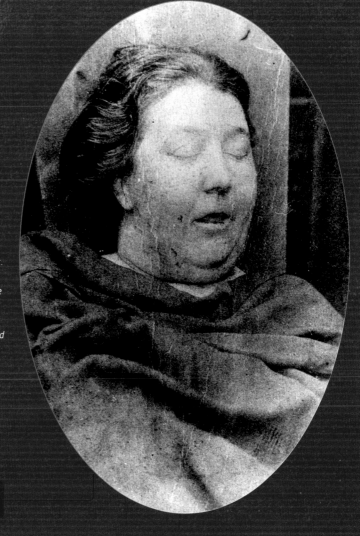

RIGHT: Mortuary photograph of Martha Tabram.

OPPOSITE: Illustration of the discovery of Martha Tabram's body by John Saunders Reeves, as published on the cover of *Famous Crimes Past and Present*, 1903.

The case was put into the hands of the head of the local CID, Detective Inspector Edmund Reid. He was an interesting character, a pioneer balloonist who in 1883 made record ascents in a balloon called *Queen of the Meadow* and received gold and bronze medals from the Balloon Association of Great Britain. He quickly learned that bayonets were common in the area – old bayonets could be bought in the local markets for a penny and were even seen as playthings for children. High hopes were placed on the evidence of Mary Ann Connolly and PC Barrett, but these hopes were soon dashed

when Barrett picked out two men at an identity parade who proved to have alibis.

Connolly was even worse. She had gone to the police station in Commercial Street and told the story of her night out with Tabram, and she agreed to attend an identification parade at the Tower of London the following day, but she didn't turn up. It was three days before the police eventually tracked her down at the home of a cousin in Feathers Court, one of the dreary streets and courts that made up the Drury Lane Rookery. Once highly fashionable, in the eighteenth century it was disreputable and rowdy, noted for its brothels and prostitutes. Plate 3 of William Hogarth's series of paintings entitled *The Harlot's Progress* (1732), in which Moll Hackabout has descended to a common brothel and is perhaps showing signs of syphilis, is set there. By the end of the nineteenth century this labyrinth of alleyways was one of the worst slums in London and eventually the target of a major clearance operation. When Connolly was finally found, she claimed that she didn't know the police needed her. Inspector Reid thought she had kept out of the way deliberately, but he did not expand on her reasons for doing so. She also behaved oddly at the identification parade, confidently parading up and down the line of men like a sergeant major inspecting the troops. Then, her arms akimbo, as if performing before the small audience of policemen and journalists, she announced, "He ain't here." Further to this, she announced that the soldiers she and Martha had been out with had white bands around their caps, which meant they were Coldstream Guardsmen, not Grenadiers stationed at the Tower of London as the police had supposed. The Coldstream Guards were stationed at Wellington Barracks, about 275 m (300 yards) from Buckingham Palace, so yet another identification parade had to be arranged. Without a moment's hesitation, Connolly picked out a Private George and a Private Skipper, both of whom had alibis.

There may have been a reason behind Connolly's behaviour, but the paucity of available information makes it difficult to understand. Her friend had been murdered in an attack so vicious that to most people, even to those hardened by the brutality of life in the East End, it was beyond shocking, and she had voluntarily given information to the police. She then disappeared, and when she was found and taken to the identification parade, behaved like an amateur comedienne. There, she changed her description of the soldiers and at another parade picked out two men who manifestly weren't the men she and Martha had spent the evening with. Her behaviour makes one wonder whether she had been with Martha at all. She certainly wasn't in evidence when Martha was seen by Ann Morris, and neither were the soldiers. Sadly, while one assumes the police

ABOVE: Inspector Edmund Reid, the officer in charge of the early Whitechapel murder investigations. He would later be joined by the better-known Inspector Frederick Abberline in September 1888.

made enquiries at the local pubs, the White Swan in particular, and presumably established as best they could the movements of the two women, the police files are sparse and the results of their enquiries, assuming there were some enquiries and Mary Ann Connolly's story wasn't simply accepted at face value, never made it into the newspapers.

The inquest into Martha Tabram's death was opened on the afternoon of 9 August 1888 in the Alexandra Room, the lecture room and library of the Working Lads' Institute in Whitechapel Road, near to Whitechapel Railway Station, today the Underground.

The inquest fell within the jurisdiction of the coroner of the South-Eastern Division of Middlesex, Wynne Baxter, but he was on holiday and it therefore fell to his deputy, George Collier. It was quickly adjourned because as that point the body had not been identified. When the inquest re-opened two

The Working Lads' Institute

The Working Lads' Institute was founded by a city merchant named Henry Hill to provide young working lads with an ennobling alternative to the corrupting influence of the music halls and pubs. There were various educational classes, a library, a fully equipped gymnasium and a swimming pool with a qualified instructor. The original site was at 12 Mount Place, off Whitechapel Road, and was opened in 1878, but the club moved to 137 Whitechapel Road in 1885. Towards the turn of the century, lack of funds threatened it with closure but the Reverend Thomas Jackson stepped into the breach, and under his auspices The Working Lads' Institute widened its brief to include the homeless and friendless lads who had no job, employment having hitherto been a prerequisite of membership. Gradually the focus moved away from providing education to social care and welfare. It moved out of the premises to Whitechapel House, Tulse Hill, in the mid-1940s and closed down for good in 1973 following a compulsory purchase order two years earlier.

The Whitechapel Murders inquests were held in the Alexandra Room, as the lecture room and library was called. As well as Martha Tabram's inquest, those of Mary Ann Nichols, Annie Chapman, Alice McKenzie and Frances Coles were held there. The room was described in one newspaper as "well and prettily furnished", the walls displaying landscapes and portraits of the Royal Family, with one particularly magnificent portrait of the Princess of Wales (Alexandra, wife of future King Edward VII) by Louis Fleischmann hanging above the seat occupied by the coroner.

RIGHT: The Whitechapel Working Lads' Institute on Whitechapel Road. The building survives to this day but is now a shop with private apartments above.

weeks later, public interest had diminished somewhat and after testimony from a handful of witnesses, mostly concerning the identification, character and history of Martha and how her body had been discovered, the jury returned a verdict of "wilful murder against some person or persons unknown" and asked that the stairs in George Yard Buildings and similar properties be lighted until after 11:00 p.m.

The police quickly came in for criticism, as they would throughout the Ripper investigation, and it is difficult to decide whether it was justified or not. The *Eastern Post* observed: "A considerable amount of mystery surrounds the whole affair, which the police have entirely failed to unravel, and the evidence they have been able to obtain has been very meagre indeed. No arrest has been made, and it would seem that as usual the 'clever' detective officers have been relying upon some of the same miserable class of the wretched victim to 'give them the clue'." While Walter Dew would dismiss these criticisms as grossly unfair, claiming that hundreds of enquiries were made, scores of statements taken, and hours of work put in every day, the fact is that the authorities had precious little to work with.

The police themselves were, for the most part, responsible for what we know of their investigation, and we know so little partly because the official records have been destroyed over the years, but also because the police refused to talk to the press. The newspapers complained about this and Walter Dew confirmed that the police kept the Press "at arm's length", a policy dictated by those on high and one which Dew thought a mistake because it turned an ally into an enemy. The fact remains that the police investigation went nowhere.

The only known line of inquiry they possessed was that provided by Mary Ann Connolly, but it petered out and Connolly herself proved difficult, unpredictable and ultimately unreliable. Whether or not the police confirmed her story about having been drinking that night with Martha and two soldiers is not known. On 24 September, two weeks after the murder, Inspector Reid wrote in a report that "inquiries" were made to find some other person who saw the deceased and Pearly Poll with the privates

on the night of the 6th but without success…". No corroborating witnesses were reported in the press or called to the inquest, so it would appear that the truth of Connolly's story was never established. Of course, it was a busy night, the end of a bank holiday, the pubs probably full and noisy and the staff very busy, so perhaps the two women and their soldier companions could have passed unnoticed. Or possibly Connolly told a concocted story just to get her five minutes of fame, and she may have disappeared when she recognized the gravity of what she had done, with her subsequent antics at the identification parades a sort of self-defence bravado.

The fury of the attack on Martha Tabram, and the focus of the knife wounds, indicate that this was not a "casual" killing. It has the look and feel of a Ripper crime, albeit one without the mutilation that would characterize later victims.

BELOW: Commercial Street Police Station, situated on a triangle of land between Commercial Street, Elder Street and Fleur-de-Lis Street, was the most prominent station in the Whitechapel case after Leman Street Police Station. In 1888 the top storey did not exist, this being added in 1906. It was closed around 1970 and now houses apartments.

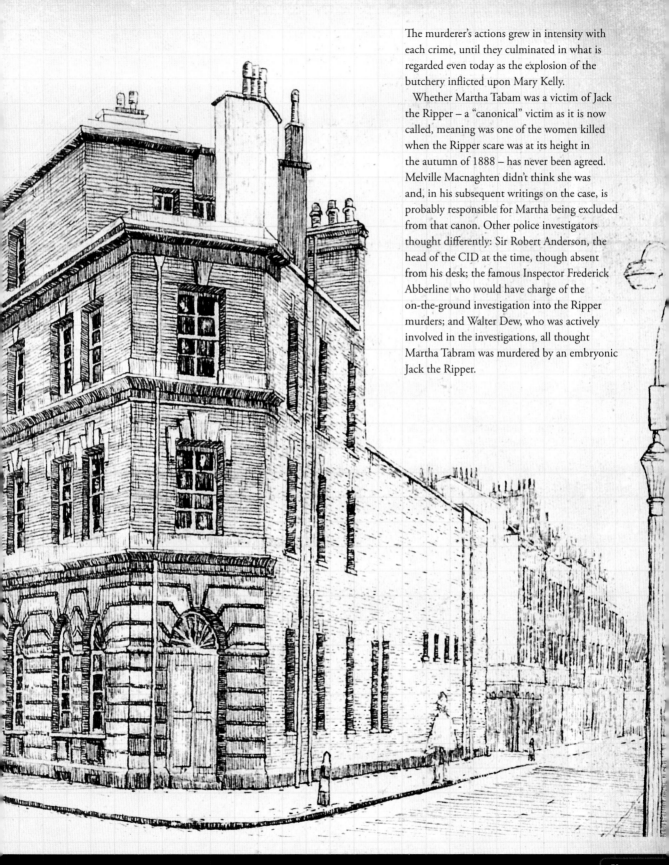

The murderer's actions grew in intensity with each crime, until they culminated in what is regarded even today as the explosion of the butchery inflicted upon Mary Kelly.

Whether Martha Tabam was a victim of Jack the Ripper – a "canonical" victim as it is now called, meaning was one of the women killed when the Ripper scare was at its height in the autumn of 1888 – has never been agreed. Melville Macnaghten didn't think she was and, in his subsequent writings on the case, is probably responsible for Martha being excluded from that canon. Other police investigators thought differently: Sir Robert Anderson, the head of the CID at the time, though absent from his desk; the famous Inspector Frederick Abberline who would have charge of the on-the-ground investigation into the Ripper murders; and Walter Dew, who was actively involved in the investigations, all thought Martha Tabram was murdered by an embryonic Jack the Ripper.

MARY ANN NICHOLS

EAGLE

Briefing

The murder of Mary Ann Nichols on 31 August 1888
drove home the commonalities of the victims of these
unusual attacks. They were undoubtedly of the same
class, coming from respectable origins but doomed
to fail by their circumstances and a proclivity for
alcohol. They appeared to be attracted to the East End
by the availability of cheap lodgings and all lodged
within a few yards of each other. Nichols, like Emma
Smith and Martha Tabram before her, had been reduced
to a life of day-to-day survival and with little or
no other options, had taken to the streets. They were
incredibly vulnerable and the places they chose to
operate were dangerous by their isolation. If these
murders were by the same hand, the killer had chosen
his target, and it was certainly an easy one.

LEFT: Buck's Row, viewed from the rear of the Board School. Left to right are Essex Wharf, the Browne and Eagle warehouses and New Cottage. Directly below are the tracks of the East London Railway.

OVERLEAF: The area surrounding Ducking Pond Row, later Buck's Row, as seen in John Roque's famous map of 1746. To the east of the White Chapel Mount is a large area of bare land that before long would be home to the London Hospital.

DEPRIVING PEOPLE OF THEIR FREEDOM AS A form of punishment is a relatively new concept; punishment in the past was usually brutal and swift, such as hanging. Other punishments were intended to be painful, such as being flogged, while a third category of punishment, reserved for less-serious crimes, was intended to humiliate the criminal, which could be very effective in a small community where everyone knew each other. A contraption known as a ducking stool was used for one of these humiliation punishments, often reserved for women (particularly acid-tongued wives) but also for people guilty of minor offences such as food adulteration. It was a seat upon which a person would be secured and then lowered into a river or pond, and held under the water until they almost drowned. There was once such a ducking pond on White Cap Green, an area of open land behind what is now Whitechapel Underground Station. It disappeared in the early years of the nineteenth century, but was recalled in the name of a nondescript little street, short and narrow, running between Brady Street and Baker's Row (today's Vallance Road). Called Ducking Pond Row, the name was corrupted over time to Duck's Row and then Buck's Row. Today it is known as Durward Street and in recent years it has been the subject of considerable redevelopment so that it is now almost impossible to imagine being beside a rippling pond sparkling in the sunlight, surrounded by fields, with a group of villagers hooting and jeering and laughing as an errant neighbour is lowered on a stool to disappear beneath the brackish water, then brought out spluttering, gasping for breath. Indeed, the area has changed so much that it is even difficult to imagine the chilly pre-dawn morning in 1888 when a discovery was made in Buck's Row that would resonate into the twenty-first century.

Buck's Row, on the whole, was considered to be a respectable street, inhabited by poor but honest working class folk. The north side was dominated by tall wool warehouses belonging to Brown and Eagle. At its western end stood Essex Wharf, the name embossed in the red brickwork on the side. This handsome building, narrow where it faced the street and expanding considerably over the land behind it, was not a wharf in the traditional sense of fronting a river or canal, but was instead the terminus of train tracks for a nearby coal depot. On the south side, at the corner with Brady Street was a beer house called the Roebuck, an unremarkable three-storey building typical of many corner pubs in the area. From the Roebuck there ran a long terrace of small two-up, two-down cottages that had been built in the mid-nineteenth century, presumably to house the workers of what was a rapidly developing industrial community. A pavement, no more than a metre (3 ft) wide, separated their front doors from the narrow road, which was maybe 6 m (20 ft) wide at the most, and their front windows were almost perpetually left in shadows by the warehouse walls opposite. The row of cottages ended in wooden gates about 2.5–3 m (8–10 ft) high fronting a stable yard known as Brown's, alongside which was a brick wall that concealed the long drop down to the tracks of the East London Railway below. Finally, the wall terminated at a large and imposing building that dominated the street and the skyline. This was the Buck's Row Board School, constructed in 1876 to replace an earlier incarnation whose playground, thanks to the restrictive space around the property, was situated on the roof, surrounded by tall iron railings.

At approximately 3:40 a.m. on 31 August

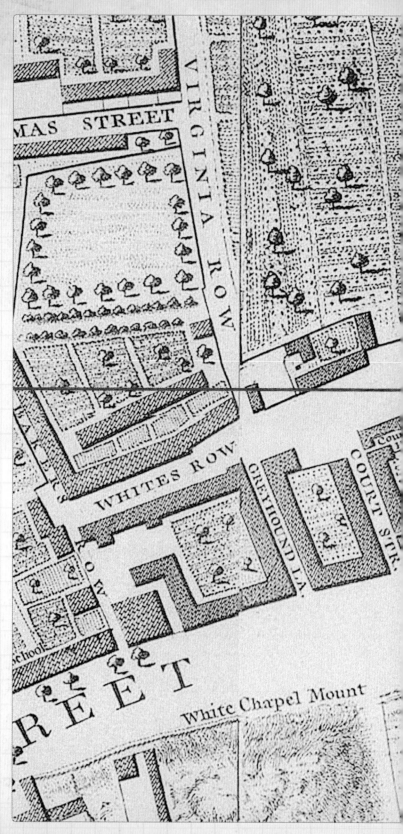

Ducking Pond

DUCKING POND ROW

Yorkshire Cᵒ

DUCKING POND LA

MILE END

MILE END

LEFT: Durward Street looking east in 1968. Nearly all the buildings in this view were nearing the end of their life at that time and would be demolished within a few years.

1888, Charles Cross was walking from Brady Street along the north side of Buck's Row on his way to work and in the pre-dawn gloom he saw something against the gates of Brown's stable yard, which he first took to be a bundled tarpaulin. Thinking it could be something of use to him, he crossed the narrow street, but as he did so he realized that it was the body of a woman. As Cross reached the middle of the road he heard the footsteps of another man approaching along the pavement behind him. He waited for him to get nearer, then said, "Come and look over here, there's a woman." This second man, whose name was Robert Paul and who was also on his way to work, looked startled and then perhaps a little wary, but he nevertheless joined Cross in a brief examination of the body. There was a street light nearby, but it didn't illuminate much in the murkiness of the little thoroughfare. The woman was on her back with her arms by her sides; her skirts had been drawn up almost to the waist and lying

close by was the woman's bonnet. Cross touched the woman's hands. They were cold and limp. "I believe she's dead," he said. Paul, touching her face and thinking it slightly warm, sought a heartbeat and thought he detected a very faint movement. "I think she's breathing," he said, "but it's very little if she is." There was nothing more they could do and after rearranging her skirts to give her a little dignity, they went on their way, agreeing to look for a policeman as they did so.

They had left the little street for no more than what must have been a few minutes when PC John Neil, 975J, patrolling his beat, entered Buck's Row from Thomas Street. Neil was a constable from J-division, a recently created division of the Metropolitan Police which served Bethnal Green and although Buck's Row was most definitely in Whitechapel, it ran just within J-division's jurisdiction. His beat – a circuit which included Whitechapel Road, Baker's Row, White's Row, Buck's

OPPOSITE: Buck's Row Board School, with the Nichols murder site marked by the gap in the fencing. By the time this photo was taken in 1990, the street and the school had been derelict for nearly two decades.

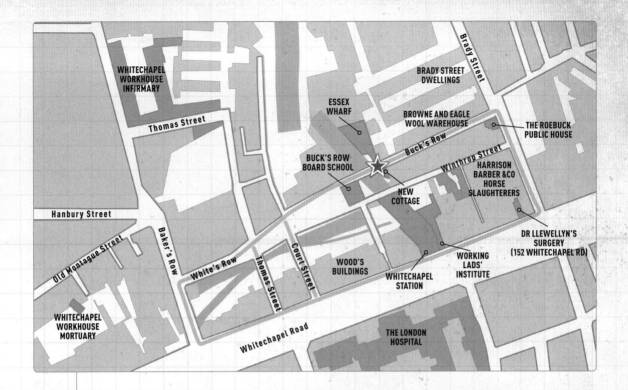

ABOVE: Map of
the Buck's Row
neighbourhood. The
blue line marks the beat
of PC John Neil on the
night of 31 August 1888.

 Murder Site

OPPOSITE: Buck's
Row looking east.
The handsome brick
building of Essex
Wharf is on the left,
New Cottage directly
opposite.

BACKGROUND INTELLIGENCE

Blitz and Rebuilding

The terrace of workers' cottages which made up the south side of Buck's Row ended in a slightly different dwelling known as New Cottage, so named as it was constructed around 1876 when the last few houses on the end of the terrace were removed to make way for the new East London Railway that ran beneath street level. Buck's Row was renamed Durward Street on 25 October 1892 following a petition by the residents to have the name changed to escape the notoriety of the Whitechapel Murders. It remains the only site where a change of title was a direct response to the Ripper crimes.

During the Second World War, a bomb landed close to New Cottage, also inflicting heavy damage to Whitechapel Underground Station. Other properties in neighbouring Winthrop Street were also affected and several had to be partially rebuilt. New Cottage was not so fortunate and was so badly damaged that it had to be torn down. In its place for many years was an empty piece of fenced-off land upon which a garage was finally constructed in the mid-1960s.

In 1970 the former Brown and Eagle warehouses on the north side were demolished.

In the meantime, the cottages had been deemed unfit for human habitation and after being cleared by 1971, they were torn down one bleak grey January day in 1972. The Roebuck pub on the corner with Brady Street survived, as did Essex Wharf, which for many years was gainfully occupied by S. Rosenberger & Coates Ltd., but the Board School closed in 1915 and was used as a warehouse for many years afterwards, eventually becoming disused and derelict. Essex Wharf followed suit and both were in a terrible state for many years. The desolation of the former Buck's Row was to last for decades; vandals eventually burnt out the school building, which became the haunt of vagrants, and for many years it remained a scene of gross urban neglect. Essex Wharf was finally demolished in 1990.

Redevelopment came in the mid 1990s with the north side becoming home to Swanlea School and the Whitechapel Sports Centre. After the demolition of the Roebuck, the south side soon gained new apartments and in 1996, the former Board School, thankfully saved, was converted into flats. It is now called Trinity Hall.

CORONER

CONSTABLE NEIL

FINDING THE BODY IN BUCK'S ROW

OPPOSITE: Lurid press illustrations like this showing the discovery of Mary Ann Nichols' body in Buck's Row, would soon become commonplace throughout the autumn of 1888.

RIGHT: A contemporary press sketch of PC John Neil.

Row and Brady Street, with occasional forays into Thomas and Court Streets (two short thoroughfares which linked the backstreets to the main road) – took him 30 minutes to walk. On passing through Buck's Row at 3:15 a.m., PC Neil had seen nothing untoward and all seemed quiet. On his next pass, he saw the bundle outside the stable gates and in the light from his lantern he could see something that Cross and Paul had failed to notice in the gloom; blood was oozing from a nasty gash to the throat. In the quiet of that Friday morning, Neil could hear the tread of another policeman passing the Brady Street entrance to Buck's Row and he flashed his light to signal for assistance. It was a PC Thain, 96J, and as he drew near PC Neil recognized him. "For God's sake, Jack, go fetch a doctor," said PC Neil, and Thain dutifully ran off to fetch Dr Rees Llewellyn from his surgery at 152 Whitechapel Road,

BACKGROUND INTELLIGENCE

Dr Ralph Rees Llewellyn (1850-1921)

The life of Dr Rees Ralph Llewellyn presents a good example of the fact that not all who lived in Whitechapel were doomed to spend their lives in poverty or gruelling labour. He was born in Whitechapel itself, the eldest son of Welsh medical practitioner Llewellyn Llewellyn, and the surgery at 152 Whitechapel Road was also the family home. Rees lived there for much of his life and following his mother's early death, went on to follow in his father's footsteps, as did his younger brother Walter. Qualified as an MRCS (Member of the Royal College of Surgeons) and LRCP (Licentiate of the Royal College of Physicians), by 1888 he had become the medical officer to the East and East Central London districts. It appears that Dr Llewellyn never married and lived most of his life with his siblings, first at the surgery in Whitechapel and later in Stamford Hill where he and Walter shared a medical practice. Stamford Hill, in north London, was then a desirable suburb on the fringes of Hackney with fine houses and was no doubt a place of choice for those with a better quality of life and of course, income. Llewellyn died there in 1921, but was buried at Tower Hamlets Cemetery, back in the heart of the district where he had served most of his years.

ABOVE: Dr Rees Ralph Llewellyn, seen here in a contemporary press illustration.

almost on the corner with Brady Street and no more than 275 m (300 yards) away.

While waiting for Dr Llewellyn to arrive, Neil was joined at the scene by three men, Charles Bretton, Henry Tomkins and James Mumford. They were employees at Harrison Barber and Co, a horse slaughterer's in nearby Winthrop Street. Mumford had spoken to PC Thain who informed him that a murder had taken place in Buck's Row and he and the two other men obviously felt compelled to satisfy their curiosity. While they were there they were joined by Patrick Mulshaw, a night-watchman who was guarding some sewage works behind the Working Lads' Institute. He had seen various constables during the night (including Neil) and although he had occasionally dozed off during his shift, he stressed that he was awake between 3:00 and 4:00 a.m. and heard nothing out of the ordinary. It was a mysterious passer-by who alerted Mulshaw to the crime; apparently, a man walked past him and said "Watchman, old man, I believe somebody is murdered down the street." The identity of this man was never ascertained.

By this time Cross and Paul had met up with PC Jonas Mizen, 56H, on the corner of Baker's Row and Hanbury Street and had informed him of their earlier discovery. On his arrival in Buck's Row he found PC Neil at the scene who, still obliged by regulations to stay with the body, instructed Mizen to fetch an ambulance. Neil was soon joined by Sergeant Henry Kirby and they woke the occupants of Essex Wharf, a man named Walter Purkiss and his family, and New Cottage, where a widow named Emma Green lived with her two sons and a daughter. Walter Purkiss's wife, Mary Ann, claimed to have been pacing her room (which overlooked the murder site) at the crucial hour. Emma Green claimed to be a light sleeper, yet nobody had heard anything unusual, and as the grey fingers of new dawn began to illuminate the murder scene, Neil looked to see if there was any evidence of wheel tracks or any suggestion that the body had been brought to Buck's Row. He saw nothing to suggest anything other than that the woman had been murdered where she lay.

Dr Llewellyn's examination of the body was typically cursory as he was required to do little more than establish that the woman was dead,

which he quickly did. The body was then lifted onto the ambulance – basically a hand-cart – and taken to the small workhouse mortuary in Eagle Place, off Old Montague Street. PC Thain, who got a lot of blood on his hands when lifting the corpse into the ambulance, noticed that there was blood on the back of the body but assumed that this had run down from the neck. He also observed a spot of congealed blood about 15 cm (6 in) in diameter which had run towards the gutter. This blood was washed away by Emma Green's son James, who threw a bucket of water over it.

The mortuary was closed and the door was locked, so the body was left on the hand-cart in the yard while the keys were obtained and the doors unlocked by a pauper inmate of the Whitechapel Workhouse named Robert Mann. The body was then placed on a slab on the floor, where at 6:30 a.m. Mann and another inmate of the workhouse, James Hatfield, stripped and washed it. Only then was the full extent of the terrible injuries discovered…

In the opinion of Dr Llewellyn, who with his assistant conducted the post-mortem, the murderer had faced the woman. He observed that bruising on her face seemed consistent with the murderer having forced back her head with his right hand, while he swiftly sliced her throat with a knife held in his left. There were two cuts in the throat: one was 10 cm (4 in) long and the other was 20 cm (8 in) long. The second wound cut all the tissue down to the vertebrae, from which it could be deduced that the knife was pointed and sharp, though the blade need not have been very long. This much had been visible when Dr Llewellyn had originally examined the body, but what nobody had realized until then and, what was particularly horrific, were the severe abdominal mutilations. The East End was a violent place and, while the shocking attacks upon Emma Smith and Martha Tabram had sent ripples of outrage throughout the immediate area, the injuries inflicted upon this woman put her murder into an altogether different category. On her left side there was a very deep and jagged wound and there were several incisions running across the abdomen. On the right side there were three or four downward cuts. All these injuries, according to Llewellyn's initial observations, appeared to be

PREVIOUS PAGES: The murder site in Buck's Row. Nichols' body was found in front of the wooden gates to Brown's stable yard and its proximity to the upstairs bedroom window of Mrs Emma Green at neighbouring New Cottage can be clearly seen.

OVERLEAF: Buck's Row looking west. The railings on top of the huge Board School contained the school playground, which by necessity was on the roof.

The Mortuary

Perhaps less surprising than it would seem, the overcrowded neighbourhoods of Whitechapel and Spitalfields offered the most rudimentary and unsatisfactory mortuary facilities. The Whitechapel Workhouse Mortuary was situated off Old Montague Street and, accessible via gates from narrow Eagle Place, was little more than a shed. The workhouse itself was some distance away in Baker's Row, but the location of the mortuary was a hangover from the days when it was actually attached to the former workhouse buildings in Whitechapel Road.

Attention to crime scenes and the examination of murder victims in the 1880s were significantly less thorough than today. Crime scenes were not always sealed off and in some cases, members of the public were able to loiter near a body as the police conducted their enquiries. The presence of the three slaughtermen from Winthrop Street at the scene of Mary Ann Nichols' murder is testament to the differing standards of the day. But if such access was deemed tacitly acceptable, the conditions at the mortuary were considered anything but.

It was described by the *East London Observer* on 1 September 1888 as "a little brick building situated to the right of the large yard used by the Board of Works for the storage of their material..." and on occasion, concern was voiced by some owing to its proximity to a playground used by adjacent Davenant Foundation School. The conditions were again brought up during the inquests into the later Ripper murders when Dr George Bagster Phillips made his point:

It was under great difficulty he could make his examination, and, as on many occasions he had met with similar difficulties, he now raised his protest, as he had previously done, that members in his profession should be called upon to perform their duties in these inadequate circumstances. There were no adequate conveniences for a post-mortem examination; and at particular seasons of the year it was dangerous to the operator.

As well as the bodies of Martha Tabram and Mary Ann Nichols, Annie Chapman (see chapters 3 and 5) and later suspected Ripper victims Alice McKenzie and Frances Coles (see chapter 10) were also taken here. Extensions to the Davenant School were built over the site in 1898 and today, a small pathway between 1980s housing covers the site.

ABOVE: A contemporary press illustration showing the entrance to the Whitechapel Workhouse Mortuary in Eagle Place, off Old Montague Street. Its inappropriate setting, next to a school playground and inhabited tenements, was a cause for concern.

Wilmott's and The White House

Wilmott's was first registered on 12 May 1852 when it was owned by Patrick Henley; George Wilmott took over in November 1863 for a mere three years. He also acquired lodging houses at Nos.11–15 Thrawl Street. He then took ownership of No.18 again in 1870 but passed it on to Joseph Davies two years later, although he kept his other properties until 1891.

A modest-sized house (when compared with other such places in the area), Wilmott's was registered to hold approximately 70 residents. The owner in 1888 was actually Alfred Wood, although the name Wilmott's was obviously retained for many years thereafter. Frances Coles, who became a much-debated victim of the Ripper in 1891 (see chapter 10), was reported to have been living at Wilmott's in July 1889.

Wilmott's survived the redevelopment of the eastern end of Thrawl Street in the early twentieth century – Keate House was built on the south-east corner with George Street in 1908, on the site of lodging houses at 16 and 17 Thrawl Street, but No.18 appears to have been converted into two smaller properties, listed as 18 and 18A. It did not, however, survive the redevelopments of the 1970s.

The White House at 56 Flower and Dean Street, immortalized in a photograph that appeared in *Living London* in 1901, allowed men and women to sleep together, raising suspicion that it was little more than a brothel. First registered on 25 September 1861, it was owned by James Smith

of 48 Flower and Dean Street. It was taken over in January 1883 by his son John, with ownership reverting back to James in July 1884. The lodging house survived when the north side of Flower and Dean Street was demolished in 1891 to make way for Nathaniel Dwellings, which opened the following year. Along with a large lodging house at No.5 (on the opposite side of the street) that was part of 19 Brick Lane, No.56 later became known as Smith's Chambers. The property was demolished in 1975.

ABOVE: An 1891 press illustration of Wilmott's Lodging House in Thrawl Street, home of Mary Ann Nichols and at some point in the future, potential Ripper victim Frances Coles.

---

have been made with a sharp knife by a left-handed man, had taken four or five minutes to inflict, had been done after death, and were done by someone who had some rough anatomical knowledge.

Among the bundle of clothing taken from the woman's body, no more than a pile of old rags in the opinion of one journalist, was a petticoat marked "Lambeth Workhouse P.R", which meant that it had come from the Lambeth's workhouse in Princess Road. Lambeth Workhouse was something of a notorious establishment, having been the subject of a controversial exposé by the journalist James Greenwood in a series of articles in the campaigning newspaper, the *Pall Mall Gazette*,

OPPOSITE: Durward Street looking east from the murder site in 1961. At the end can be seen Brady Street, from where PC John Thain was attracted by PC Neil's lamp signal.

in the mid-1860s. Commissioned to write the articles by his brother Frederick, the then editor of the newspaper, James had disguised himself as a pauper and entered Lambeth workhouse for a night in January 1866. His revelations of the squalid conditions, neglect and maladministration he encountered in the 14 hours he stayed there caused a sensation and the exposé is recognized even today as an example of pioneering undercover journalism. The Princess Road workhouse had ceased to be the main Lambeth workhouse, however, in 1887–88 as a new establishment had been built in Renfrew Road and all who were able-bodied were transferred there. The aged and infirm remained at Princess Road, which was refurbished and reopened during 1887–1888. The 200 men and 150 women moved back to Princess Road encountered a particularly harsh regime. In 1895 Charles and Sydney Chaplin, with their mother, were inmates there for a short while before their mother was committed to Cane Hill Lunatic Asylum and the children transferred to Hanwell School for Orphans and Destitute Children. Charles, of course, went on to be the great star of silent comedy.

The Matron of the workhouse was brought in to view the woman's body but she failed to recognize it. Nonetheless, it was later established that the woman had been a resident at the workhouse many times over the years. One of a stream of visitors who went to the mortuary that day recognized the deceased as a woman named Polly who lived at 18 Thrawl Street, Spitalfields, a doss-house commonly known as Wilmott's. People from the lodging house were brought to the mortuary and although several people recognized the body as that of Polly, it was not until the evening that a young woman named Mary Ann Monk came from Wilmott's and rather haughtily identified the body as that of Mary Ann Nichols, with whom she had been an inmate of the Lambeth Workhouse some six or seven years previously. According to Monk, they

had last seen each other in mid July 1888 when they drank together in a pub on New Kent Road, south London.

Mary Ann Nichols was 1.57 m (5 ft 2 in) tall, had a dark complexion, brown hair which was turning grey, and brown eyes, and her teeth, some of which were missing, were a little discoloured. Her features were small and delicate and she had high cheekbones and a youthful appearance, which despite her condition, made her look ten years younger than her 43 years of age. Friends spoke of her cleanliness, her reticence to discuss her past and her general air of melancholy. Her only possessions when she died were a comb, a small white handkerchief and a piece of broken mirror.

Born on 26 August 1845, she was the daughter of a blacksmith named Edward Walker and the second of his three children. She had married a printer named William Nichols at St Bride's Fleet Street in 1864 and together they had five children between 1866 and 1879, but the marriage had been marked by a series of separations and finally collapsed for good in 1880. William Nichols later attributed their marital troubles to Mary Ann's heavy drinking. Her own father acknowledged that Mary Ann drank heavily, but claimed that the marriage

---

BACKGROUND INTELLIGENCE   ## The Frying Pan

The Frying Pan pub stood at 207 Brick Lane on the northern corner of Brick Lane and Thrawl Street and although the current building dates from around 1891, records show that the pub itself goes back to at least 1811 when the owner was an Ann Pybus of 22 Red Lion Street, Spitalfields. In the late nineteenth century it was renumbered as 13 Brick Lane and, perhaps owing to its proximity to the notorious doss-houses of Thrawl Street and its environs, was known for its clientele of prostitutes, a state of affairs that apparently continued into the twentieth century. The landlord in 1888 was William Farrow and the pub was owned by Truman, Hanbury, Buxton & Co, the famous brewery which sat at the northern end of Brick Lane. Owing to its less than salubrious location, the Frying Pan appeared in several Old Bailey criminal cases; one significant incident

took place in 1862 when five men and two women were convicted of stealing money from the then landlord, James King. King had left a bag of money and various other valuables in his upstairs room only to find that the room had been rifled through and everything taken while the staff were downstairs working and the pub was still open. These items exceeded the sum of £500, which would be the equivalent today of around £30,000!

The interior of the Frying Pan was significantly altered in 1966 and it eventually closed its doors for the last time in 1991. It was swiftly converted into a balti restaurant, The Sheraz, but the original name – as Ye Olde Frying Pan – can still be seen in the terracotta relief design at the top of the building. The restaurant owners, aware of the brief link to the Ripper murders, mention the connection with Mary Ann Nichols' alleged visit in their menu.

came to an end after William Nichols took up with another woman, and it was noticeable that the couple's eldest son would have nothing to do with his father at his mother's funeral. Whatever the truth was, Mary Ann Nichols left her family and in September 1880 went into Lambeth Workhouse.

The workhouse would be her home on and off for several years, the known exceptions being a brief sojourn with her father early in 1883, when her drinking caused friction and precipitated her eventual departure. She also had a relationship with a man named Thomas Stuart Drew, apparently a beau before her marriage to Walker who had been recently widowed. This relationship ended in 1887 and at the end of that year, when she was discovered destitute and sleeping rough in Trafalgar Square, Mary

Ann was again sent to Lambeth Workhouse. A possible new future opened before her because the Matron of the Workhouse, Sarah Fielder, found Mary Ann a job as a domestic servant with Samuel and Sarah Cowdry at Ingleside, Rose Hill, Wandsworth. It was an opportunity for Mary Ann to start life afresh and in a letter to her father she wrote expressing her pleasure at the job:

I just write to say you will be glad to know that I am settled in my new place, and going all right up to now. My people went out yesterday and have not returned, so I am left in charge. It is a grand place inside, with trees and gardens back and front. All has been newly done up. They are teetotallers and religious so I ought to get on. They are very nice people, and I have not too much to do. I

OPPOSITE: Women and children relax on the pavement in front of No. 56 Flower and Dean Street, the notorious "White House", circa1902. It is very likely that the adults in this photograph were prostitutes.

RIGHT: The corner of Whitechapel Road and Osborn Street, circa 1890, where Ellen Holland met Mary Ann Nichols at approximately 2:30 a.m. on the morning of 31 August 1888. Little over an hour later, Nichols was dead.

RIGHT: Whitechapel Road in 1899, showing the haymarket. The obelisk proved to be an obstruction to motorized traffic in the early twentieth century and was later removed.

hope you are all right and the boy has work.
So good bye for the present.
from yours truly,
Polly

Sadly, for reasons unknown, but perhaps easily guessed at, she stole clothing worth more than £3 (about £177 today) and absconded.

She very soon afterwards sank into the stews of the East End, living at Wilmott's at 18 Thrawl Street, where she shared a room with three other women, one named Emily Holland. On 24 August, she stayed the night at a doss-house known as The White House at 56 Flower and Dean Street.

Thursday, 30 August 1888, dawned bright and warm, a very welcome change to the bad weather of that appalling summer, but as the morning progressed the skies began to hint in a very foreboding manner that it would not last. Soon after noon they darkened threateningly, and when a storm broke over London at 2:30 p.m. it was dramatic. Loud explosions of thunder and extremely vivid flashes of lightning accompanied a torrential downpour that was unremitting for several hours. It was so bad in some parts of the country that there was severe flooding which left several families homeless. How Mary Ann Nichols spent that afternoon isn't known for certain, but it was probably in the local pubs. Indeed, according to a report made by an Inspector Helson, Mary Ann was seen leaving a pub on the corner of Thrawl Street and Brick Lane called The Frying Pan at

OPPOSITE: The Frying Pan pub on the corner of Brick Lane and Thrawl Street, from which Nichols was reported to have been seen emerging on the morning of her death.

about 12:30 a.m. on 31 August This was the only account of such a sighting and one must assume that, as it appeared in a police report, the information may have been the result of on-the-ground enquiries made soon after the murder. Between 1:20 and 1:40 a.m. Mary Ann Nichols was in the kitchen at Wilmott's and had been warming herself by the communal fire when she was approached by the lodging house deputy and asked for the 4d for her bed. Nichols didn't have the money and the deputy told her that she knew the rules and would have to leave. Apparently a little worse for drink, she appeared to be unconcerned and according to one newspaper said, "I'll soon get my doss money. See what a jolly bonnet I've got now." She indicated a little black bonnet which nobody had seen before and which in a few hours would be lying on the ground next to her fingertips in Buck's Row.

Earlier that evening there had been a fire at the London docks in nearby Wapping. The docks had been closed at 4:00 p.m. as was customary and there were few people around. At about 8:30 p.m., somebody smelled burning and shortly afterwards there was an immense burst of flames from the top of one of the huge South Quay Warehouses in the centre of the docks. Some 137 m (150 yards) long, its ground floors were stacked from floor to ceiling with brandy and gin, and through the iron-barred windows a raging furnace could be seen within. Fierce explosions followed, accompanied by huge

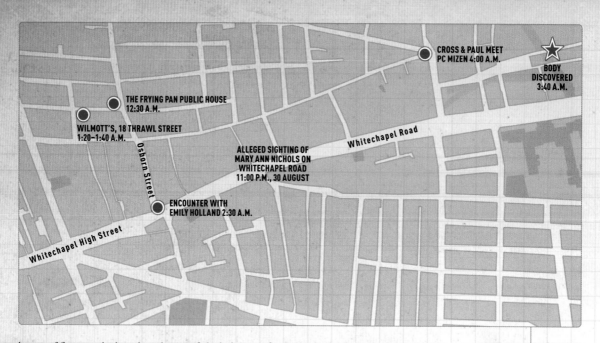

CROSS & PAUL MEET
PC MIZEN 4:00 A.M.

BODY
DISCOVERED
3:40 A.M.

THE FRYING PAN PUBLIC HOUSE
12:30 A.M.

WILMOTT'S, 18 THRAWL STREET
1:20–1:40 A.M.

Osborn Street

ALLEGED SIGHTING OF
MARY ANN NICHOLS ON
WHITECHAPEL ROAD
11:00 P.M., 30 AUGUST

Whitechapel Road

ENCOUNTER WITH
EMILY HOLLAND 2:30 A.M.

Whitechapel High Street

bursts of flame as the barrels and cases of alcohol fuelled the conflagration. Upwards of a dozen fire streamers on the Thames fired cascades of water at the building, battling to contain the blaze before it spread. By 11:00 p.m., the fierceness of the fire had diminished sufficiently for it to be seen that in a few hours it would be extinguished altogether, and by midnight several of the fire engines, their crews exhausted, were returning to their stations. But then the alarm was raised that another and even worse fire had broken out at the Ratcliffe Dry Dock. That fire started in a warehouse belonging to J F Gibb and Co. It was stuffed to the gills with flammable material and it was not long before the flames had leapt across to the masts and rigging of the *Cornuvia*, a vessel moored nearby, and to a large warehouse some 37 m x 14 m (120 ft x 45 ft) containing 726 tonnes (800 tons) of coal! It caught quickly and threw out an enormous heat. Gallon s of water seemed as first to have no effect. Various surrounding buildings were damaged, some badly, and it was only the efforts of the firemen that prevented their complete destruction. Other buildings were damaged by smoke and water. These fires provided a wonderful free entertainment and thousands of people came from miles around to stand and gawp. Watching the glow of the blaze from as far away as Holloway in North London was a man named John Pizer, who in a few days

was famously destined to get caught up in the Jack the Ripper story. Closer to the unfolding events was Mary Ann Nichols' friend from the doss-house, Emily Holland.

At about 2:30 a.m., Emily was returning home from the fires when she turned into Osborn Street, as Emma Smith had done so fatefully a few months earlier (see chapter 2). Mary Ann was coming towards her, she was staggering somewhat and appeared to be quite drunk, and as she got to the corner of Osborn Street and Whitechapel Road, she slumped against the wall of a grocer's shop. Emily stopped and they chatted for a few minutes. Emily tried to persuade Nichols to return with her to Wilmott's, assuring her that she'd be able to get her a bed on the promise of having the necessary funds later, but Mary Ann seemed confident that she would quickly find someone with a willing 4d. The couple parted and Nichols turned into the broad thoroughfare of Whitechapel Road, walking east.

The police report that claimed that Mary Ann was seen leaving The Frying Pan also stated that she had been seen walking along Whitechapel Road at about 11:00 p.m. that night, and was possibly soliciting. It is quite possible that, knowing the places off the main road where she could hopefully earn her night's doss-money, she returned. Whatever the case, after meeting Emily Holland, Mary Ann Nichols would never be seen alive again.

ABOVE: Map of the area traversed by Mary Ann Nichols during her last hours.

★ Murder Site
● Key Location

OPPOSITE: The mortuary photograph of Mary Ann Nichols.

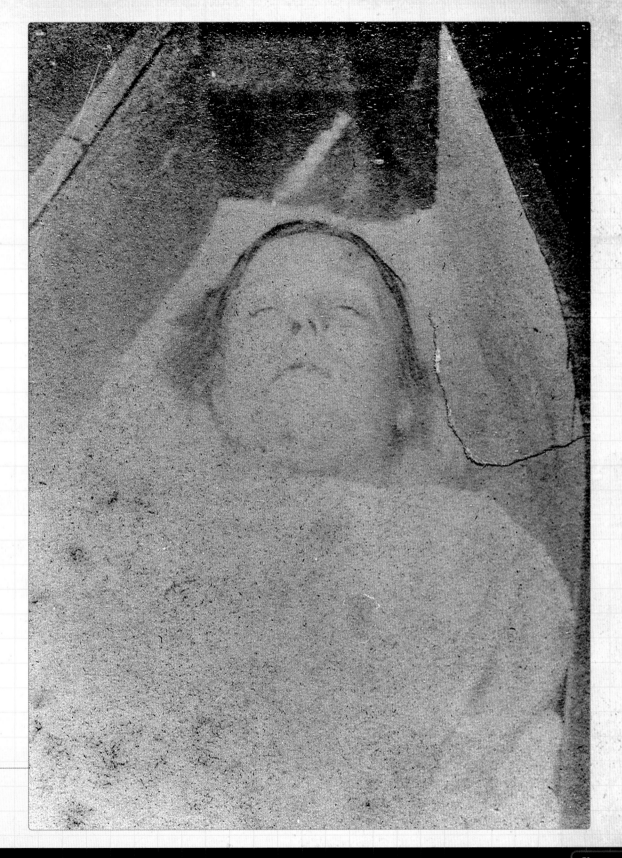

The next murder by the "Whitechapel fiend" was a turning point in the case. Although the circumstances of the victim were similar to those that had gone before, the scene and timing of the crime demonstrated an increased daring and the injuries inflicted on the poor woman were of unprecedented violence. The East End reeled from these events and with the idea that a maniac was on the loose now well and truly accepted by both the public and the authorities alike, panic and fear replaced the existing apprehension. The press, both domestic and international, responded accordingly, reporting and commenting in a way that fed that fear.

LEFT: Hanbury Street looking west towards Commercial Street. The turning on the right is John Street, home of John Richardson.

BELOW: John and Annie Chapman, photographed circa 1869, the year of their wedding. This remains the only published image of any of the Whitechapel murder victims when alive.

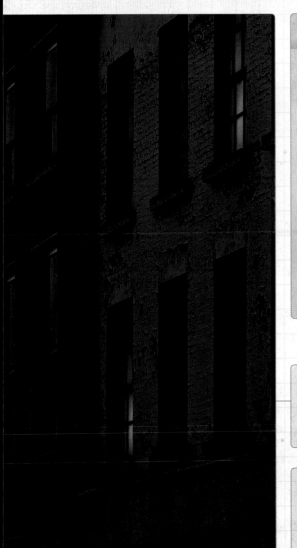

HANBURY STREET, WHERE ANNIE CHAPMAN was murdered, been known previously as Lolesworth Lane. That's what it was called in about 1648 when a document of that time described it as "newly named or known", but it soon became known as Brown's Lane after a prominent resident named William Brown who owned three houses, a yard, two sheds, a cow-house, a garden and an orchard there. He also rented a large open field which he probably used for pasture and which was known as Lolesworth Field. It, too, had an alternative name, Spital Field, because it had once adjoined a hospital. It would give its name to the whole area and was where Spitalfields Market would be built.

By 1677 the whole north side of Brown's was built up, as is shown on the map created by John Ogilby and William Morgan which dates from that time. Development of the south side followed and it was around 1740 that a carpenter named Daniel Marsillat leased some land from the owner Granville Wheler and built an uninspiring three-storey house with a roof garret used for silk weaving. Sometime in the mid-1800s the street would be renamed Hanbury Street and the house given the number 29.

In 1888, above the single front door there was a notice which, in straggling white letters, read "Mrs A. Richardson, packing-case maker". The

RIGHT: Contemporary press sketch of John Davis, the 56 year-old man who discovered Annie Chapman's body. Davis lived in the third-floor front room of No.29 with his wife and three sons.

door opened into a hallway; on the left there was a staircase leading up and on the right a passage about 7.5 m (25 ft) long and 1 m (3 ft) wide ran the length of the house to a rear door. The floorboards were bare and creaked as you walked along them. The rear door had no lock on it and opened into a yard. Two stone steps led down into the yard, which was around four metres (13–14 ft) square, unevenly paved with stones, and separated from the neighbouring yard by an old and rotten fence about 1.7 m (5 ft 6 in) high. At the bottom of the yard was an outside lavatory on the right, and on the left was a work shed. There was no exit.

It had once been a family home, but for the previous 15 years it had been rented by a 66-year-old widow named Amelia Richardson who sub-let the rooms she did not use herself. She seems to have taken care over who she let rooms to, since the residents were decent and hard working. A short woman with dark hair streaked with grey, the widow had taken over her husband's business as a packing-case manufacturer after he died in the middle of 1882. She used the cellar and rear yard of the house to carry out this work, employing one of her sons and another man. She lived with her

OPPOSITE: The back yard of 29 Hanbury Street as it would have been at the time of the murder. Next door is the yard of No.27, the home of Albert Cadosch.

RIGHT: Map of the Spitalfields area showing key sites in the Annie Chapman case.

 Murder site

BREWERY CLOCK

Commercial Street

29 HANBURY STREET

Hanbury Street

SPITALFIELDS MARKET

THE TEN BELLS PUBLIC HOUSE

THE PRINCE ALBERT PUBLIC HOUSE

Church Street

CHRIST CHURCH

Brushfield Street

CROSSINGHAM'S 35 DORSET STREET

Dorset Street

THE BRITANNIA PUBLIC HOUSE

grandson, James, in the first floor front room and used the back room downstairs for cooking. She also held weekly prayer meetings in this room.

In the front room facing the street lived Harriet Hardiman, a 49-year old widow who shared the room with her 16-year-old son William. The room doubled as a small shop from which Harriet sold cat's meat (meat for cats, not meat from cats, it was horseflesh). Tragedy had dogged the family in recent years: Harriet's husband, Edward, had died in 1880; her 28-year-old daughter, Sarah, had died in the house in 1885; her grand-daughter, Harriet Maria, had died on 18 June 1888 from the consequences of congenital syphilis contracted from her mother; and Harriet's daughter-in-law, Harriet Maria's mother, Sarah, would be dead within the week.

On the first floor, the back room was occupied by James Waker and his son Alfred, who was 31-years-old and weak minded but inoffensive. James Waker had lived at 29 Hanbury Street for some years and had seen two grandchildren born there.

On the second floor lived Robert Thompson, his wife and daughter, and two young women named Cooksley, while in the front room of the third floor lived John and Mary Davis and their three adult sons. John Davis was a carman (delivery driver) at Leadenhall Market. Their neighbour on that floor was 71-year-old Sarah Wilcox (the newspapers consistently referred to her as Cox), whom Mrs Richardson charitably allowed to live there for no payment.

John Davis had gone to bed early, at 8:00 p.m on 7 September, but suffered a restless night and at 5:45 a.m. he heard the clock on Christ Church. A witness, one Mrs Long (see page 93) heard the clock on the brewery chime... and Albert Cadosch, another witness who lived next door (see page 93), saw Christ Church Clock chime the quarter hour. Davis got up, made and drank a cup of tea, and went downstairs. The front door was wide open, thrown back against the wall, but the rear door was closed and he pushed it open. Two stone steps led down into the yard from the back door and between them and the rickety fence was a small recess. In it Davis saw the body of a woman, horribly mutilated.

The body was that of Annie Chapman. She is the only victim of Jack the Ripper of whom there is a photograph taken when she was alive. She was born in 1841 as Annie Eliza Smith, the illegitimate

ABOVE: Christ Church Spitalfields, photographed in 1909. Amelia Palmer gave Annie Chapman money a few days before the murder after they met outside.

child of George Smith, a soldier in the Second Regiment of the Life Guards, and Ruth Chapman, who would marry shortly after her birth. In 1869 she married John Chapman, a relative of her mother's, who was a coachman and from time to time the couple lived in some pleasant and wealthy accommodations. For example, when their second daughter was born they were living at 17 South Bruton Mews, which runs parallel with Bruton Street where the future Queen Elizabeth II would be born at No.17 on 21 April 1926.

Sometime before 1880 John got the job of coachman and domestic servant working for Sir Francis Tress Barry at his house, St Leonard's Hill Mansion in Clewer, Berkshire. The mansion, to which John Chapman was attached, living in an apartment over the stables, is today part of the Legoland theme park. Sir Francis Tress Barry's immense wealth was derived from mining interests in Portugal. He was a Conservative MP, representing Windsor in the House of Commons from 1890 to 1906, and rubbed shoulders with royalty, the Prince and Princess of Wales having been guests at their home in 1881. It is far from

OPPOSITE: Crossingham's Lodging House at 35 Dorset Street, Annie Chapman's doss-house of choice. To the left can be seen Little Paternoster Row, looking towards Brushfield Street.

ABOVE: A rare colour photograph of 29 Hanbury Street taken by John Gordon Whitby in 1961. By now, the house had gained an extra door leading into the shop below.

OPPOSITE: The front of 29 Hanbury Street as it would have looked in September 1888.

surprising, therefore, that Annie began to prove an embarrassment when her heavy drinking took a serious hold. She became known to the police as a drunk and even found herself taken into custody for drunkenness, albeit never being charged before the local magistrate. Eventually, as the *Windsor and Eton Gazette* (15 September 1888) tactfully put it, "her dissolute habits made it imperatively necessary that she should reside elsewhere than on the gentleman's grounds." She and John Chapman separated and Annie headed back to London.

John Chapman continued to live in Clewer with the children, who received good educations. Both the daughters attended school (one educated at a very respectable ladies school in Windsor, paid for by an aunt), while the son, John Alfred, was said to be a cripple who was for some time treated in a London hospital. John Chapman sent Annie a weekly allowance of 10s (in terms of today's wages, about £30). It was a hefty chunk of John's earnings, probably half of what a good labourer would hope to make and almost certainly more than a farm labourer would ever anticipate. Annie would have lived reasonably well on it, but at Christmas 1886 the money stopped. John Chapman was dead. He'd been forced through ill-health to resign his job

earlier in the year and he died on Christmas Day 1886 of cirrhosis of the liver, ascites and dropsy. His allowance died with him and Annie, clearly an alcoholic, was thrown to her own devices.

A curious story emerged several years later when the Reverend James Patterson received a long letter from one of his parishioners warning that alcoholic wine used at services was dangerous, claiming that the mere taste of alcohol on her husband's lips had been the dreadful ruin of his sister. The relevant part of the letter explained:

Just before I was six years old, my father cut his throat, leaving my mother with five children, three girls older, and one younger than myself. My eldest sister took to drink when she was quite young. Fourteen years ago I was converted. Twelve years ago I heard a sermon on "Christians and Total Abstinence". I signed the pledge with two of my sisters and we tried to persuade the one given to drink to give it up. She was married and in a good position. Over and over again she signed the pledge and tried to keep it. Over and over again she was tempted and fell. At last, of her own accord, she went into a home for the cure of the intemperate, her husband paid 12d per week and she stayed one year. She came out a

Crossingham's

Standing on the north side of Dorset Street, at the corner with Little Paternoster Row, Crossingham's was first registered on 5 March 1887 and had four floors, which accommodated 114 people. The basement, with a fire in the grate, was a communal area where lodgers could gather, chat, cook and eat their food. It was owned by William Crossingham and was one of several lodging houses he owned in the area, the most prominent of the others being Commercial Street Chambers which stood at 15–19 Dorset Street. The deputy of No.35 was Timothy Donovan. It was at Crossingham's that Mary Connolly, the drinking companion of Martha Tabram, had been living before the murder of her friend (see chapter 3), and Mary Ann Nichols (see chapter 4) may have been a regular as her death certificate gives it as her address. William Crossingham died of kidney disease at his home in Romford on 28 February 1907 and all his properties (which included more lodging houses in White's Row and Little Paternoster Row) were passed over to William Hunnible who continued to run them as lodging houses.

Crossingham's was demolished along with the entire north side of Dorset Street in 1928.

RIGHT: A contemporary press illustration of Dorset Street, showing Crossingham's Lodging House at No.35.

changed woman – a sober wife and mother, and things went on very happily for a few months. Then her husband had a severe cold, but his duty compelled him to go out, so to fortify himself against the cold, he took a glass of hot whiskey. He was careful enough not to have it in her presence for fear it should be a temptation. He drank it and came to kiss her before starting. In that kiss the fumes of alcohol were transmitted and all the old cravings came back. She went out soon after her husband and in less than an hour was a drunken mad woman. Poor thing! She never tried again, she said it was no use, no one knew the fearful struggle, and that unless she could keep out of sight or smell, she could never be free. For years we wrestled with God in prayer for her, never doubting that he would give the needed strength some day. She could not keep sober, so she left her husband and two children, one a dreadful cripple, through her drink. She

has had eight children, six of these have been victims to the curse. Her husband allowed her enough to live on while he lived, but he died two years after she left him. A white-haired, broken-hearted man only 45. We never knew where she lived, she used to come to us at home now and then, we gave her clothes and tried in every way to win her back, for she was a mere beggar. She said she would always keep out of our way, but she must and would have the drink. I need not follow her history for if you read the life of "Annie Chapman", one of the worst victims in the terrible Whitechapel murders, you read the end of my sister's life.

The authenticity of this letter is unknown, although many of the details are true – John Chapman was only 44-years-old when he died and Annie did leave her children, but it is not confirmed that George Smith, Annie's father, cut his throat – and if the story is accurate it suggests

PREVIOUS PAGES: A wide view of Hanbury Street looking west, showing No.29 and further along, the Black Swan pub at No.23 and the Weaver's Arms on the corner of John Street.

that Annie Chapman valiantly struggled against her illness and failed.

The loss of that weekly 10s would have made Annie's situation desperate and she appears to have tried to support herself doing crochet work or by selling flowers and matches on the street or at the markets, notably Stratford Market where she went every Friday, She had already begun living with a sieve maker known as Jack Sivvey or Sievey. Whether or not the loss of her allowance contributed to the end of their relationship is not known, but they separated late in 1887 or early 1888 and he moved to Notting Hill. Annie had then taken up with a bricklayer's labourer named Edward Stanley, who had known her when she lived in Windsor. They had a casual relationship, mostly spending the weekends together, lodging at different doss-houses in the area.

As for her drinking, at the time of her death Annie Chapman seems to have got it under control, at least to a degree. There is always a reluctance to speak ill of the dead, but several people who knew her said that while Annie had a taste for rum and even acknowledged that she was addicted to drink, several also said that she seldom drank, that she drank mostly on Saturdays, and that it didn't take much to get her drunk. She otherwise worked hard, was clever and respectable, and never used bad language. However, a close friend named Amelia Farmer said she didn't think Annie Chapman was "very particular what she did to earn a living and at times used to remain out very late at night."

Annie Chapman's last days alive were reasonably well accounted for by police and journalists. On Saturday, 1 September 1888, she met Ted Stanley at the corner of Brushfield Street and the two of them went to 35 Dorset Street where they spent the night. Although there is some confusion about it, there was almost certainly a fight that night, between Annie and a woman named Eliza Cooper in the Britannia pub on the corner of Dorset Street. Annie and Ted Stanley were drinking with Cooper and a man known as Harry the Hawker, when Chapman caught Cooper trying to palm Harry the Hawker's 2s piece, switching it for a penny. Cooper struck Chapman in the face and chest. Cooper was clearly something of a dangerous character as she is almost certainly the same Eliza Cooper who was fined £5 (the equivalent of about £300 today) and bound over to keep the peace for six months at Clerkenwell Police Court on 15 October 1888 for assaulting one Thomas Wilne on Clerkenwell Road.

Annie and Stanley spent that night at 35 Dorset Street and the next day Stanley left her between 1:00–3:00 p.m. Annie was sporting a black eye and the following day she showed her friend Amelia Farmer some bruising on her chest and on her temple. She was evidently feeling sorry for herself

BACKGROUND INTELLIGENCE — The Casual Ward

During the nineteenth century the long-held belief that the poor were responsible for their poverty began to change as it was realized that some cases of poverty were caused by circumstances over which the individual had no control. What the Victorians were unable to decide was how to distinguish between those who genuinely needed assistance and those who didn't. One way to tell was to make the assistance so unpleasant that only the truly needy and desperate would take it, so the conditions in the workhouse were extremely unpleasant. But for many people such as Annie Chapman the only thing that stood between them and the workhouse was the daily 4d that would secure a bed in a common lodging house. Anything that prevented one from getting the money, be it age, infirmity, or, as in Annie's case, illness, led to the workhouse. The casual ward (for the "casual poor") was a part of the workhouse set aside for vagrants and was often purpose-built. The conditions there were worse than in the workhouse itself and for uncertain reasons it was commonly called "the spike". The American author Jack London devoted a whole chapter to the Whitechapel spike in his famous personal exploration of the East End, *The People of the Abyss* (1903). Appropriately dressed, he had queued several times in the hope of obtaining entry, and eventually got in. He found the place so vile in every respect that he could not bear to spend the required two-and-a-half days there. Much to the consternation of the friends he'd made, he seized the first opportunity to flee. "I have been to the spike, and slept in the spike, and eaten in the spike," he later wrote, "also, I have run away from the spike."

and said she was going to see if she could get a pair of boots from her sister to enable her to go hop-picking. Whether or not she did visit her sister is unknown, but she doesn't seem to have got any boots and the following day, when Farmer met Annie outside Christ Church, Annie complained of feeling so unwell that she was thinking of going into the casual ward for a day or two. Farmer gave her friend 2d (about 50p today) and told her not to spend it on rum, but to get some food and a cup of tea.

Annie went to the casual ward on Wednesday and stayed there until she returned to Crossingham's on the Friday with some medicine and a box containing a few pills, but she wasn't feeling any better and told Amelia Farmer that she had to pull herself together and find the money for her lodgings. What Annie did not know was that she was dying, her lungs and the membranes of her brain in the advanced stages of a disease which would, if it had been allowed to take its course, have killed her. Annie's personal journey however, was about to end abruptly, cut short by Jack the Ripper's knife.

As that Friday slipped into Saturday she came back to 35 Dorset Street and shared a pint of beer with a painter named William Stevens. Stevens saw Annie with her box of pills. The box broke and she wrapped the pills in a torn piece of envelope lying on the kitchen floor, on which Stevens noticed a red postmark. The time was about 12:30 a.m. and Annie left the kitchen soon after, but returned about three-quarters of an hour later, and was seen heading down to the kitchen by Crossingham's deputy Timothy Donovan, who sent the night watchman, John Evans, to get her bed money. Annie hadn't got it, but was unperturbed and told Donovan not to let the bed as she'd soon be back. John Evans had followed Chapman up from the basement kitchen and walked with her to the street door. He saw her enter Little Paternoster Row and head towards Brushfield Street, where she turned towards Christ Church. And that is the last anyone is known to have seen Annie Chapman alive.

John Fennell Richardson stood outside 29 Hanbury Street. He was a tall but stout man, with dark brown hair and a brown moustache, and he spoke with an unprepossessingly hoarse voice. He was the son of Amelia Richardson, 35 years old and married, with a home of his own nearby at 2 John Street and a family of two boys and a daughter he'd named Amelia after his mother. The front door was shut but unlocked and easily swung open. He walked along the bare, creaking floorboards of the passage to the rear door, also shut but opening to his push. He stood on the top step looking into the rear yard, looking to his right to check that the cellar was securely locked. It had been broken into not long before and saws and hammers stolen, and as these were expensive to replace he had made it his custom to swing by the house on market mornings. He noted to his satisfaction that the padlock was securely fastened on the cellar door. He then sat on the second step and cut a bit of leather from his shoe which had been irritating his toe. He then tied up his boot and went out of the house. He did not close the rear door, allowing it to swing shut behind him, but he was sure that he closed the front door. He probably hadn't been at the house for more than three minutes.

Although John Richardson didn't see anything, his testimony is among the most important in the Annie Chapman murder case. Very few of the timings are likely to be anywhere near precise, but Richardson was at 29 Hanbury Street sometime between 4:40 a.m. and 4:50 a.m. and he wasn't in the house above a few minutes. The sun rose that morning at 5:23 a.m., so it was still dark while

KEY EVIDENCE Medical Evidence

Three witnesses, Timothy Donovan, William Stevens and John Evans, all thought Annie was drunk when she left 35 Dorset Street. Annie had even shared a pint with Stevens, and admitted to Donovan that she had been to the Britannia. However, Dr George Bagster Phillips, who performed the post-mortem, declared that there was no alcohol in her stomach. It may be that he classified only spirits as alcohol, as many did, beer being thought of as merely a nourishing and healthy food.

ABOVE: The back yard of 29 Hanbury Street in the mid-1960s, a few years before demolition.

Richardson was at the house and it is possible that in the yard even nearby objects would have been shrouded in the pre-dawn gloom and difficult to see unless specificially looked for. The yard door opened to the left and would have partially obscured the recess next to the steps where Annie Chapman's body was later found; if the door was closing back on Richardson (and he said the door closed of its own accord) the door may have hidden a lot from view; and as Richardson's attention was directed away from the recess to the cellar, the body could have been there and Richardson may not have seen it. However, Richardson was adamant that the body was not there and that he would have seen it if it had been.

In the house next door lived a young man named Charles Albert Cadosch – apparently everyone called him Albert and it seems to have been the name he preferred, even though it was his second name. He was 28 years old, a glass cutter by trade, and had a growing family, although tragedy had struck three years earlier when his eldest child,

Isabella, had died aged only seven. He got up about 5:15 a.m. and went to the rear of the yard to use the outside toilet. As he returned across the yard to the back door he heard talking coming from the yard of No.29. He couldn't distinguish any words except "No", which he thought was spoken by a woman. He didn't pay much attention at the time, not even when he returned to the yard a few minutes later and heard a soft fall against the fence. Had he looked over the fence he may have come eye-to-eye with Jack the Ripper; instead he went back into the house, passed through the passage to the front door, and went off to work. Significantly, he did not see anybody as he left the house and as he passed Christ Church he noticed that the time was 5:32 a.m.

Mrs Elizabeth Long, who worked as a cart-minder at Spitalfields Market, lived in Church Row, which is now called St Matthew's Row after the church. Mrs Long's walk to work took her into Hanbury Street and on entering it she heard the clock on the nearby brewery strike 5:30 a.m. John Davis above heard Christ Church clock chime. Outside No.29

ABOVE: Hanbury Street in 2010. All houses on the north side, including No.29, were replaced by extensions to the Truman brewery in 1970. The brewery itself closed down in 1989 and now houses shops and a flourishing Sunday market.

OPPOSITE: Aerial view of the yards behind the north side of Hanbury Street. Visible are the backs of Nos. 31, 29 and 27.

Mrs Long saw a man and a woman talking. The man was facing away from her, so she couldn't get a good look at him, although she seems to have caught a glimpse of his profile as she walked past. She thought he looked "very dark" like a foreigner, by which she meant a Jew, and he wore a brown deer-stalker hat and a dark coat, although she wasn't certain about the coat, and he presented what she described as a shabby, genteel appearance. He appeared to be a little taller than the woman and aged about 40. The couple were talking loudly and he heard the man say "Will you?" and the woman reply "Yes". Mrs Long then passed them by and never looked back. When she viewed the body of Annie in the mortuary she was certain that she was the woman she'd seen.

It was round about then that John Davis was making and drinking some tea in preparation for the working day ahead, then going downstairs. He noted the front door swung back against the wall – John Richardson was certain that he'd closed it after him – and padded down the hall in the direction of the back yard and towards the discovery that

would ensure his immortality. Horrified at the sight that met his eyes, Davis ran back through the hall passage to the front door and dashed into the street. He saw Henry Holland, a thin and sickly looking youth, and summoned him into the yard. Davis then saw two men, James Kent and James Green, outside the Black Swan, a pub just three doors away on the same side of the street. They worked for Joseph and Thomas Bayley who ran a business making packing cases from the pub's rear yard and Davis summoned them to view the horrible scene he'd discovered. The men all gazed down at the still corpse of Annie Chapman, something lying beside her and drawn over her shoulder which Davis would later struggle to explain. "It was part of her body. I did not examine the woman, I was too frightened at the dreadful sight."

As if suddenly galvanized, the men went rushing off to find a policeman. There wasn't one immediately visible, so James Kent went to the pub for a stiff brandy and then went to look for something with which to cover the body. Green, seeing no policeman, went back to the workshop at the back of the Black Swan. Holland eventually found a policeman in Spitalfields Market, but the man was on fixed point duty and unable to leave his position. Holland was so angered by this that he made a formal complaint at the police station in Commercial Street that afternoon. He looked around for another policeman, didn't see one and went back to 29 Hanbury Street. Only John Davis seems to have thought of going directly to the police station, but before he got there an inspector, Joseph Chandler, on seeing some men running towards Hanbury Street, had stopped one and been told of the murder. He was entering the house when Holland returned, joining what by now was a largish crowd outside the house and in the passage. In fact the noise was such that Mrs Richardson, assuming from the agitation that the house was on fire, sent her grandson to investigate, and on learning of the murder, went downstairs, before suddenly remembering that she was improperly

attired and scuttling back to her room.

Dr George Bagster Phillips was summoned from his surgery at 2 Spital Square and arrived at 29 Hanbury Street, where he made a thorough examination of the body. The time was by now about 6:30 a.m.

Annie Chapman's body was lying on the ground in the recess between the yard steps and the fence. Her head was towards the house and her feet towards the yard. Her legs were drawn up, the feet resting on the ground and her knees turned outwards. The body was terribly mutilated. The abdomen was opened and the murderer had severed the intestines from the abdominal wall, removed them from the body and placed them over Annie's shoulder. From the pelvis the murderer had also removed the uterus and its appendages, the upper portion of the vagina and the posterior two-thirds of the bladder, but as no trace of these body parts could be found in the yard or yards of

BACKGROUND INTELLIGENCE

Dr George Bagster Phillips

Dr George Bagster Phillips, probably the most prominent doctor in the Ripper investigation, was appointed Police Surgeon to H Division in 1865. He was born in 1835, the son of an ironmonger named Henry Phillips and his wife Sarah (formerly Bagster). At the age of 16 he was apprenticed to a chemist and druggist named Gilkes in Leominster, Hertfordshire. He moved back to London for medical school, graduating in 1861, and began practising from 2 Spital Square. In 1880 he married Eliza Toms and settled into a life of domesticity and routine, never changing homes, and dying of apoplexy in 189. He left effects valued at £3,824 (worth almost £230,000 today), which was sufficient to enable his wife to enjoy a reasonably comfortable existence. She died in 1940.

Walter Dew recalled Dr Phillips in his book *I Caught Crippen* (1938) as "an elderly man", though Phillips was just over 50 years old at the time of the Ripper murders, so Dew's memory probably reflects his own youth at the time. He also remembered Phillips as "ultra-old-fashioned both in his personal appearance and his dress. He used to look for all the world as though he had stepped out of a century-old painting. His manners were charming; he was immensely popular both with the police and the public, and he was highly skilled." In his obituary that appeared in The Lancet on 13 November 1897, his assistant in 1888, Dr Percy John Clark,

LEFT: Contemporary press illustration of Dr Phillips.

described him as "a modest man who found self-advertising abhorrent. Under a brusque, quick manner engendered by his busy life, there was a warm, kind heart, and a large number of men and women of all classes are feeling that by his death they have lost a very real friend."

RIGHT: Hanbury Street and the immediate vicinity as it would have been in 1888, showing key locations.

 Murder site

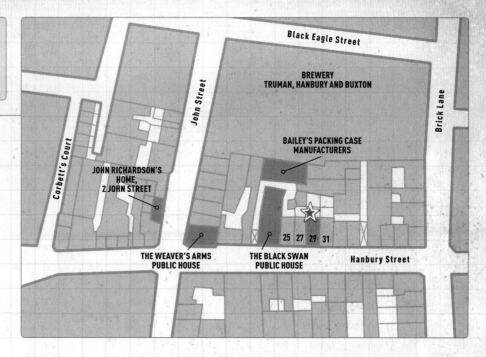

the neighbouring properties, it had to be assumed that they had been taken away by the murderer, although at the inquest on 13 September 1888 Dr Phillips acknowledged that the body parts "might have been lost" when the body was moved to the mortuary. Annie's left arm was resting across her left breast. Her face was on its right side and swollen, her tongue, also swollen, protruded between her teeth. The throat was deeply cut, the jagged incisions reaching right round the neck commencing from left to right and cut down to the spine as if an effort had been made to sever the head from the body. There was blood spatter on the fence. The injuries to the abdomen and throat had probably been done with the same very sharp knife, which must have been at least 13–15 cm (5–6 in) long, probably more, and most likely the sort of knife used by doctors, although a well-ground-down slaughterman's knife could have done the job.

Dr Phillips noted older bruising, probably the consequences of the fight Annie had had, but there was fresh bruising on the face, especially about the chin and the sides of the jaw, from which he concluded that the murderer had taken hold of Annie's chin to push the head back and had commenced the incision from left to right. The swollen face and protruding tongue indicated that she had been suffocated before the incisions had been made.

The stomach contained a little food, probably a baked potato she was eating when she left the lodging house in Dorset Street, but there was no sign of fluid and Dr Phillips was convinced that she had not taken any strong alcohol for some hours before her death.

Rigor mortis, the stiffening of the muscles in the body which normally appears about two hours after death, was beginning to set in and Dr Phillips therefore thought Annie had been dead for at least two hours by the time he came to examine her.

Dr Phillips was particularly impressed by how cleanly the incisions were cut. The rectum was avoided and the vagina divided low enough to avoid injuring the cervix uteri (the narrow lower end of the uterus), and from this he concluded that the murderer had considerable anatomical knowledge. Dr Phillips thought it would have taken the murderer at least a quarter-of-an-hour to have inflicted all the injuries and that, had he been working in the methodical way of a surgeon, it would have taken him the best part of an hour. The examination at the scene of the crime and the autopsy afterwards had been very thorough and Dr Phillips was evidently a very capable doctor, so his attribution of anatomical knowledge and a degree of surgical skill has to be treated seriously. Jack the Ripper was working at speed, in conditions of poor visibility and under inevitable pressure from the danger of being discovered in the act, but the manner of the incisions displayed knowledge and the use of the knife suggested skill. Thus began the theory, which has lasted to this day, that Jack the Ripper was a doctor.

However, several of Dr Phillips's conclusions have been questioned, notably the absence of any sign of fluid in Annie's stomach and his conviction that she hadn't drunk any alcohol for some hours. Alcohol was detected by smelling the stomach contents, which can't have been very pleasant, and the use of the term "strong alcohol" suggests that Dr Phillips was looking for spirits and, as far as we know, Annie had been drinking beer. One can only assume that she had rid herself of the liquid in the usual fashion.

Dr Phillips' estimate of the time of death is another matter, and raises huge problems. Rigor mortis is not the most accurate way of determining the time of death, but Dr Phillips arrived at the scene at 6:30 a.m. and estimated from its onset that death had occurred two hours earlier, at about 4:30 a.m. This means that the body would have been there when John Richardson was sitting on the step between 4:45 a.m. and 4:50 a.m. cutting the piece of offending leather from his shoe. It also makes the testimony of Albert Cadosch and Elizabeth Long worthless, while at the same time raising the question of who Cadosch heard in the yard of 29 Hanbury Street and why, if the body was there at that time, they didn't report finding it. The coroner, Wynne Baxter, a solicitor, not a doctor, thought Dr Phillips' estimate of the time of death was wrong, but the police, perhaps understandably and perhaps rightly, gave priority to Dr Phillips, which lost them any potential clues that Cadosch or Long may have provided.

Albert Cadosch and Mrs Long's timings present their own problems too, because if it was Annie Chapman that Albert Cadosch heard in the yard before 5:30 a.m., it can't have been Annie Chapman that Mrs Long saw standing on the pavement outside 29 Hanbury Street after 5:30 a.m. Albert Cadosch's timings would also make it likely that he'd have seen the couple outside the house and Mrs Long in the street, yet he saw neither. Both timings were estimates based on different clocks, Cadosch seeing the clock on Christ Church as he passed by, and Mrs Long hearing the striking of the brewery clock in Brick Lane. However, if Mrs Long had heard the brewery clock strike the quarter hour instead of the half hour, the stories could be reconciled.

As soon as Dr Phillips completed his examination of the body, it was removed from the house, but with some difficulty. News of the murder had spread and a crowd estimated to be several hundred in number and described as very excitable, had gathered in the street. Public feeling, and in some measure hostility, towards the police, who would in due course come in for considerable criticism from the press, was beginning to mount.

Annie Chapman's body was taken to the Whitechapel mortuary where it was placed into the care of Robert Mann, who had charge of the mortuary and who had received Mary Ann Nichols' body. Once again the body was left on the ambulance in the yard of the mortuary until taken inside by two nurses, where it was stripped and washed on the instructions of the Clerk to the Board of Guardians (the authority which administered workhouses in accordance with recommendations made by the poor law commission).

Meanwhile, Inspector Chandler had searched the yard and found a few remaining items of Annie Chapman's possessions, including a screwed up piece of paper containing two pills. It was a portion of envelope and on one side there was the seal of the Sussex Regiment, and on the other the letter "M" in what appeared to be the handwriting of a man, and a post office stamp dated "London, 28 August 1888".

This looked like an important clue, especially given the belief at the time that Martha Tabram had been murdered by a soldier. The Sussex Regiment was stationed at the famous military camp at Aldershot, the "Home of the British Army". The camp was divided by the Basingstoke Canal into the north camp and south camp, the 1st Battalion being stationed at north camp. The police visited the camp and made inquiries, only to discover that envelopes bearing the regimental crest were widely available in the camp and also at the post office in the neighbouring town. The lead was a dead end, and it fizzled out altogether when it was learned that Annie Chapman had picked the piece of envelope from the floor in the lodging house when her box of pills broke.

OPPOSITE: The mortuary photograph of Annie Chapman.

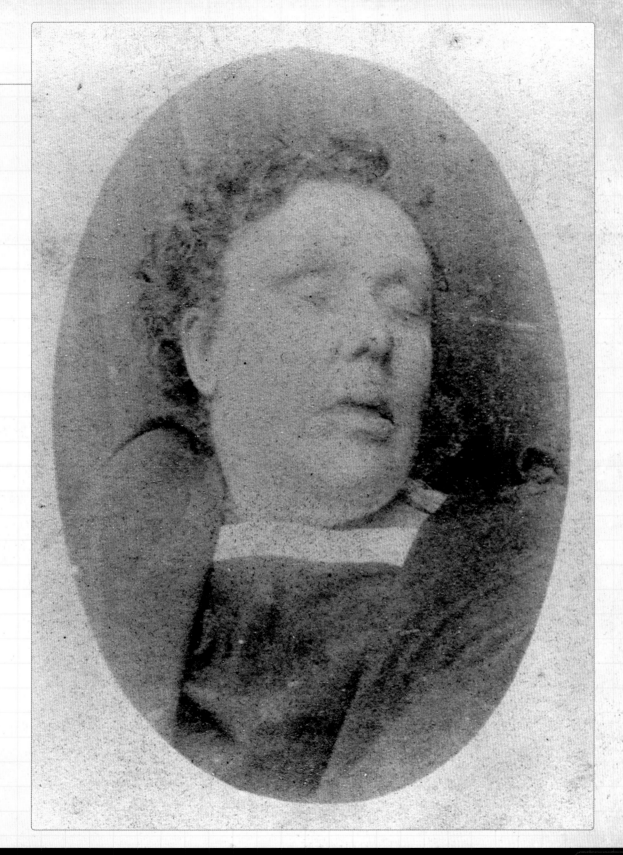

For the avid reader in late-Victorian Britain, there appeared to be no end of newspapers, journals and gazettes through which literate citizens could furnish themselves with the daily or weekly events of the time. The reduction and eventual abolition of newspaper tax in 1855, bolstered by steady improvement in printing methods, meant that a vast number of publications graced the news-stands. They catered to every requirement, locality and political tendency and, helped by an increase in literacy levels following the introduction of compulsory education, were assured of a growing readership.

SOME NEWSPAPERS, SUCH AS *THE TIMES*, THE *Daily Telegraph* and the *Daily News* followed the long-standing tradition of the broadsheet, offering readers lengthy and supposedly reliable news articles crammed into large pages of tightly columned text. Some, such as the *Illustrated London News* and the *Penny Illustrated Paper*, had taken advantage of the new printing revolution and offered their readership handsome engravings depicting more grandiose and often sensational events for their delectation. Other newspapers, however, chose to dispense with the sober reporting championed by the broadsheet mainstays and used their circulation and influence to further sociological and often political causes. By the autumn of 1888, two papers in particular had become the firebrands of what would soon be called "the new journalism".

Founded in 1865, the *Pall Mall Gazette* began as a paper for the higher echelons of society, written by members of their own class. By the time of William Thomas Stead's editorship (1883–1889), the paper had metamorphosed into a radical, free-thinking journal. Stead was not afraid to get his hands dirty to expose a wrong or champion a cause and in 1885 he self-penned a series of hard-hitting articles. Among them was "The Maiden Tribute of Modern Babylon", which exposed the scandalous trade of "buying" children for the purposes of prostitution. In order to demonstrate the truth of his revelations, he arranged the "purchase" of Eliza Armstrong, the 13-year-old daughter of a chimney sweep. Stead's willingness to put himself in jeopardy to prove his point landed him in deep water and he was given a three-month prison sentence. The irony was that he was convicted on technical grounds – he had failed to first secure permission for the "purchase" from the girl's father. The result of Stead's campaign resulted in the age of consent for girls being raised from 12 to 16 that same year. Despite Stead's punishment, it was an outcome of which he was particularly proud and he was known to wear his prison uniform on the anniversary of his incarceration. Perhaps his most noted claim to fame, however, is that he sailed across the Atlantic aboard the ill-fated RMS *Titanic* in April 1912, becoming one of the many who perished on that fateful voyage.

The Star, an evening newspaper founded in 1788 by John Murray, was the newspaper which garnered considerable notoriety and popularity above all others on the back of the Whitechapel Murders. In 1888, its newly appointed editor was Thomas Power "T P" O'Connor, considered today as a leading light of the "new journalism" and who described his journal's style of reporting as one which was intended to "hit the reader right between the eyes". The murders of Emma Smith (see chapter 2) and Martha Tabram (see chapter 3) had, relatively speaking, scant newspaper coverage outside of the local East London press, though the area was served by no less than six different newspapers at that time and many were moved to comment on the growing feeling of outrage and unease created by these unique crimes. The murder of Mary Ann Nichols (see chapter 4) took the reporting to another level, with the *Illustrated Police News* devoting a full-page front-cover illustration to the discovery of her body in Buck's Row by PC Neil. The national press was now also quick to devote increasing column inches to the events surrounding this most ferocious homicide – the Nichols inquest was reported in detail across the spectrum of newspapers. While the traditional broadsheets attempted to keep to the reporting and express opinion only in the voices of those who wrote to the papers themselves, the *Pall Mall Gazette* and, most obviously, *The Star*, saw the developing situation as a way not just of

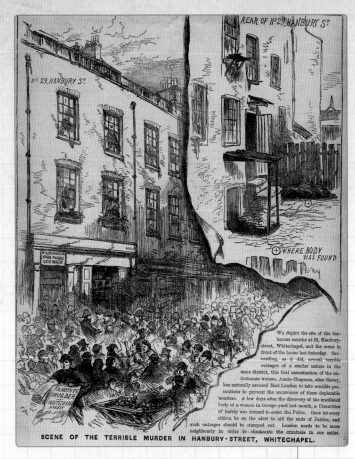

N° 29, HANBURY ST.

REAR OF N° 29, HANBURY ST.

WHERE BODY WAS FOUND

We depict the site of the barbarous murder at 29, Hanbury-street, Whitechapel, and the scene in front of the house last Saturday. Succeeding, as it did, several terrible outrages of a similar nature in the same district, this foul assassination of the unfortunate woman, Annie Chapman, alias Sievey, has naturally aroused East London to take sensible precautions to prevent the recurrence of these deplorable murders. A few days after the discovery of the mutilated body of a woman in George-yard last month, a Committee of Safety was formed to assist the Police. Once let every citizen be on the alert to aid the ends of Justice, and such outrages should be stamped out. London needs to be more neighbourly in order to checkmate the criminals in our midst.

SCENE OF THE TERRIBLE MURDER IN HANBURY-STREET, WHITECHAPEL.

exposing the injustices meted out upon the East End poor, but also as a way of bringing to book those they felt were responsible for the status quo. The murder of Annie Chapman (see chapter 5) triggered a deluge of anger and frustration from the radical press and with the situation suddenly becoming a political fight as much as a criminal case, the developing events in the East End slums began to attract the interest of the press from overseas. The phenomenon of the Whitechapel Murders now began in earnest.

By the first week of September, *The Star* was repeatedly commenting on Sir Charles Warren's leadership of the Metropolitan Police with undisguised contempt. It even published interviews with police officers who appeared to offer less than complimentary opinions of their chief and his methods. Along with the marginally less noisy *Pall Mall Gazette*, it described him as a "maladroit martinet" and a "puritan Jingo", terms that were no doubt intended to be cutting, if not downright offensive to the Commissioner and his supporters. With the murders of the three East

ABOVE: This illustration from the contemporary press showing Hanbury Street after the murder of Annie Chapman is a clear indicator of the sensation and fear felt among the population of the East End at that time as it shows crowds filling the entire street and surrounding thoroughfares.

PREVIOUS PAGES AND OPPOSITE: "Blind Man's Buff", the satirical cartoon published in *Punch* in September 1888 more than amply demonstrated the press attitude to the seemingly ineffective police investigation, even at this early stage.

ABOVE: A press illustration of John Pizer, one he claimed had little bearing on his real appearance. It appeared to show a Jewish archetype more than anything else.

End "unfortunates" receiving an astonishingly quick surge in publicity which had now spread overseas, the paper commented that:

The murderer must be a Man Monster, and when Sir Charles has done quarrelling with his detective service he will perhaps help the citizens of East London to catch him.

The quote above undoubtedly made reference to the less-than-happy situation in the upper ranks of the Metropolitan Police at that time. Only a month before Warren had seen the departure of the Assistant Commissioner James Monro, the man in charge of the Criminal Investigation Department (CID). Warren's belief that he himself should have a great deal of say in the running of both the uniformed and detective branches had caused friction between the two, to the point where, in August 1888, Monro resigned. His replacement was Dr Robert Anderson, a strong character with well-developed religious beliefs who had come to London from Ireland in 1867 as deputy head of the anti-Fenian intelligence branch and who was later Secretary to the Prison Commissioners from 1887–1888. His new role as Assistant Commissioner of the Metropolitan Police CID would begin on the first day of September 1888. However Anderson had already been complaining to Warren about his ill-health. On Warren's recommendation, the man who was set to take on overall responsibility for the Whitechapel Murders case commenced his tenure with a long recuperative holiday in Switzerland. He left on the day Annie Chapman was murdered.

Despite the vilification of the upper ends of the police hierarchy in their current incarnation, as far as the men on the ground were concerned there was at least some good news with the arrival of Inspector Frederick Abberline from Scotland Yard (see chapter 3). Abberline, who stands today as probably the best-known of the police officers involved in the Ripper case, was a Dorset-born clockmaker who joined the Metropolitan Police in 1863, rising swiftly in the ranks to become Inspector in 1873, the same year he took up his duty in H-Division, Whitechapel. He was sent to central office in Whitehall in 1887, and had by then become an exceptionally popular officer, acquiring enormous knowledge of the East End, its people and of course, its criminal fraternity. Because his role would be to coordinate individual investigations on the ground, he became the natural choice when the murder of Annie Chapman required a professional with serious local clout. By the time Abberline began his new role, *The Star* had already given him something else to chew over, throwing another variable into the already confusing mêlée; the suspect known only as "Leather Apron".

Leather Apron was the *soubriquet* given to a local man who, for some time previously, had gained a reputation for accosting prostitutes, demanding money with the threat of violence or even death if they did not comply. It was generally accepted that he was a Jew, his face being of "a marked Hebrew type"(as described in *The Star* on 5 September 1888). The apron, which he wore as he committed his acts of extortion, was part of his work-wear and the sharp leather-knife he carried was the tool of his trade as a slipper-maker. The first appearance of this mysterious individual came in the 4 September edition of *The Star*, and

PUNCH, OR THE LONDON CHARIVARI.—September 22, 1888.

BLIND-MAN'S BUFF.

(As played by the Police.)

"TURN ROUND THREE TIMES, AND CATCH WHOM YOU MAY!"

kick-started a wave of fear, which escalated into aggression on the streets when it was mixed with the sensation of the Hanbury Street murder. Leather Apron fitted nicely with the notion that the murderer had to be "an outsider". The indigenous East Enders felt that surely only a foreigner would do such terrible things, and the 40,000 strong Jewish community east of the Tower of London, with their alien dialect and customs, their tendency to establish ghettos and, relevantly, their kosher slaughterhouses, made for a convenient scapegoat. That said, the idea that the killer was not from the area was also held by those who came from wealthier parts of the capital, those fun-seeking outsiders, also often from wealthier parts of London, who enjoyed rubbing shoulders with the rougher element of society, and even the criminal fraternity, who, outraged by the murders as much as anyone else, felt that these crimes were too much even by their standards. The buck was being well and truly passed.

The search for Leather Apron was, however, proving fruitless. It has been suggested that he did not really exist and was merely a name given to somebody or something that created great fear in the district but could not really be pinned down. As a result, anybody, whether innocent or otherwise could be a Leather Apron without even trying. One example came in the form of local street criminal George Cullen, commonly known as Squibby. A boisterous and powerful man, Cullen had been wanted for street gambling and on 1 September, he verbally threatened and threw a stone at a police officer, but he missed his target and hit an innocent passerby. He escaped arrest on that occasion, but on the day of Annie Chapman's murder, he was seen in the street by Walter Dew who promptly gave chase. Assuming that Dew was in pursuit of Leather Apron, a heated crowd, already in a state of great anxiety following the latest atrocity, followed suit and Cullen had to be escorted to safety away from the baying mob who, one might imagine, would have torn the man limb from limb had they been given the chance. This was only one of a number of incidents reported by the press. Some involved physical violence and it would sometimes take only the slightest suspicion to release the fervent anger of a mob.

One very interesting incident also took place on the day of the Hanbury Street murder. Mrs Fiddymont was the wife of the proprietor of the Prince Albert pub, which stood at the corner of Brushfield Street and Steward Street, near to Spitalfields Market. She stated that at 7 a.m. on 8 September 1888 she was standing in the "first compartment" of the bar talking with her friend Mary Chappell when a man entered the pub whose appearance alarmed her. He was wearing a stiff brown hat, a dark coat and no waistcoat; his hat was pulled down over his eyes and his face was partly concealed. He asked for half a pint of "four ale" (a cheap mild ale) and she served the drink while looking at him through the mirror at the back of the bar. Mrs Fiddymont was struck by the fact that there were blood spots on the back of his right hand. She also noticed that his shirt was torn. The man drank the beer in one gulp and immediately left and Mary Chappell, also suspicious, followed him into Brushfield Street and, noting that he was heading in the direction of Bishopsgate, pointed him out to a

BELOW: The now infamous *Punch* cartoon "The Nemesis Of Neglect" allied the murders with the long standing poverty and vice of the East End which the magazine felt had gone unchecked for too long.

PUNCH, OR THE LONDON CHARIVARI.—September 29, 1888.

THE NEMESIS OF NEGLECT.

"THERE FLOATS A PHANTOM ON THE SLUM'S FOUL AIR,
SHAPING, TO EYES WHICH HAVE THE GIFT OF SEEING,
INTO THE SPECTRE OF THAT LOATHLY LAIR.
FACE IT—FOR VAIN IS FLEEING!
RED-HANDED, RUTHLESS, FURTIVE, UNERECT,
'TIS MURDEROUS CRIME—THE NEMESIS OF NEGLECT!"

ABOVE: Sergeant William Thick, whose arrest of John Pizer was an early breakthrough in the case. Unfortunately, Pizer was innocent and was released.

bystander, Joseph Taylor, who promptly followed him. Inspector Abberline later stated in a report that this man was identical in description to one Jacob Issenschmidt, a man who was known by some in the area as "the mad pork butcher". Issenschmidt was, for a brief period of time, a suspect, however his mental instability saw to it that he was later incarcerated in an asylum, his presence there exonerating him from the subsequent murders in the series.

Mrs Fiddymont, Chappell and Mr Taylor later attended two identity parades, the first including another suspect, William Piggott, and the second with a slipper-maker named John Pizer. In the first line-up, only Chappell picked out Piggott, but she then stated that she was not sure if he was the man seen in the Prince Albert. With Pizer, no identification was made, but ironically, Pizer's presence in that parade was the result of an important lead regarding the identity of the mysterious Leather Apron.

Before the identity parade took place, Pizer had been arrested at his home at 22 Mulberry Street, Whitechapel, a small house close to St Mary's church where he lived with his family. The arresting officer was Sergeant William Thick, an experienced and highly regarded officer whose knowledge of the criminals of the East End made

him believe he possessed inside knowledge as to the identity of the elusive Leather Apron. On 10 September, Sergeant Thick knocked on Pizer's door, only to be greeted by the man himself. He promptly arrested him on suspicion of the murder of Annie Chapman. Pizer had been earmarked as Leather Apron on 7 September by a police report made by Inspector Joseph Henry Helson and perhaps armed with this crucial information, Thick, whose knowledge of the area was considerable, knew exactly where he could find him. He was sure, too, that Pizer was the miscreant he was after and indeed, once questioned, it was apparent that much local suspicion as to the identity of Leather Apron had been aimed at Pizer in particular. Ironically, it was partly this notoriety which helped exonerate him of the murder of Annie Chapman in any case, for at that time, under the recommendation of his brothers, he holed himself away at 22 Mulberry Street for fear of personal injury, staying there from 6 September until his arrest. It also transpired that on the night of 31 August, as Mary Ann Nichols met her doom and the fires raged at the London Docks, Pizer was several miles away from the theatre of crime in Holloway, North London. That night, he had chosen to stay at Crossman's lodging house, known as The Roundhouse, and at about

BACKGROUND INTELLIGENCE

Jack London Meets Sergeant Thick

The American author and journalist Jack London (1876-1916) is probably most famous for his novels *Call of the Wild* (1903) and *White Fang* (1906). However, one of his most impressive works was his non-fiction *The People of the Abyss*, published in 1903, which was a grueling expose of the social conditions that hid behind the wealth and pomp of London.

Jack London was a Socialist, joining the Socialist Labor Party in 1896, and *The People of the Abyss* was the result of London's investigative foray into the slums of the capital, much of it set in Whitechapel. He slept in doss-houses, spent time in a workhouse and even slept rough on the streets to get a feel for the plight of the poorest classes of the East End. Sometimes the experience became too much for him, but what he produced, though depressing, is still held up as a major work of social journalism. It was while setting himself up in Whitechapel that London had

the opportunity to meet Sergeant William Thick and walk the streets with him, even though that meant waiting at his home for him and his two daughters to return from church.

On meeting Thick, London described him as "shades of Old Sleuth and Sherlock Holmes!" While settling down to a simple meal of bread and marmalade, London noted the simplicity of Thick's family life and the small but respectable home in which they resided. Indeed Thick, no doubt using his local knowhow and influence which came from many years as a respected (and often feared) policeman, soon acquired the author a room in a house on the same street.

London referred to Thick as "Johnny Upright", a well-known nickname that was apparently derived from the upright bearing of both his stature and his police methods. He was also described by Walter Dew in his memoirs as "an unholy terror to the local lawbreakers".

ABOVE: Jack London, photographed in 1905.

Who Wrote the "Dear Boss" Letter?

Despite it being generally accepted as containing the first use of the name "Jack the Ripper", opinion on the letter's veracity weighs heavily in favour of it being a contemporary hoax, most likely written by a journalist. Robert Anderson believed this to be the case, and stated so in his memoirs, as did Melville Mcnaghten:

This document was sent to Scotland Yard, and (in my opinion most unwisely) was reproduced, and copies of same affixed to various police stations, thus giving it an official imprimatur. In this ghastly production I have always thought I could discern the stained forefinger of the journalist indeed, a year later, I had shrewd suspicions as to the actual author! But whoever did pen the gruesome stuff, it is certain to my mind that it was not the mad miscreant who had committed the murders. The name "Jack the Ripper", however, had got abroad in the land and had "caught on"; it riveted the attention of the classes as well as the masses.

The identity of the alleged journalist author has often focused on an individual known for many years only as "Best", whose culpability for writing the Dear Boss letter was brought to the public attention in 1966. In recent years he has been identified as Frederick Best, a reporter for *The Star*. Thomas Bulling, a journalist employed by the Central News Agency, himself has also been accused of being the creator. This information was brought to light by the discovery of a letter written in 1913 by Chief Inspector John Littlechild, formerly of Special Branch:

With regard to the term "Jack the Ripper" it was generally believed at the Yard that Tom Bullen (sic) of the Central News was the originator, but it is probable Moore, who was his chief, was the inventor. It was a smart piece of

journalistic work. No journalist of my time got such privileges from Scotland Yard as Bullen.

According to the opinion of an American newspaper report of April 1891, Charles Moore, the General Manager of Central News, was the author who created the undoubted sensation in order to generate publicity for his agency. The report claimed that his friends observed that the communications (described as "postal cards") did not surprise him as much they might have done, and that the handwriting of the letter resembled Moore's. This allegation was attributed to a Mr Brisbane, "who was a London journalist at the time of some of the atrocious

Dear Boss

25. Sept. 1888.

I keep on hearing the police have caught me. but they wont fix me just yet. I have laughed when they look so clever and talk about being on the right track. That joke about Leather apron gave me real fits. I am down on whores and I shant quit ripping them till I do get buckled. Grand work the last job was. I gave the lady no time to squeal. How can they catch me now. I love my work and want to start again. You will soon hear of me with my funny little games. I saved some of the proper red stuff in a ginger beer bottle over the last job to write with but it went thick like glue and I cant use it. Red ink is fit enough I hope ha. ha. The next job I do I shall clip the ladys ears off and send to the

"The "Dear Boss" letter."

police officers just for jolly wouldnt
you . Keep this letter back till I
do a bit more work . then give
it out straight My Knife's so nice
and sharp I want to get to work
right away if I get a chance .
Good luck .

yours truly
Jack the Ripper

Dont mind me giving the trade nam

wasnt good enough
to post this before
I got all the red
ink off my hands
curse it
No luck yet. They
say I'm a doctor
now ha ha

Whitechapel Murders".

It has also been noted that a journalist
would be more likely to send such a
communication to the Central News Agency (a
press organization not necessarily recognized
by the wider public), which is what happened,
as opposed to a specific newspaper or the
police. The original letter was missing for
many years until it was sent anonymously
from Croydon with other official documents in
1987. It now resides at the National Archives
in South London along with over 200 letters
that followed the in the wake of the Dear Boss
letter's original publication.

1:30 a.m. he decided to take a stroll down Seven
Sisters Road to view the great red glow that was
visible from the fires even at that distance. While
there, he struck up a conversation with a police
officer, giving Pizer a most reliable alibi which
could be checked.

John Pizer later took the unprecedented
step of appearing at Annie Chapman's inquest
to exonerate himself of the murders and
subsequently, owing to the accusations against
his character, he was able to make claims for libel
damages. The owners of *The Star*, for one, were
made to pay for their sensationalism.

By the middle of September 1888, frustration
hung in the air. Any evidence picked up at the
Hanbury Street crime scene only led to dead
ends for the investigating officers. Rumours
were common, while hysteria and interference
from time-wasters and pranksters made a sober
judgement of the situation difficult at best. The
radical press now fervently decried the apparent
impotence of the police and regularly used the
situation as a stick with which to beat them with,
and taking the worst of it all was Sir Charles
Warren. Popular satirical magazines such as *Punch*
lampooned the relationships between the officials
and made a point of suggesting that the crimes
were a by-product of the awful conditions to be
found in the East End which had gone unchecked
for so long. Cartoons like "Blind Man's Buff",
showing a blindfolded police officer reaching
out for somebody to arrest, have remained
iconic images of the Whitechapel Murders to
this day. One more than any other encapsulated
the fear, the danger and the social conscience
that the murders pricked. On 29 September,
Punch published a poem entitled "The Nemesis
of Neglect", a lengthy verse which espoused the
wrongs of the slums and how failure to right them
had resulted in the visitation of awful crime. The
final verse was particularly powerful:

> Dank roofs, dark entries, closely-clustered walls,
> Murder-inviting nooks, death-reeking gutters,
> A boding voice from your foul chaos calls,
> When will men heed the warning that it utters?
> There floats a phantom on the slum's foul air,
> Shaping, to eyes which have the gift of seeing,
> Into the Spectre of that loathly lair.
> Face it – for vain is fleeing!
> Red-handed, ruthless, furtive, unerect,
> 'Tis murderous Crime – the Nemesis of Neglect!

The poem was accompanied by a most evocative illustration; it depicted a translucent phantom floating through a slum alley, large knife drawn, staring out like some form of supernatural predator, its eyes piercing and its jaw hanging loose in a horrifying gape. The left hand was extended with the bony fingers posed into a claw. On its forehead was the word "CRIME". This illustration was without doubt one the most striking images from those fearful times. It was the perfect embodiment of a murderer who was fast becoming the uncatchable, much-feared lurker in the shadows.

As witty satirists joined forces with indignant moralizers within the media, a new ingredient presented itself which lifted these murders from the merely horrific to the almost mythical. On 27 September, the Central News Agency in New Bridge Street, London, received a letter addressed to "The Boss, Central News Office, London City" and bearing an EC postmark. Written in red ink, it claimed to have been penned by the killer himself:

25 Sept 1888
Dear Boss,
I keep on hearing the police have caught me but they wont fix me just yet. I have laughed when they look so clever and talk about being on the right track. That joke about Leather Apron gave me real fits. I am down on whores and I shant quit ripping them till I do get buckled. Grand work the last job was. I gave the lady no time to squeal. How can they catch me now. I love my work and want to start again. You will soon hear of me with my funny little games. I saved some of the proper red stuff in a ginger beer bottle over the last job to write with but it went thick like glue and I cant use it. Red ink is fit enough I hope ha. ha. The next job I do I shall clip the ladys ears off and send to the police officers just for jolly wouldn't you. Keep this letter back till I do a bit more work, then give it out straight. My knife's so nice and sharp I want to get to work right away if I get a chance. Good Luck.
Yours truly
Jack the Ripper
Dont mind me giving the trade name

Written in crayon at right angles to the main body of the letter was the afterword:

PS Wasnt good enough to post this before I got all the red ink off my hands curse it No luck yet. They say I'm a doctor now. ha ha

The letter was not the first missive claiming to be from the killer as a letter dated 24 September had been received by Sir Charles Warren a few days previously, but, like its less famous forebear, the "Dear Boss letter" was initially taken lightly. Nonetheless it was sent on to Scotland Yard on 29 September with a covering note from Thomas Bulling of the Central News Agency:

The editor presents his compliments to Mr Williamson & begs to inform him the enclosed was sent the Central News two days ago, & was treated as a joke.

Despite press and police knowledge of the letter, the public would remain none the wiser for

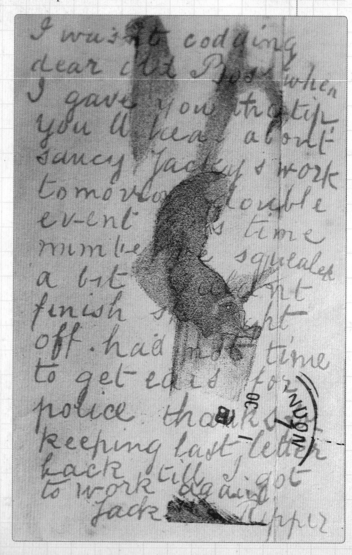

BELOW: The "Saucy Jacky" postcard, received by the Central News agency on 1 October, the second communication to bear the name "Jack the Ripper" and evidently written by the same author as the "Dear Boss" letter.

The Central News Agency

Based at 5 New Bridge Street, close by Blackfriars Bridge in London, the Central News Agency became a major player during the events surrounding the Whitechapel Murders. Formed in 1863 as the Central Press, and renamed in 1871, it immediately strove to undercut its two main rivals, Reuters and the Press Association, and its tendency to find and distribute sensational stories meant it was often looked down upon by more responsible journalists. Its notoriety was ensured during the Ripper crimes, when its receipt of the "Dear Boss Letter" made it the source of major press and public interest.

Its methods came under scrutiny many years later when *The Times* compared telegrams received by the agency with the subsequent reports based on those communications. It appeared that many of these missives were embellished by the Central News Agency. One commentator noted that after seeing a news report about a naval battle in the Far East, more than two-thirds of the final report had been prepared in London, and was fleshed out with information that had not been contained in the original telegram.

RIGHT: The offices of the Central News Agency on New Bridge Street, London, seen at the centre of this photograph from the 1900s.

several days. Those who were party to its content generally felt that it was a hoax, including the press agency, which would later be accused of creating the artefact in the first place. The ominous request to "Keep this letter back till I do a bit more work, then give it out straight" was respected, however, and indeed, there was not long to wait. Once the Whitechapel killer had struck again, the contents of the letter were released to the general media in both print and facsimile forms, accompanied by a second missive received on 1 October. A postcard, seemingly smeared with blood, and again slipped into the postbag of the Central News, referred to the content of the previous missive and appeared to have been written in the same hand:

I was not codding dear old Boss when I gave you the tip, you'll hear about Saucy Jacky's work tomorrow double event this time number one squealed a bit couldn't finish straight off. had not the time to get ears for police. thanks for keeping last letter back till I got to work again. Jack the Ripper

"Saucy Jacky's work" this time was, as stated, a double murder. On the early morning of 30 September 1888, Elizabeth Stride and Catherine Eddowes would become the next unwitting victims of the man who, within a few days, would be known to the world as "Jack the Ripper". Their deaths would throw up more questions for the authorities and even more consternation from the public and with a sudden twist of fate, create yet more problems for the already battered Metropolitan Police and their counterparts in the City of London.

ELIZABETH STRIDE

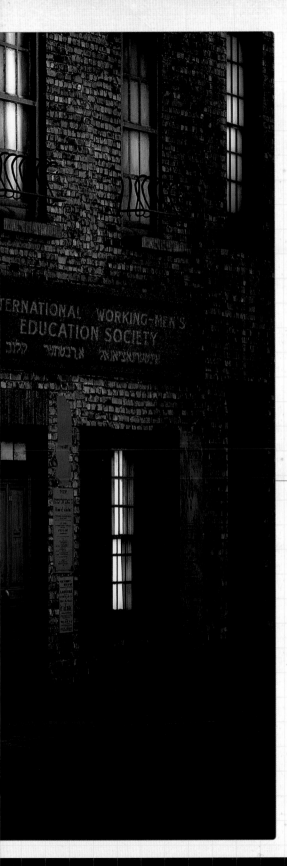

LEFT: Berner Street showing
the entrance of Dutfield's
Yard between Nos.42 and
40 Berner Street (the
International Working-
Men's Education Society).

Briefing

In the days that followed the murder of Annie Chapman, the criticism of the police in most newspapers grew. Journalists blamed the police for the murderer not having been brought to justice, and complained that the police treated reporters with a disdain that would be dismissed as beneath contempt were it not almost criminally senseless. The police had prevented journalists from visiting the mortuary and the house where Annie Chapman had been murdered. A policeman at the mortuary had lied to them, inspectors and even constables had wilfully misled them, and they had denied reporters information which, it was felt, would have allayed alarm somewhat had it been made public.

LEFT: Berner Street showing the entrance of Dutfield's Yard between Nos.42 and 40 Berner Street (the International Working-Men's Education Society).

UNFAVOURABLE COMPARISONS WERE MADE between the British police and the police in New York who apparently enlisted the services of journalists and encouraged their active participation in investigations. Some newspapers were extremely outspoken in their criticism. *The Star* in particular observed that the clumsiness of the police had made the name of the commissioner, Sir Charles Warren, a "stink in the nostrils of the people of London". To have public officials derided in such language in a newspaper was unusual and must have been thrilling to many readers. Journalists clamouring for interviews, pursuing their own investigations, criticizing the police and later the government in no uncertain terms, and believing they had the right to do this, was a new and very exciting phenomenon, but nobody was prepared for what was about to happen next.

Arbeter Fraint, which means "Worker's Friend" in Yiddish, was a weekly Yiddish newspaper founded in 1885 by Morris Winchevsky (a pseudonym, one of many he used; his real name was Lippe Benzion Novochovitz) for a Jewish radical, anti-religious and, later, an anarchist readership. It would be suppressed by the British Government on the outbreak of the First World War, but in the late 1880s it was an important and influential publication.

PREVIOUS PAGES: Aerial view of Berner Street, close to the junction with Fairclough Street.

In the same year that it first saw the light of day, radicals acquired a property at 40 Berner Street and set up the International Working-Men's Education Club (this was how most people referred to the International Working Men's Education Society). Pretty much forgotten today, it was an important gathering place for radicals, Anarchists and Social Democrats, who had meetings and gave lectures there, held concerts and dances and staged occasional plays. In 1886, the club took over publishing *Arbeter Fraint*, and its editorial and printing offices were in the yard accessed along a narrow passage running along the side of the house. It was in this passage, against the wall and close to the street gate, that the body of Elizabeth Stride was found at 1:00 a.m. on 30 September 1888.

Elizabeth Stride was Swedish. She was born on 27 November 1843 on a small farm called Stora Tumlehead in the district of Torslanda on Hisingen, Sweden's fourth largest island, which is largely rural until the advent of industry in the nineteenth century. Elizabeth was the daughter of Gustaf Ericson and his wife Beata, and the second of their four children, there being an elder sister, Anna Christina and two younger brothers, Carl and Svante. When she was 17 years old she moved to Gothenburg and worked as a maid as well as looking after the four children of a man named Lars Fredrik Olofsson. By the end of 1865 she had given birth to a stillborn girl and had twice been admitted to hospital for the treatment of a venereal disease.

OPPOSITE: Berner Street looking north near the junction with Fairclough Street. At the corner is the Nelson Beer House, with the entrance to Dutfield's Yard a few doors further up.

The police had registered her as a professional prostitute. Her life was going horribly wrong.

In 1866 Elizabeth's mother died and although it was no doubt a tragedy for Elizabeth, a small inheritance enabled her to travel to London. It is uncertain what she did in London in the first years she was there. Charles Preston, from whom she had borrowed a clothes brush before going out on the last night of her life, said she had once told him that she had gone into service and worked for a foreign gentleman, and Michael Kidney, with whom Elizabeth lived on and off for the last years of her life, said she had lived with a family near Hyde Park. She would later give her address as 67 Gower Street, a highly respectable district in Bloomsbury, not far from the British Museum.

On 7 March 1869 Elizabeth married John Thomas Stride at St Giles-in-the-Fields church in London's West End, and together they opened a coffee shop in Upper North Street, Poplar, moving a year or two later to 178 Poplar High Street. Things seemed to be going right for Elizabeth, but the marriage was a troubled one and by 1881 it had come to an end. Elizabeth gravitated towards Whitechapel and eventually took lodgings at 32 Flower and Dean Street, a doss-house that would prove to be her preferred abode for much of her remaining years. In November 1884 she went to prison for seven days for being drunk and disorderly, and for soliciting.

BACKGROUND INTELLIGENCE — The Princess Alice Disaster

A story Elizabeth appears to have been fond of telling people was that she and her husband and children had been aboard the pleasure steamer *Princess Alice* when it struck another vessel and sank with a horrendous loss of life.

On 3 September 1887, the *Princess Alice* was taking a "moonlight trip" down the Thames from London Bridge to Gravesend and back, laden with over 800 passengers. As she approached North Woolwich Pier where some passengers were due to disembark, the SS *Bywell Castle*, a coal boat bound for Newcastle, came into view. In an attempt to avoid each other in the poor light, the captains of both vessels misjudged their routes and the much heavier *Bywell Castle* hit the *Princess Alice*, effectively cutting the latter in two. It sank in four

minutes. Most of the dead went down with the boat but it is believed that many also died as a result of swimming in water that had been contaminated with 341 million litres (75 million gallons) of raw sewage, which had been pumped out of Crossness and Barking sewer outfalls only an hour earlier. It was the greatest ever Thames shipping disaster and 650 people perished. Not one of them, however, was named Stride.

It appears that Elizabeth told many people of her experience that night and the story crops up time and time again in interviews with those who knew her. But, of course, it was a falsehood. In reality, John Stride died in October 1884 of heart disease, several years after the couple had parted, and they had no children.

Dr Thomas Barnardo

Dublin-born Thomas Barnardo is famous today for the work he did to assist destitute children. He opened his first home for boys in Stepney in 1870, and is still remembered for the work in this area that continues to be done by the charity that bears his name. On 6 October 1888 he wrote a long letter to *The Times* about the children who lived in common lodging houses. Below is an extract from that letter.

Only four days before the recent murders I visited No. 32, Flower and Dean-street, the house in which the unhappy woman Stride occasionally lodged. I had been examining many of the common lodging-houses in Bethnal-green that night, endeavouring to elicit from the inmates their opinions upon a certain aspect of the subject. In the kitchen of No. 32 there were many persons, some of them being girls and women of the same unhappy class as that to which poor Elizabeth Stride belonged. The company soon recognized me, and the conversation turned upon the previous murders. The female inmates of the kitchen seemed thoroughly frightened at the dangers to which they were presumably exposed... One poor creature, who

had evidently been drinking, exclaimed somewhat bitterly to the following effect:– "We're all up to no good, and no one cares what becomes of us. Perhaps some of us will be killed next!" And then she added, "If anybody had helped the likes of us long ago we would never have come to this!"... I have since visited the mortuary in which were lying the remains of the poor woman Stride, and I at once recognized her as one of those who stood around me in the kitchen of the common lodging-house on the occasion of my visit last Wednesday week.

Dr Barnardo was not above making up stories to get publicity for the important and life-saving work to which he devoted his own life. Little John "Carrots" Somers, the 11-year-old boy who was turned away from a Barnardo's home that was full and whose death a short time later led to the famous Barnardo's statement "No Destitute Boy or Girl Ever Refused Admission", is thought by many not to have existed. The deputy of 32 Flower and Dean Street was emphatic that Stride had not stayed there on the night of Barnardo's visit, but it is an enduring and touching story nevertheless.

Around 1885 she met and began living with a waterside labourer named Michael Kidney. It seems to have been a stormy, and even violent relationship: Stride on one occasion in early 1887 accused Kidney of assault, but she failed to turn up in court to press the prosecution. Elizabeth frequently left Kidney, who, at the inquest on 3 October 1888 was reported as estimating that in the three years they'd lived together they had been apart for five months, and he blamed her drinking. "It was drink that made her go away," he said, and her regular appearances before the magistrates during 1887/88 for being drunk and disorderly and using obscene language suggested that drink had a hold on her, and that she could be difficult. Kidney and Elizabeth may have had one of their quarrels on 25 September 1888. He claimed they had been on good terms, but her friend, Catherine Lane, into whose care Elizabeth had entrusted a piece of velvet on the night she died, said that Stride had told her that she'd left Kidney following a row. Whatever the cause, Elizabeth went to her old lodging at 32 Flower and Dean Street.

Elizabeth was around 1.65 m (5 ft 5 in) tall (accounts differ), but was nicknamed Long Liz.

Other nicknames appear to have been Annie Fitzgerald, Epileptic Annie (owing to her tendency to pretend to have an epileptic fits when drunk), Hippy Lip Annie (the meaning of which is uncertain; "hippy" might mean large hipped, while the lip could refer to Stride's lower lip: her admittedly unflattering mortuary photograph suggests that she had an unnaturally large or swollen lower lip), and Mother Gum, because when she laughed the whole of the upper gum was displayed. Friends and acquaintances said she was of good character, but there was a strong aversion to speaking ill of the dead, and Elizabeth's court appearances suggest a personality at odds with the very quiet woman described by the lodging-house deputy, Elizabeth Tanner. Tanner said that Elizabeth worked when work was available, often doing cleaning work for the Jews – she could speak Yiddish according to Michael Kidney. In the *Morning Advertiser* on 2 October 1888, a bedmaker at the lodging house, Mrs Ann Mill, said of Stride that "a better hearted, more good-natured cleaner woman never lived".

During the afternoon of Saturday 29 September 1888 Elizabeth had cleaned the rooms at 32

OPPOSITE: The view looking south along Berner Street from the direction of the International Working-Men's Education Society

OVERLEAF: This view of Berner Street shows (left to right) Nos. 46 to 32, including Matthew Packer's premises at 44 and Fanny Mortimer's house at 36.

32 Flower and Dean Street

This large lodging house began as a single property before being integrated with No.33 in 1853. Originally registered in 1852 in the name of Joseph Goodman, from 1871 the owner was John Satchell who had recently acquired 19 George Street, once the home of Martha Tabram (see chapter 3). No.32 Flower and Dean Street was licensed to accommodate 77 lodgers at this time and, when required, was Elizabeth Stride's house of choice from 1882. Following her murder, a sketch of the rather tatty-looking house was published in the press, describing it as "lodgings for travellors Etc with every accommodation".

John Satchell gave up No.32 in March 1891 as new developments were about to change the north side of Flower and Dean Street and it was demolished soon after.

LODGINGS
FOR
TRAVELLORS & ETC
WITH EVERY
ACCOMMODATION

**RIGHT: An illustration of
32 Flower and Dean Street
from *Famous Crimes Past
and Present* (1903), based
on a contemporary press
sketch.**

Flower and Dean Street and been paid 6d (£1.50 in today's money) for her labours. She had then gone to the pub, the Queen's Head on the corner of Commercial and Fashion Streets. She had returned to the lodging house, leaving a piece of velvet for safekeeping with Catherine Lane and, rather touchingly, borrowing a clothes brush from Charles Preston to smarten herself up. Thomas Bates then watched her leave. She seemed happy.

It was 11:00 p.m. and raining quite hard as two men named Best and Gardner were going into the Bricklayer's Arms at 34 Settles Street. A man and a woman came out of the pub and lingered in the doorway as if reluctant to go out into the rain. The man was kissing and cuddling the woman, which astonished the men because he was respectably dressed and his behaviour seemed inappropriate. The two men made a few good-natured remarks and the couple dashed off into the rain. When Best and Gardner later viewed the body of Elizabeth Stride, they were certain she was the woman they had seen. They described the man as 1.65 m (5 ft 5 in) in height, well dressed in a black suit and coat and wearing a black billycock hat (as bowler hats, popular at the time, were generally called). He had a thick, black moustache, but otherwise he had no facial hair at all, not even eyebrows.

The next possible sighting of Elizabeth Stride is extremely controversial: Matthew Packer sold fruit and vegetables through the open bottom half of a sash window at his home at 44 Berner Street. He

**OVERLEAF: Berner Street in
1909, showing the former
Nelson Beer House and
the entrance to Dutfield's
Yard. This was one of
many photographs taken in
the neighbourhood taken in
the lead-up to its imminent
demolition later that
same year.**

claimed that between 11:00 p.m. and midnight on the 29 September, a man and a woman had come to his shop and bought some black grapes. It was a dark night and the only light was provided by an oil lamp just inside the shop window, but Packer was able to describe the man as middle-aged, about 1.7 m (5 ft 7 in) tall, stout and square built, wearing dark clothes and a "wideawake" hat (a type of low-crowned felt hat popular among Quakers, sometimes called a Quaker hat, and not dissimilar to a cowboy hat). He looked like a clerk, but had a rough voice. The woman, said Packer, was middle-aged, wore a dark dress and jacket, and there was a flower pinned to her bosom (Packer said it was white). Packer took the money for the grapes and watched as they crossed the road, where they stood in the pouring rain for more than half-an-hour. They moved off at about 12:15 a.m. or a little earlier, said Packer, who closed his shop just after.

For most of the time that Packer was supposedly selling grapes to a couple who he then watched standing in the rain eating them, William Marshall was standing in the doorway of his home at 64 Berner Street. He estimated the time to be about 11:45 p.m. when he saw a man and a woman three doors away, and after viewing Elizabeth's corpse in the mortuary he was certain that she was the woman he had seen. Marshall said Elizabeth was wearing a small crepe bonnet, but he did not see any flower pinned to her bosom. It was the man's behaviour which attracted Marshall, however. Like Best and Gardner, Marshall thought the man did not look the type to be kissing and cuddling her as he was; he was very decently dressed in a black coat and light trousers, and he was wearing a round cap with a small peak like the ones worn by sailors. He had the appearance of a clerk and his voice was mild, sounding like that of an educated man. He was of middling height and middle-aged, and rather stout. The couple stood there for about ten minutes, then Marshall overheard the man say, "You would

BELOW: The former Queen's Head pub on the corner of Commercial Street and Fashion Street, photographed in 2009. After its closure in 1927, it became a confectioner's and later a bank.

Matthew Packer's Story

Matthew Packer changed his story in almost every interview he gave, and he gave quite a few, apparently relishing his five minutes of fame. His timings changed frequently, so much so that a police report observed that his account would have no worth as evidence. The official records also show that Sergeant Stephen White interviewed Matthew Packer at 9:00 a.m. on the morning of the murder (30 September) and that at that time Packer claimed not to have seen anyone in the street that night: "I saw no one standing about, neither did I see anyone go up the yard. I never saw anything suspicious or heard the slightest noise. And I knew nothing about the murder until I heard of it this morning." Packer also told Sergeant White that he had shut early, having done no business because of the heavy rain. It appears that the rain had begun about 9:00 p.m. and stopped about 11:00 p.m. Packer had therefore closed *before* 11:00 p.m., two hours before the murder and before Stride had left the Bricklayer's Arms – if, indeed, it had been Stride whom Best and Gardener had seen. Furthermore, while Packer claimed to have watched the man and the woman standing in the pouring rain for half an hour, Dr Blackwell who examined Stride where she was found, stated that her clothes were not wet.

As interest in Packer's story dwindled, he claimed that two men had visited his shop, one of them saying that he thought the man who had bought the grapes was his cousin, an Englishman who had spent many years in the United States. What truth was in the story is unknown, but the press quickly reported that it led nowhere. The police may have taken it a little more seriously than the press indicated, as Irish–American Francis Tumblety would later claim that he was arrested on suspicion of being involved in the murders because he wore an American–style slouch hat.

Eventually Packer began to complain that he had neglected his business for a week to help the police and received no remuneration.

BELOW: Matthew Packer shown giving evidence to the police in a contemporary press sketch.

say anything but your prayers," and the couple walked away in the direction of Fairclough Street. At no time between 11:30 p.m. and midnight, said Marshall, did it rain.

Crucial to Elizabeth Stride's story is what people saw going on the street, what people didn't see and the times. For example, it is possible that a man named Israel Schwartz witnessed an assault on Elizabeth Stride. Whether or not the man Schwartz saw attack her was her murderer is not known, nor is it absolutely certain that he witnessed an assault on Stride or, indeed, that he witnessed any assault at all.

As described above, No.40 Berner Street had been converted from a house into the International Working-Men's Education Society generally more simply referred to as the Berner Street Club. That evening the Chair was taken by a young man named Morris Eagle, who opened the discussion at 8:30 p.m. The topic that night was "Why Jews Should Be Socialists", and there was a good turnout, with about 100 people in attendance.

The house had three storeys. At the front there was a single window and a door which led into a hallway with a staircase half-way along leading to the first floor. There were three doors along the hallway, one opening onto the front room which was used as a dining room, the second to the rear room which was used as a kitchen, and the second opened into an outdoor passage that ran from a gate to the rear of the house. On the first floor there was now a single room, with three windows looking out onto a rear yard. At one end was a stage, and in front of it were rows of plain, backless benches which could just about seat 150 people. On the third floor were the private rooms of the Club's steward, Louis Diemshitz and his wife.

The talk finished at about 11:30 p.m. and most of those who had attended left the Club by the street door. About 20 to 30 people stayed behind to talk. Some started singing. At the side of the house there was a passage. It was between 2.7 and 3.7 m (9 and 12 ft) wide and had two large wooden gates that folded backwards from the street. The left gate had a small wicker gate set into it and in white paint on the gates was written "W. Hindley, Sack Manufacturer. A. Dutfield, Van and Cart Builder". Arthur Dutfield was no longer there, but had given his name to the yard. Walter Hindley had a workshop facing the gates, and adjoining it was an unused stable. Beyond that were the two-roomed offices of *Arbeter Fraint*. Before you got that far there was the rear door of 40 Berner Street, and two lavatories were opposite.

Morris Eagle left the club by the front door between 11:30 p.m. and 11:45 p.m. to take his fiancée, Kate Kopelansky, home. He apparently saw nothing in the street to attract his attention. At about 12:10 a.m. William West left the house by the side entrance and returned some literature to the printing office of *Arbeter Fraint*. As he returned to the Club he looked towards the open gates but he saw nothing unusual. The passage was unlit and West was short sighted, so even if the body of Elizabeth Stride had been there, it is unlikely that he'd have noticed it. Back in the club, West collected his brother

and, with another member of the club, Louis Stansley and they went into Berner Street. He didn't see anyone in the street.

Charles Letchford, a 21-year-old who lived at 30 Berner Street, came along the road at about 12:30 a.m. He said that "everything seemed to me to be going on as usual", which as far as one can tell from the press reports means that nothing much was happening. His sister was standing at the door of the house and, although not stated, it is to be assumed that she had seen nothing.

Charles Letchford and his sister must have gone indoors by the time the beat of 26-year-old PC William Smith, 452H, brought him into Berner Street at about 12:35 a.m. He saw a man and a woman, who he noticed had a flower pinned to her jacket and who he later identified as Elizabeth Stride, standing on the pavement opposite the Club. The man was about 1.7 m (5 ft 7 in) tall, and wore a dark overcoat and dark trousers and was wearing a hard felt deerstalker hat. He was clean shaven, appeared respectable, and PC Smith guessed his age to be about 28. He had a newspaper parcel in his hand. This was a very

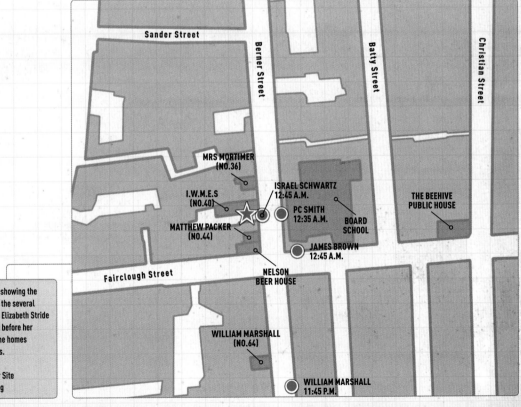

RIGHT: Map showing the positions of the several sightings of Elizabeth Stride in the hours before her death and the homes of witnesses.

⭐ Murder Site
◉ Sighting

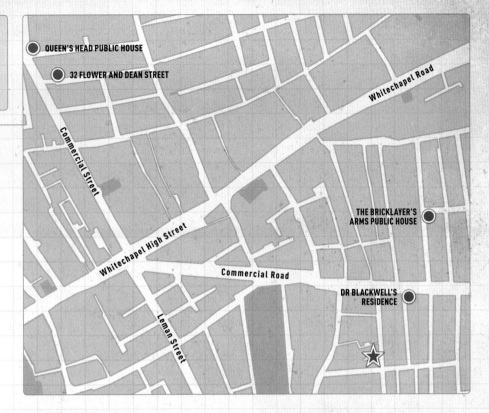

RIGHT: Map showing the relative positions of key places in the final hours of Elizabeth Stride.

⭐ Murder Site
● Key Location

QUEEN'S HEAD PUBLIC HOUSE

32 FLOWER AND DEAN STREET

Whitechapel Road

Commercial Street

Whitechapel High Street

THE BRICKLAYER'S ARMS PUBLIC HOUSE

Commercial Road

Leman Street

DR BLACKWELL'S RESIDENCE

LEFT: Looking down Dutfield's Yard. The murder site would have been on the right hand side, just past the open gate by the ventilation grate near the ground.

important sighting.

Morris Eagle returned to the Club at about 12:35 a.m., planning to have some supper. He must have been lost in thought or been naturally unobservant because he was unable to recall whether there was anybody in the street. Finding the street door locked, he went through the gateway into the passage alongside the house. Perhaps unsurprisingly he did not notice anything as he said it was dark and a body might have been lost in the shadows. Eagle went upstairs and joined a friend singing a Russian song. About five minutes later Joseph Lave, a printer and photographer who had recently arrived in London from the United States and who was temporarily living at the club, escaped the smoke-filled upstairs room and strolled around the yard and as far as the street. It was very quiet, he said, and he did not mention seeing anyone.

As Joseph Lave was escaping the smoke, James Brown left his home at 35 Fairclough Street to get some supper from a chandler's shop (as a general grocer was known) at the corner. He was in the shop for no more than a few minutes and returning to his house he saw a man and woman standing against the wall by the Board School in

Fairclough Street. The man had his arm up against the wall, and the woman was facing him, her back to the wall. Brown heard the woman say, "No, not tonight, some other night" and he turned to look. It was dark where they were standing, but Brown reckoned the man was about 1.7 m (5 ft 7 in) tall, and stout. He was wearing a hat, but Brown couldn't describe it. Most significantly, however, the man was wearing a long coat which almost reached down to his heels. Brown thought the woman was Elizabeth Stride, but wasn't certain and he did not see a flower pinned to her breast. He had reached home and nearly finished his food when he heard cries of "Police" and "Murder", but saw nobody when he opened a window to see what was going on, though he later saw a policeman at the corner of Christian Street being summoned to Berner Street.

Another important witness, but one not called to give evidence at the inquest, was Fanny Mortimer, who lived with her husband and children at 36 Berner Street, three doors away from the club. She claimed to have been standing at the door of her home for some time and to have returned inside and begun preparing for bed when she heard a pony and cart pass by outside. It appears that the only pony and cart known to have passed down Berner Street did so shortly before 1:00 a.m. During the time she was standing there she had seen nobody in the street except a young man carrying a shiny black bag who had walked down Berner Street from Commercial Road. This man was Leon Goldstein. He had been to a coffee shop in Spectacle Alley, a narrow and gloomy little passage that ran off the south side of Whitechapel High Street, where he had collected empty cigarette packets, and he was returning along Berner Street shortly before 1:00 a.m. to his home at 22 Christian Street, with the packets in his bag. He was a member of the International Working-Men's Education Society and William West had later gone with him to Leman Street Police Station where he'd identified himself as the man seen by Mrs Mortimer.

Mrs Mortimer's story has a problem about timing: in early newspaper reports, where she isn't named, she is credited as saying that she had gone to her front door after hearing the measured, heavy tramp of a policeman passing the house on his beat. She estimated that she had been standing at her door for about ten minutes before returning indoors, and to have heard the passing pony and cart four or five minutes later. The problem is that the only policeman to have passed her house on his beat was young PC William Smith, 452H, whose beat had taken him past her house at 12:35 a.m. If she had gone out after hearing PC Smith pass by then she would have been at her door for the full half hour between 12:30 a.m. and 1:00 a.m., which is indeed what later press accounts report Mrs Mortimer as saying. However, Mrs Mortimer cannot have been at her door for the whole half hour because she would have seen several people in the street if she had been, among them Charles Letchford's sister, Morris Eagle returning to the Club at 12:35 a.m., and possibly Joseph Lave at or about 12:40 a.m. She saw none of them and none of them saw her.

Even more important than Mrs Mortimer's testimony is that of another witness, who likewise was unaccountably not called to give evidence at the inquest: Israel Schwartz, a man with a strong Jewish appearance, lived with his wife at 22 Ellen Street. At 12:45 a.m. he turned into Berner Street from Commercial Street. A short way ahead there was a man walking on the same side of the street and beyond him, outside the gates of the International Working-Men's Education Society, a woman was standing. The man stopped and spoke to the woman, then he tried to pull her into the street but was apparently unable to do so and instead turned her round and threw her down onto pavement. The woman screamed three times, but not very loudly. Schwartz sought to avoid the altercation and crossed to the opposite side of the road, for the first time seeing another man who was apparently lighting his pipe. The man who threw the woman down shouted out "Lipski!", the name of a Jew who the previous year had been convicted of murder and hanged and whose name was now used as an insult epithet. Schwartz wasn't sure to whom the word had been addressed and it wasn't apparent to him whether the first and second man were acquainted or together. In one of the few surviving official reports on the Stride murder, Inspector Abberline wrote that he had questioned Israel Schwartz very closely about to whom he thought "Lipski!" had been shouted, but he was unable to say. However, Abberline concluded from Schwartz's strong Jewish appearance that it had probably been addressed to him. Schwartz walked away, but he was feeling alarmed, especially as he couldn't speak English, and on realizing that the second man was following him, he started running.

Israel Schwartz identified the woman as Elizabeth Stride. He described the man who had assaulted her as aged about 30 years old, 1.65 m (5 ft 5 in) tall, with a fair complexion, fair hair and a small brown moustache. He was dressed in a dark jacket and trousers, and wore a black cap with a peak. He was noticeably broad shouldered – for which reason he is known among students of the Ripper mystery as the "Broad-Shouldered Man". The second man, often referred to as "Pipeman", was about 35 years old, 1.8 m (5 ft 11 in) in height, with a fresh complexion and light brown hair and moustache. He was dressed in a dark overcoat and was wearing an old hard black felt hat with a wide brim. He was holding a clay pipe in his hand.

Hardly any newspapers reported Schwartz's story, but it appears that a journalist working for *The Star* was in Leman Street Police Station when Schwartz turned up to give his account.

ABOVE: An extremely unflattering portrait of Elizabeth Stride from the contemporary press of 1888.

OVERLEAF: An overhead view of Dutfield's Yard showing the murder site and the side entrance to the International Working-Men's Society.

The *Star* added some important information: Schwartz was Hungarian, was well-dressed, and appeared to be an actor or associated with the theatre. He did not speak English, but was accompanied by a friend who interpreted for him. According to the journalist, Schwartz and his wife had been living in Berner Street and were moving that day, but he'd had to go out and walked home down Berner Street to check that his wife had successfully moved. The version as reported in *The Star* said that the man walking in front of him seemed a little drunk. Schwartz saw him stop to talk to the woman, place his hand on her shoulder and push her back into the passage. Not wanting to get involved, Schwartz had crossed the road, but the noise of the quarrel caused him to look back. He was just stepping from the kerb when the second man came out of the doorway of The Nelson, a beer house at the corner of Berner Street and Fairclough Street only a few doors away. This man shouted out a warning to the man assaulting the woman – *The Star* reporter makes no mention of "Lipski" being called out – and rushed towards Schwartz, who was positive he saw a knife in the man's hand.

The differences between the police statement and the press report are not great, and the police report which has survived is not a verbatim account of what Schwartz said, but a summary of his statement made by Chief Inspector Donald Swanson. It is therefore subject to all sorts of possible error, not least Swanson misinterpreting or misrepresenting of the original statement. Similarly, *The Star's* journalist was receiving the story via an interpreter in unknown conditions and he may not have been able to question Schwartz closely about the details, as the police were. Then there is Schwartz himself to add to the mix, for we have no idea whether he welcomed or was uncomfortable with the anticipated publicity his story might bring, and whether he would have exaggerated or played down parts or all of his story accordingly. For example, it seems likely that if the second man really did have a knife in his hand, Schwartz would have told this to the police. However, the perils of interpretation could turn a clay pipe into a knife. It is tempting to assume that Schwartz changed his story to make his running away look less cowardly; one could give him a metaphorical white feather for running away from a man with a pipe, but running away from a man with a knife who looked like he intended to use it is far more understandable. Schwartz also played down the altercation, telling the journalist that the man only pushed the woman, whereas to the police he said that she was swung round and thrown to the ground. The impression given to the journalist appears to be that Schwartz crossed the road to avoid a minor domestic incident, whereas to the police he described what was a serious assault (albeit not dramatically so by the standards of the time). Again Schwartz presents a less cowardly face to the journalist. Similarly, to the journalist Schwartz said he heard the altercation behind him, turned to look and was stepping from the pavement (presumably with the intention on intervening) when he saw the second man with a knife and concluded that discretion was the better part of valour, whereas to the police he admitted that he ran off when he thought he was being followed.

Less easy to explain is the location of the man with the pipe. The newspaper explicitly states that he emerged from the doorway of the pub on the corner, but the police reports are ambiguous. The police summary by Swanson reads:

BELOW: Showing the murder site marked by the cross, this illustration of the inside of Dutfield's Yard is from *Famous Crimes Past and Present*, published in 1903.

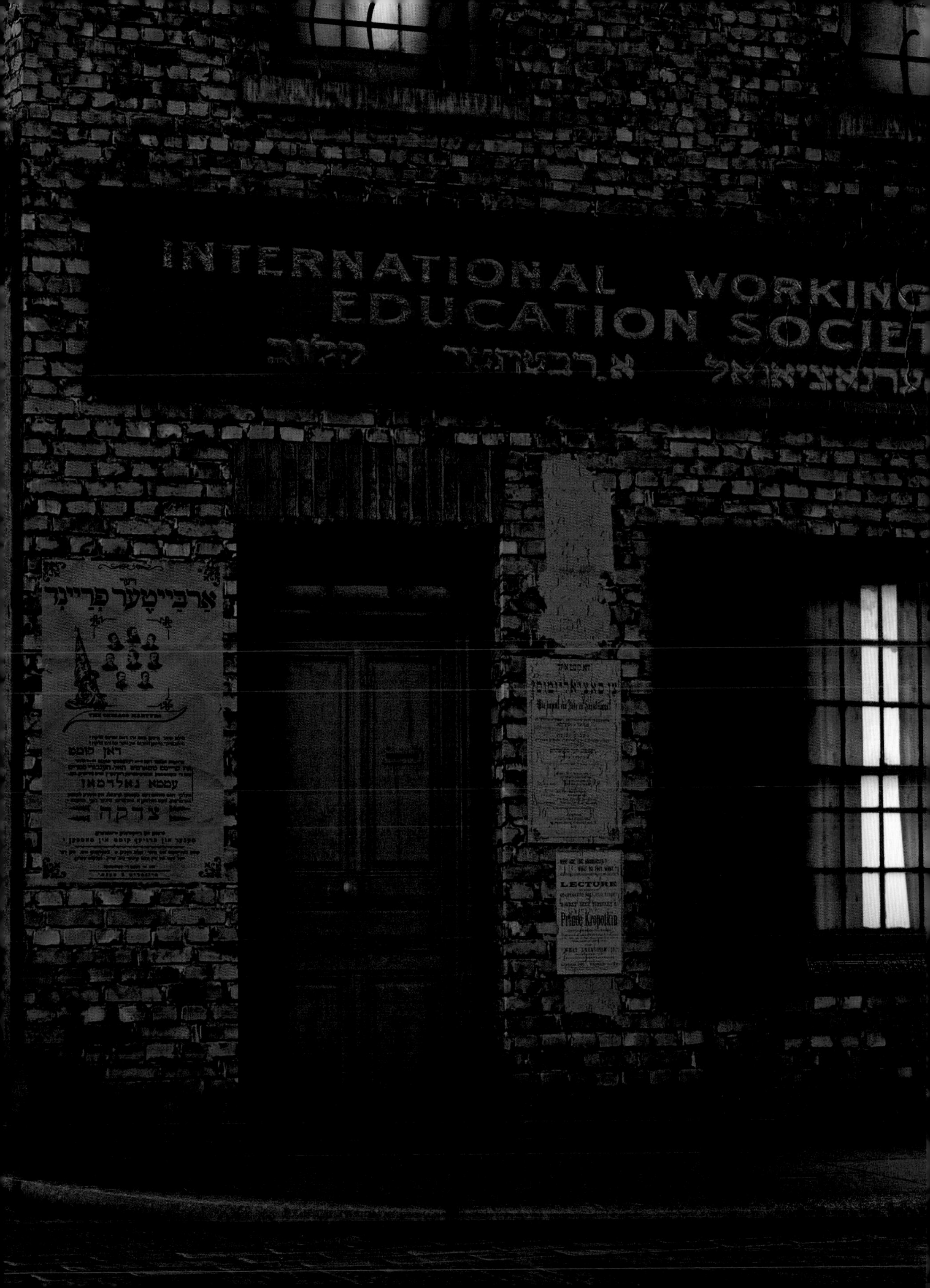
INTERNATIONAL WORKIN
EDUCATION SOCIE
ארבייטער פריינד
LECTURE
Prince Kropotkin

*On crossing to the opposite side of the street, he
saw a second man standing lighting his pipe.
The man who threw the woman down called
out, apparently to the man on the opposite side
of the road "Lipski". Inspector Abberline said:
"There was only one other person to be seen in
the street, and that was a man on the opposite
side of the road in the act of lighting a pipe.'*

It is not clear from whose perspective Swanson
and Abberline intended the man "on the opposite
side of the road" to be, the attacker's or Schwartz's.
Both were writing about Schwartz and may have
meant that the man was on the opposite side
of the road to him, which wouldn't necessarily
contradict the newspaper account, whereas if
they'd meant opposite to the attacker it would
mean that Schwartz and Pipeman were on the
same side of the road, opposite the pub.

Given that Israel Schwartz saw a woman he
identified as Elizabeth Stride being assaulted outside
the gates leading into the passage where her body
would be found within 15 minutes, his testimony
should have been considered crucial, yet he was
not called to give evidence at the inquest. The
surviving police documentation sheds no doubt
on the veracity of his statement, which was clearly
accepted during and after the inquest, so his absence
seems inexplicable – unless we accept the statement
by Assistant Commissioner Robert Anderson in a
report to Commissioner Sir Charles Warren dated
5 November 1888 and repeated almost verbatim by
Warren in a letter to the Home Office the following
day. Anderson wrote, "I have to state that the
opinion arrived at in this Dept. upon the *evidence
of Schwartz at the inquest* in Eliz. Stride's case is…"
(the authors' italics). So, did Schwartz give evidence
at the inquest? We may never know.

Just to complicate matters, the *New York Times*
reported on 2 October 1888 that "…two people
at least saw a man and the woman together in the
Berner Street gateway, and one saw him throw
her down. He went away and left her there, but it
was half-an-hour before it was known that she had
been murdered." This story is significant because
only Schwartz and Pipeman saw a couple in the
gateway and the report says that only one of them
saw Stride thrown to the ground (which *The Star*
report doesn't mention).

What seems to be the case is that at 12:45 a.m.
a woman was assaulted outside the gates leading
to the passage running along the side of the club.

Minutes later Mrs Mortimer came to her door and
all was quiet in the street at that time. Consideration
must be given to the possibility that the footsteps
Mrs Mortimer heard passing by were not those
of a policeman, but of the Broad-Shouldered
Man leaving the scene. If so, Elizabeth Stride was
either dead or in the passage, out of Mrs Mortimer's
range of vision, and perhaps in the company of
her murderer.

Or, of course, the woman wasn't Stride, the
altercation was all over and those involved had left
Berner Street before Mrs Mortimer opened her
door, which, if the timings are remotely accurate,
would mean that Stride and her murderer entered
Berner Street together or independently and went
into the passage in the four minutes after Mrs
Mortimer had gone indoors.

Louis Diemshitz, steward of the International
Working-Men's Education Society, sold cheap
jewellery at the markets and it was his custom on
Saturdays to travel by pony and cart to the market
at Westow Hill, near Crystal Palace. He was 26
years old, an ardent Socialist who would remain
with the movement and become a noted speaker
at Socialist events. He had been steward of the
club since or almost since it opened. He didn't
usually return home until after midnight and as
he passed a tobacco shop in Commercial Street
he noted that the time was 1:00 a.m. or a minute
or two after. He turned into Berner Street, passed
Mrs Mortimer's house, and turned through the

ABOVE: PC William Smith
who believed he saw
Elizabeth Stride with a man
at 12.30am on the morning
of 30 September 1888.
The couple were standing
on Berner Street opposite
Dutfield's Yard.

BELOW: A contemporary
press sketch of the moment
Louis Diemschitz discovered
the body of Elizabeth Stride.

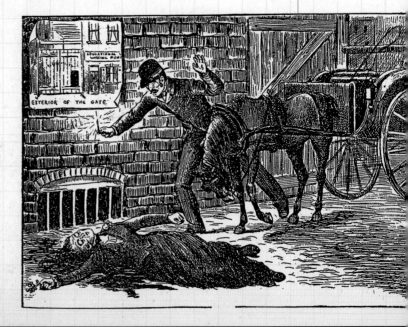

ABOVE: By the time of Stride's death, any reports of a new murder would immediately attract hundreds of onlookers to the scene, a situation that would be impossible today.

open gates into the passage at the side of the Club, but his pony shied and looking down Diemshitz saw something on the ground. Getting down from the cart he struck a match and saw a woman, who he thought was drunk or dead. He rushed up the passage to the side door and found his wife in the ground-floor front-room. "There is a woman lying in the yard, but I cannot say whether she is drunk or dead," he told her, then disappeared upstairs and informed the people in the concert room, among them Morris Eagle and a young man called Isaac Kozebrodsky, who both returned downstairs to the passage with Diemshitz. Eagle struck a match and to their horror they saw blood trickling down the gutter almost from the gate to the club. Diemshitz and Kozebrodsky ran for a policeman, heading off towards Fairclough Street, while Eagle turned in the opposite direction towards Commercial Road, all the time shouting "Police!"

Edward Spooner was standing for about half-an-hour with a young lady outside the Beehive pub on the corner of Fairclough Street and Christian Street. Just after 1:00 a.m. he saw Diemshitz and Kozebrodsky running up the street shouting

KEY EVIDENCE   Problems of Identification

Identifying a murder victim was a priority for the police and often presented a serious problem, rarely more so than in the case of Elizabeth Stride because a very distressed woman named Mary Malcolm saw the body in the mortuary and declared with absolute certainty that it was her sister, Elizabeth Watts. She met her sister every Saturday about 4:00 p.m. on the corner of Chancery Lane.

According to Mrs Malcolm, her sister was married to the son of Edward Watts, a long-established wine and spirit merchant in Bath, the marriage having produced two children, but she was an alcoholic and the marriage had effectively come to an end because of this and her infidelity. There were a lot of similarities with Elizabeth Stride: like Stride, her sister would fake epileptic fits when drunk; she had appeared before the magistrates for drunkenness; she was also known as "Long Liz"; and she had lived with a man who ran a coffee house in Poplar.

The only trouble was that a news agency tracked down Elizabeth Watts and she was

alive and well, and the respectable and hard-working wife of a crippled labourer named Joseph Stokes. A London journalist called "Elise" who wrote the "A Lady's Letter From London" column for the New Zealand newspaper Te Aroha News said that a friend had attended Elizabeth Stride's inquest and thought Mrs Malcolm was a "gin-sodden virago" and that:

from first to last this woman's transparent object was to turn the catastrophe to account somehow... Not a word of honest pity for the dead woman's shocking fate crossed her lips. Her own goodness and generosity to her poor sister was the never-ending theme of her discourse, or would have been, if the coroner had not cut her short.

Whether or not Mrs Malcolm really did meet with someone every week, her story fitted the facts and the press and the authorities were for some time convinced that Stride was Mrs Malcolm's sister, even preferring Mrs Malcolm's identification over that of others.

"Murder" and "Police". They ran past him towards Grove Street, but soon stopped and turned back and as they passed Spooner again, he asked them what had happened. On being told, he returned with them to Berner Street. There were about 15 people milling around in the passage and as one of the crowd lit a match, Spooner lifted Stride's chin. The body was still warm and blood was flowing from the neck wound. Spooner said there was a red and white flower pinned on Stride's jacket, and in her right hand there was a piece of paper doubled up.

Morris Eagle returned to the passage with two policemen, PC Henry Lamb, 252H, and PC Edward Collins, 12HR. Lamb flashed his light on the body and immediately sent Collins to fetch the doctor and Eagle to the police station. He instructed Spooner to shut the gates, then went inside the club and examined the hands and clothing of the people inside for any marks of blood. On going back outside, he examined the outside toilets and woke up the residents of the cottages in the yard. He appears to have been a very thorough policeman.

PC Collins returned to the passage with Edward Johnston, the assistant of Dr Frederick Blackwell, whose surgery was nearby on Commercial Road. Blackwell, who had been asleep in bed, arrived at precisely 1:16 a.m. and estimated that Stride had been dead for 20–30 minutes by the time he arrived – putting the time of death at between 12:45 a.m. and 1:00 a.m.

Poor Elizabeth Stride was lying on her left side close to the wall, her feet towards the street, about 1 m (3 ft) from the gate. Her hands were cold, but her face, neck, chest and legs were warm. Her right hand was open, lying across her chest and smeared inside and out with blood. The left hand was lying on the ground, was partially closed and contained a small packet of cachous – pills used to freshen the breath – wrapped in tissue paper. A number of the cachous were in the gutter. Stride's clothing was dry and there was a flower pinned to her dress. Her bonnet was on the ground, close to her head. Blood was running in the gutter into a drain from a clean 15 cm (6 in) incision in the neck. It commenced on the left side, 5 cm (2 in) below the angle of the jaw and had nearly cut the windpipe in two. It terminated on the opposite side of the neck, 2.5 cm (1 in) below the angle of

the right jaw. Elizabeth would have bled to death comparatively slowly, unable to make any sound.

At the post-mortem the doctors found a bluish discolouration over both shoulders, especially the right, and under the collar-bone and in front of the chest. They appeared to have been made by the pressure of two hands, and while it was not certain that they were recent or connected with the crime, Dr George Bagster Phillips (see chapter 5), who attended the post-mortem, was of the opinion that the murderer had seized Stride by the shoulders, forced her to the ground, and cut her throat from left to right. If the incision was made away from the murderer, he would probably not have been blood-stained. It was a neat theory, but he acknowledged that it failed to account for Elizabeth's blood-stained hand and wrist. Dr Blackwell believed that the murderer had pulled back Elizabeth's head with the check silk scarf she was wearing around her neck and that she had grasped at the front of it; Blackwell pointed out that the cut throat exactly

ABOVE: Dr Frederick Blackwell's surgery was at 100 Commercial Road, minutes from Berner Street. He arrived at 1:16 a.m. to pronounce Elizabeth Stride dead.

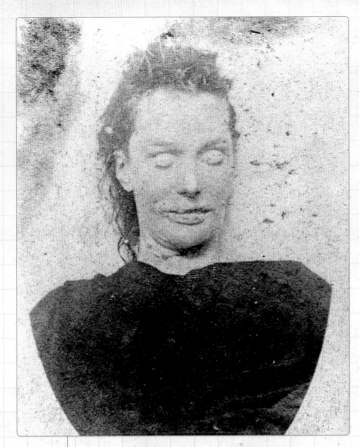

corresponded with the lower edge of the scarf, which was slightly frayed.

What appears clear, especially from Edward Spooner's statement that blood was flowing from Elizabeth's throat when he reached the passage, is that she had been very recently murdered, that her killer may have been disturbed by the arrival of Louis Diemshitz, and might even have been hiding in the darkness of the passage when Diemshitz discovered the body, fleeing only when he went into the club for help.

On the face of it, *if* the woman who Schwartz saw assaulted was Elizabeth Stride and if the Broad-Shouldered Man was her murderer, then the assault would have taken place in the few brief minutes *after* Mrs Mortimer had returned indoors. It is possible that the assault happened before she came to the door and that Stride was killed some five or ten minutes after the incident Schwartz witnessed. Alternatively, the woman he saw assaulted may not have been Elizabeth Stride.

At 4:30 a.m. the body of Elizabeth Stride was removed to the mortuary and at 5:30 a.m. PC Collins washed away all traces of blood. From the discovery of the body to the completion of the at-scene investigation, only a few hours had elapsed.

ABOVE: The mortuary photograph of Elizabeth Stride.

RIGHT: Elizabeth Stride's body was taken to the mortuary in the grounds of the church of St. George-in-the-East. It later became a nature study centre and is shown here derelict in 2009.

OPPOSITE: A sketch made during the Stride inquest of Louis Diemschitz.

CATHERINE EDDOWES

LEFT: "Ripper's Corner", Mitre Square, as it would have been on the "double event" of the murders of Elizabeth Stride and Catherine Eddowes. The rear of Mr Taylor's shop overlooks the murder site.

OVERLEAF: Busy Aldgate High Street, photographed around 1900.

Briefing

On that Saturday evening, 29 September 1888, when Elizabeth Stride, having brushed her clothes and smartened up, was out and hopefully enjoying the last few hours that remained of her life, a woman named Catherine Eddowes was getting drunk. At 8:30 p.m. PC Louis Robinson, 31 City, noticed a small group of people gathered outside No.29 Aldgate High Street, and on going over to investigate he found a woman slumped on the pavement, evidently very drunk. He asked if any of those gathered around knew who the woman was. No-one did, so he heaved her to her feet and leant her against the shutters of the shop, but she began to slide sideways.

FORTUNATELY PC GEORGE SIMMONS, 959 CITY, arrived and together they were able to take her to Bishopsgate Police Station, where the station sergeant, James Byfield placed her in a cell to sleep it off. Policemen checked on her at several times during the evening: PC Robinson 31 City, at 8:50 p.m. and afterwards, PC George Henry Hutt, 968 City, who had taken charge of the prisoners at 9:45 p.m. and visited them several times during the course of the night.

Saturday 29 September passed into Sunday 30 September and at 12:55 a.m. Sergeant Byfield told PC Hutt to check on the prisoners to see if any of them were in a fit state to be released. He found Eddowes awake and, if not sober, capable, so she was brought from the cells. She gave her named as Mary Ann Kelly and her address as 6 Fashion Street. One being told the time, she said, "I shall get a damned fine hiding when I get home, then." Hutt said, "Serve you right; you have no right to get drunk," and he pushed open the swing door. "This way, missus," he said and she walked down the passage to the street door. "Please, pull it to," said Hutt. "All right," she replied. "Good night, old cock." She went out into the street and turned towards Houndsditch, the opposite direction to her quickest route back to the common lodging house she called home.

OPPOSITE: Bishopsgate Police Station as it would have been in 1888. From here, Catherine Eddowes was released to her fate. The station was rebuilt in the 1930s.

BELOW: A contemporary press illustration of John Kelly, produced during the inquest into Catherine Eddowes's death.

Catherine Eddowes was born in Wolverhampton on 14 April 1842, but had been taken by her family to London when her father obtained employment there. Her mother had died in 1855 and her father in 1857, neither living beyond their 40s. Their large family was split up and Catherine went back to Wolverhampton to live with an uncle and aunt, William and Elizabeth Eddowes, but it seems that she was caught stealing from her employers and ran away to Birmingham to another uncle. She thereafter flitted between Birmingham and Wolverhampton, eventually meeting up with a man named Thomas Conway, a former soldier who had served for over two years in India before being invalided out in 1861. They began to live together and made what living they could by selling booklets known as chapbooks on the streets. One of their books apparently retold the story of Christopher Charles Robinson, who was hanged at Stafford Gaol in 1866 for the murder in Wolverhampton of his fiancée Harriet Seager. Catherine was allegedly a relative of Robinson and Conway was one of an estimated 4,000 people who attended the public hanging.

They had a daughter, Catherine Ann Conway, and further children followed, but Catherine had begun to drink heavily and this exacerbated her fiery temperament, which set her partnership with Thomas Conway on a course for disaster. There were rows, blows were occasionally exchanged, and sometimes Catherine would leave for two or three months. By 1880 there was no coming back, the relationship had collapsed completely, and Catherine walked out on her family. She went to the East End, where a sister was living, and moved into Cooney's lodging house.

From 1881, 55 Flower and Dean Street had been the home of John Kelly and it was there that he met Catherine. "We got throwed together a good bit and the result was that we made a regular bargain," he explained to a journalist. "We have lived here ever since, as the people here will tell you, and have never left here except when we've gone to the country together hopping [hop picking]... Well, Kate and me lived on here as best we could. She got a job of charring now and then and I picked up all the odd jobs I could in the Spitalfields Market. The people here were very kind to us."

As Kelly said, he and Catherine would go hop picking once a year. It was hard work, but for an estimated 50,000 and 60,000 people every year it provided a welcome break in the countryside. In 1888 Kelly and Eddowes walked to Kent and stopped off in Maidstone, where Eddowes purchased a pair of boots from Arthur Pash's shop in the High Street and a jacket from William Edmett's pawnbrokers and clothes shop. They then went on to Hunton, a village about 8 km (5 miles) from Maidstone, where they hoped to be hired to do some hop picking, but the weather that year had been appalling and hop crops across the county had been almost wiped out. There was no work and Eddowes and Kelly returned to London, travelling part of the way with another couple who

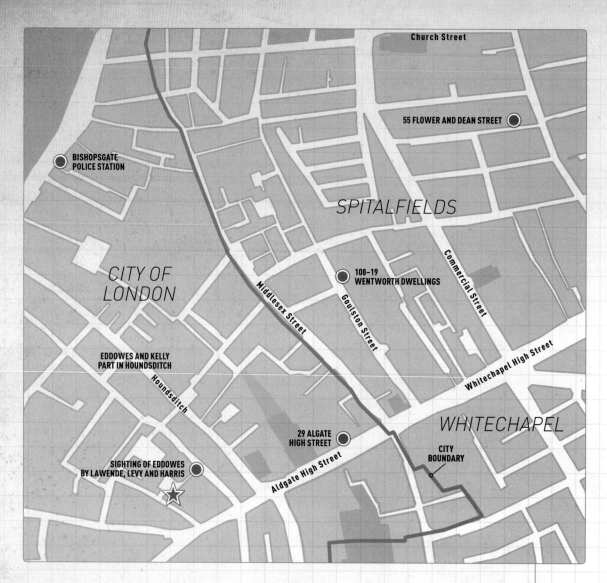

Church Street

55 FLOWER AND DEAN STREET

BISHOPSGATE
POLICE STATION

SPITALFIELDS

*CITY OF
LONDON*

108–19
WENTWORTH DWELLINGS

Commercial Street

Middlesex Street

Goulston Street

EDDOWES AND KELLY
PART IN HOUNDSDITCH

Houndsditch

Whitechapel High Street

WHITECHAPEL

29 ALGATE
HIGH STREET

CITY
BOUNDARY

SIGHTING OF EDDOWES
BY LAWENDE, LEVY AND HARRIS

Aldgate High Street

ABOVE: Map of the area
relating to the Eddowes
murder, showing key sites.

★ Murder Site
◉ Key Location

were heading to Cheltenham and who generously gave Catherine a pawn ticket for a shirt they had pledged with Jones's in Church Street (today's Fournier Street in London) in the name of Emily Burrell. They reached London on the afternoon of Friday 28 September. They had no money, but Kelly managed to earn 6d (about £1.50 today) and Eddowes took 2d (approximately 50p today) saying that she would get a bed in the casual ward in Shoe Lane. She told Kelly to use the rest of the money to get a bed at Cooney's.

Catherine got into some trouble at the casual ward and appears to have been turfed out. She returned to Cooney's at 8:00 a.m. and Kelly's boots were pawned at Smith's pawnbroker's in Church Street, where she pledged them in the name of "Jane Kelly", giving her address as 6 Dorset Street.

Kelly bought some food and a little tea and sugar and after they had breakfasted Catherine said she would try to borrow some money from her daughter in Bermondsey. Catherine parted from Kelly at 2:00 p.m. in Houndsditch and promised to be back in a couple of hours. According to Kelly, he warned her about the Whitechapel Murderer, but she'd said "Don't you fear for me. I'll take care of myself, and I shan't fall into his hands." Wherever Catherine went that Saturday afternoon, it almost certainly wasn't to see her daughter in Bermondsey (see box on page 149).

Catherine was wearing a chintz skirt buttoned at the waist, over which she wore an apron and a brown linsey bodice (linsey was a coarse twill or plain woven fabric woven with a linen warp and a woollen weft) with a black velvet collar and brown metal buttons down the front. She also wore a black jacket edged with imitation fur around the collar and cuffs, the pockets trimmed with black silk braid and imitation fur. She had a piece of red silk gauze around her neck as a scarf and on her head she wore a black straw bonnet, trimmed with green and black velvet and black beads, and tied with strings under the chin. On her feet, incongruously, she was wearing a pair of men's lace-up boots.

Apart from the fact that she got hold of enough money to buy (or found someone willing to treat her to) enough alcohol to get falling-down drunk, we do not know how Catherine spent the afternoon and early evening, but by 8:30 p.m. she was incapable and locked in the cells of Bishopsgate Police Station to sober up, to be released at 1:00 a.m. on Sunday morning. She was seen turning towards Houndsditch, a main road connecting Bishopgate and Aldgate. Running almost parallel with Houndsditch was Duke Street, from which a narrow passage led into a gloomy square overshadowed by warehouses. It was called Mitre Square.

In about 1108 Queen Matilda, the wife of Henry I, founded a priory of Austin canons in Aldgate and in due course two of her children were buried there. It became a great centre of learning, but in February 1532 it was dissolved and sold or given to favoured merchants and courtiers. Nothing of the priory survives today except some pointed arches inside an office building, but a street called Mitre Street follows the line of the nave of the priory church and the former cloister was where Mitre Square is today, with an entrance to the square being in Mitre Street. By the mid-1670s, the area had become known as Duke's Place and was also the site of St James's Church. It soon became commercial and by the time the church was demolished in the 1870s, tall warehouses had begun to take over the sides of the square, which earned its present name some time before 1830.

Mitre Square measured about 23 x 24 m (77 x 80 ft) and had three entrances, including the one from Mitre Street already mentioned. One at the far end on the left or north-eastern side was an archway leading through a passage 17 m (55 ft) long and 1.5 m (5 ft) wide to a street market called St James' Place. There was a fire brigade station there, but no one there that night saw or heard anything unusual. A night-watchman named James Blenkinsop was on duty taking care of some ongoing street improvements. He would later tell police that at about 1:30 a.m. a respectably-dressed man stopped and asked if he'd seen a man and a woman go through the passage. Blenkinsop hadn't and nothing more is known about him. He did not

---

BACKGROUND INTELLIGENCE — Cooney's Lodging House

A five-storey building with a single room on each floor, Cooney's was on the north side of Flower and Dean Street, close to the Brick Lane junction, and it was one of the largest common lodging houses in the area. It became a registered lodging house in October 1871, when it was owned by a man named Jimmy Smith. John Cooney married Smith's daughter, Elizabeth, and took over the house in May 1884, retaining ownership until 1891 when re-development forced him to relinquish it and it was demolished. Cooney acquired a large number of other houses in the area, as well as the Sugar Loaf pub in Hanbury Street (which was frequented by his cousin, the renowned music-hall performer Marie Lloyd), and he became a very wealthy man.

In his book, *East End Underworld: Chapters in the Life of Arthur Harding* (1981), Arthur Harding, a villain and a violent criminal who was a child at the time of the Whitechapel murders, recalled that Jimmy Smith begun his business by selling over-priced coal to the poor people – getting rich "out of swindling poor people out of small sums" – but he became "the governor about Brick Lane" and "the man who straightened up the police". He was a bookmaker and all the local bookies paid him money while he in turn paid off the local police – constables got a shilling a day and sergeants and inspectors received more, and at Christmas a bonus such as a crate of whisky. Harding's account is not altogether trustworthy since he had a complaint against the police and wanted to expose what he saw as widespread venal corruption, but we so rarely hear the criminal voice that it is important to note his opinion.

When asked her name at Bishopsgate Police Station, Catherine Eddowes said it was Mary Ann Kelly and that she lived at 6 Fashion Street. When she pawned John Kelly's boots she did so in the name of Jane Kelly and gave her address as 6 Dorset Street, and a woman named Mary Price, who lived at 36 Flower and Dean Street, having seen Catherine's body in the mortuary, identified her as a woman she knew as Jane Kelly. Two other women were equally sure that Eddowes was a woman named Annie who lived in or over a shop in a court near to Dorset Street.

The *Daily Telegraph* later reported that enquiries were made at 6 Dorset Street, and it was discovered that nobody named Jane Kelly appear at the inquest.

lived there. The irony is that the next victim was a young woman who lived at 26 Dorset Street who was named Mary Jane Kelly (see chapter 9). One wonders whether anyone directed the attention of the police to Mary Jane Kelly, and if they possibly even questioned her.

Mary Jane Kelly's room was partitioned off from the rest of the house and was accessed through a door down a passage leading into a court. The front room of the house (No. 26 Dorset Street) was used to store market carts and also by homeless people as a place to sleep. One press interview claimed that Eddowes had at one time used this room, commonly known as "The Shed".

OPPOSITE: Mitre Square during the mid-1960s, as seen from the entrance from Church Passage (today's St James's Passage).

On the right was Church Passage, 26 m (85 ft) long and 1.8 m (6 ft) wide, which led into Duke Street. PC Edward Watkins, 881 City, usually entered Mitre Square through Duke Street, but on that particular night he varied his beat – he described as doing it "left-handed" – and entered the square at about 1:30 a.m. through the carriageway from Mitre Street. He saw nothing to excite his attention as he turned his lantern light into all the corners, just as he usually did.

Meanwhile, three men left the Imperial Club at 16–17 Duke Street. They were Joseph Lawende, Joseph Hyam Levy and Harry Harris. Lawende walked a little ahead of his companions and on looking across the road to the entrance to Church Passage he noticed a man and a woman with her back to him. The woman put her hand on the man's chest, not to push him away but in a friendly way. Lawende walked past and did not look back, but he had noticed that she was wearing a black jacket and a bonnet which he later identified as those worn by Eddowes. He said the man was taller than the woman and wearing a cloth cap with a peak, but was adamant that he wouldn't be able to recognize him if he saw him again. During his testimony at the inquest on 11 October 1888, Joseph Hyam Levy said he had noticed the couple and had paid them scant attention, but acknowledged that he had said, "I don't like going home by myself when I see these sorts of characters about. I'm off." As the couple were only talking together and doing nothing alarming, threatening

or even morally distasteful, it is difficult to explain Levy's reaction to them. One can only suppose that he was offended by what he imagined they were doing. The third man, Harry Harris, saw nothing.

PC James Harvey, 965 City, walked down Duke Street about five minutes after Lawende, Levy and Harris had passed by. The man and the woman Lawende and Levy had seen at the entrance to Church Passage had gone and Harvey walked down the passage as far as the entrance of Mitre Square. He neither saw nor heard anything to arouse his attention. By now PC Watkins's beat was bringing him back to Mitre Square. He reached the entrance to the square at about 1:44 a.m., stopped to look up and down Mitre Street, then turned into the square. He flashed his light into the dark corner and it shone on the body of Catherine Eddowes. "She was ripped up like a pig in the market," he later graphically told a journalist for *The Star* newspaper, adding, "I have been in the force a long while, but I never saw such a sight." Shaken, he quickly crossed the road to a warehouse owned by a large wholesale grocery company called Kearley and Tonge where he knew that the night-watchman, an ex-policeman named George Morris, would be around to get some help. Morris, who was sweeping a corridor when PC Watkins knocked, quickly went to look at the body, and then ran into Mitre Street and on into Aldgate, blowing his old police whistle.

PC Harvey and PC Frederick Holland, 814 City, went to Watkins' assistance and Holland then went to fetch Dr George Sequeira from his surgery at 34 Jewry Street. He reached Mitre Square at 1:55 a.m.

OVERLEAF: This aerial reconstruction of Mitre Square shows how poorly lit much of it was. The murder site, seen to the left, received very little illumination at all.

OPPOSITE: Mitre Square circa 1925, virtually unchanged since the time of the Whitechapel Murders. The site of Eddowes' murder is behind the car.

BACKGROUND INTELLIGENCE — Catherine Eddowes and her Daughter

Catherine Eddowes comes across as a pleasant and jolly woman, as seemingly reflected by her cheery "Goodnight, old cock" as she left Bishopsgate Police Station. But there was a dark side to her character, as is revealed by the alleged causes of the breakdown of her marriage, her fondness for drink and her relationship with her eldest child, Catherine Ann Conway, who by 1888 was calling herself Annie and living with a man named Louis Phillips and their children. Her relationship with her mother had deteriorated considerably since 1886 when Catherine had assisted with the Annie's confinement when her

third child was born. Since that time, Catherine had become such a persistent scrounger that Annie and her family had moved home a couple of times to avoid her, each time keeping their address a secret. As far we are aware, Catherine didn't know where Annie lived, but must have known she no longer lived in Bermondsey. It's possible that on that Saturday afternoon, Catherine did intend to go to Bermondsey and make enquiries about Annie, it's equally possible that John Kelly lied about Catherine saying she was going to visit her daughter so that he could avoid admitting that she was going to prostitute herself.

ABOVE: The Church Passage entrance to Mitre Square in the mid-1960s, showing just how narrow the passage was. This is where PC James Harvey walked at 1:40 a.m. on the night of the "double event", at which time he saw and heard nothing unusual.

OPPOSITE: The corner of Church Passage and Duke Street where Catherine Eddowes was seen with a man by three witnesses, taken from a 1908 illustration. To the right is the Great Synagogue.

News of the discovery spread. Three plain-clothes detectives named Daniel Halse, Edward Marriott, and Robert Outram who had been talking at the southern corner of Houndsditch were quickly on the scene. Inspector Edward Collard, on duty at Bishopsgate Police Station, sent telegraphs to his superiors and a constable to fetch the police surgeon, Dr Gordon Brown, and then headed for Mitre Square himself. Dr Brown, Superintendent James McWilliam and Superintendent Foster followed in quick succession.

Catherine Eddowes had been ferociously attacked. She was stretched out on her back, her head resting on a coal hole and turned towards her left shoulder. Her bonnet was lying in a pool of blood which had run from the wound in her neck, and her throat had been cut some 15–18 cm (6 in–7 in) from the left ear to about 8 cm (3 in) below the lobe of the right ear. The left carotid artery had been cut, causing almost instantaneous death. There was a quantity of clotted blood on the pavement on the left side of the neck, round the shoulder and upper

ABOVE: Mitre Square looking from the former Kearley and Tonge warehouses towards the murder site. Taken in 1967, this photograph shows early signs of the redevelopment that would follow in the next decade.

OVERLEAF: A nocturnal view looking towards the entrance of Mitre Square from Church Passage which gives an idea of just how dark and isolated Mitre Square must have seemed at that time.

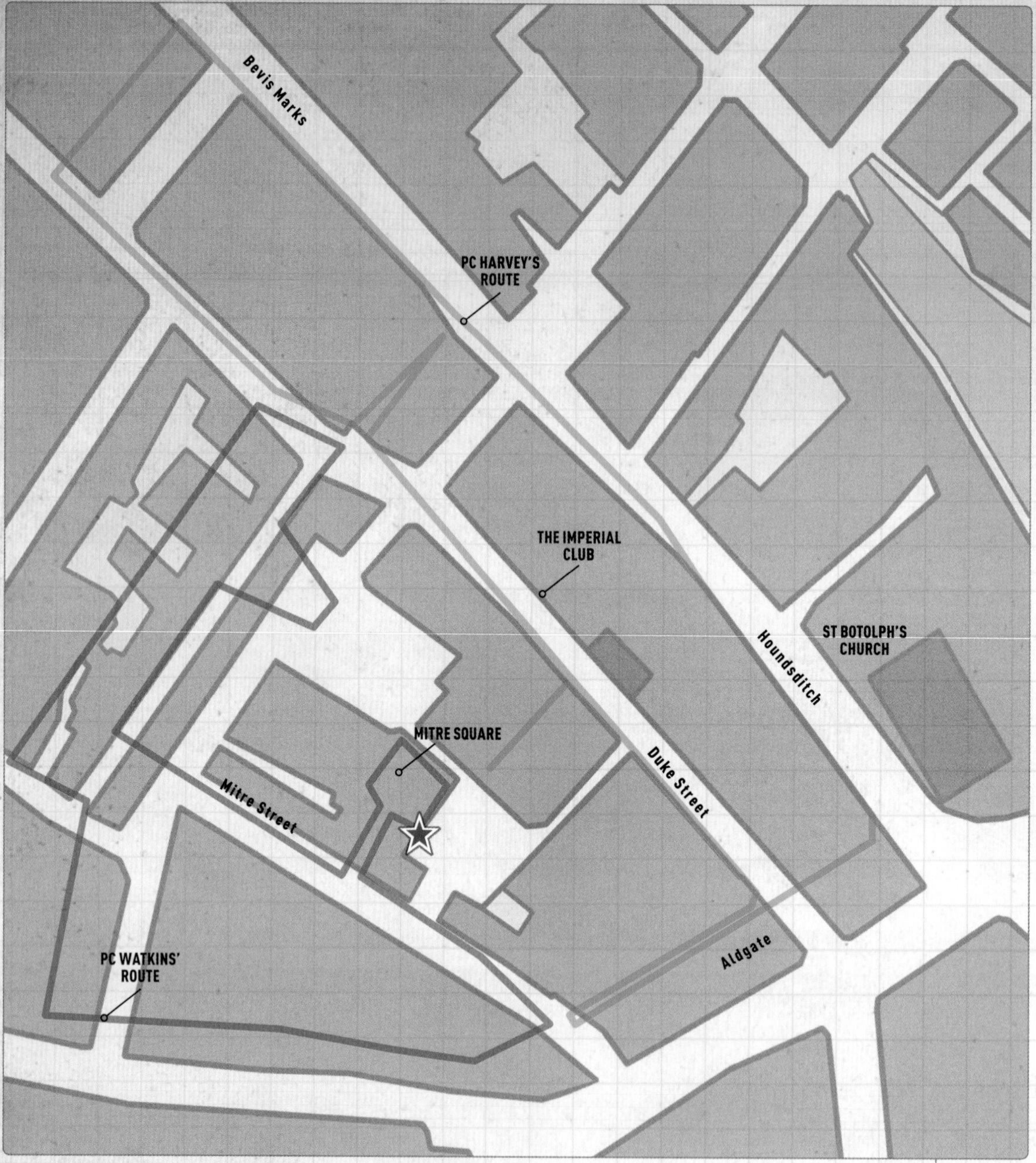
Bevis Marks
PC HARVEY'S ROUTE
THE IMPERIAL CLUB
Houndsditch
ST BOTOLPH'S CHURCH
MITRE SQUARE
Mitre Street
Duke Street
Aldgate
PC WATKINS' ROUTE

ABOVE: Map of the Mitre Square area showing the beats of Watkins and Harvey.

☆ Murder site

part of arm. Several buttons were found in the blood after the body was removed.

Her arms were laid by her side, palms upwards and fingers slightly bent. Near the right hand there was a thimble. The left leg was extended straight down, in a line with the body, and the right leg was bent at the thigh and knee. The abdomen and face had been appallingly mutilated, the intestines pulled out and laid over the right shoulder, and a piece of the intestines about 60 cm (2 ft) long had been detached and placed between the body and left arm. Dr Gordon Brown thought the murderer had done this deliberately. The left kidney and all but a small portion of the uterus had been removed and were missing, presumably taken by the murderer.

The face had been disfigured, and the murderer had left peculiar nicks to the lower eyelids and two inverted V's on the cheeks below the eyes. It had taken time to do this, from which it can be inferred that the murderer was either unconcerned about discovery or knew he had the time. The lobe and auricle of the right ear was cut – several portions of the ear fell from the clothing when the body was undressed at the mortuary – and the tip of the nose was completely cut off.

On the left side of the body a policeman found a small mustard tin containing the pawn ticket for John Kelly's boots and that for the flannel shirt given to Eddowes by Emily Burrell when she and Catherine parted company on the road back from hop picking in Kent. He also found three small black buttons generally used for women's boots, a small metal button and a metal thimble.

Eddowes was dressed in a black cloth jacket, brown linsey bodice, chintz skirt, black straw bonnet, silk scarf and men's boots. Underneath, she wore a grey petticoat, a very old green alpaca skirt and a very old blue skirt, a white calico chemise and a man's white front-buttoned vest. In addition to the pawn tickets, buttons and thimble, scattered about her person were:

1 black straw bonnet trimmed with green and
    black velvet with black beads, black strings
1 black cloth jacket, imitation fur edging around
    collar and sleeves
2 outside pockets, trimmed with black silk braid
    and imitation fur
1 chintz skirt with three flounces and brown
    button on waistband
1 brown linsey dress bodice, black velvet collar,
    with brown metal buttons down front
1 grey petticoat with white waist band
1 very old green alpaca skirt
1 very old ragged blue skirt with red flounce and
    light twill lining
1 white calico chemise
1 man's white vest, button to match down front,
    two outside pockets, no drawers or stays
1 pair of mens' lace up boots, mohair laces,
    right boot had been repaired with red thread
1 piece of red gauze silk found on neck
1 large white handkerchief
Unbleached calico pockets
1 blue stripe small bag, waist band and strings
1 white cotton pocket handkerchief, red and
    white bird's eye border
1 pair brown ribbed stockings, feet mended with
    white
12 pieces of white rag, some slightly
    bloodstained

RIGHT: PC James Harvey, taken from a group police photograph of about 1887, the officer who may well have come the closest to catching the Ripper in the act.

FAR RIGHT: Contemporary press illustration of PC Edward Watkins. He patrolled Mitre Square every fifteen minutes and on the night of the murder was working 'left-handed'; in other words, walking his beat backwards.

BELOW: A detailed illustration of Mitre Square from *Llloyds Weekly News*. In the absence of on-the-scene photography, illustrators would invariably have to document the sites for publication by drawing them "from life".

OPPOSITE: The entrance to Church Passage from Duke Street. Catherine Eddowes and her companion, possibly the Ripper himself, stood beneath the lamp.

1 piece of white coarse linen
1 piece of blue and white skirting (3 cornered)
2 small blue bags
2 short clay pipes (black)
1 tin box containing tea
1 sugar
1 piece of flannel and 6 pieces of soap
1 small tooth comb
1 white handle table knife and 1 metal teaspoon
1 red leather cigarette case, white metal fittings
1 tin match box, empty

1 piece of red flannel containing pins and needles
1 ball of hemp
1 piece of old white apron

Dr Gordon Brown thought Catherine had died some 40 minutes before he arrived (sometime after 1:40 a.m.) and allowing that the murderer must have been working at speed, he estimated that it would have taken at least five minutes to inflict all the injuries. In his inquest testimony, Brown said he thought the murderer must have possessed "a good deal of knowledge as to the position of the organs in the abdominal cavity and the way of removing them", it being his opinion that the removal of the kidney, which was covered by a membrane and easily overlooked, "would require a great deal of knowledge as to its position". This did not necessarily suggest a doctor, as a butcher would have possessed the necessary anatomical knowledge and skill. Dr George Bagster Phillips, who attended the autopsy, agreed with Brown, although Dr Sequeira felt that the murderer displayed no special knowledge and would have had enough light to work by, thus reducing the level of skill needed. Catherine was already on the ground when the fatal wound was inflicted and a sharp pointed knife with a blade at least 15 cm (6 in) long had been used. The murderer would not necessarily have been covered with blood.

As soon as the medical examination was completed, the body was placed on the ambulance and taken to the mortuary at Golden Lane, where it was stripped by the mortuary keeper, Mr Davis. Detective Halse, who had accompanied the body, noticed that a piece of Eddowes' apron had been torn away.

PC Alfred Long, 254A, who had served for 12 years with the 9th Lancers, being awarded a Distinguished Conduct Medal following his participation in the Second Afghan War (1878–1880), was among the many policemen from other divisions who had been drafted into Whitechapel to supplement policing there. His beat brought him into Goulston Street at 2:20 a.m., at which time he didn't see anything to attract his attention, but when he returned through the street at 2:55 a.m. he noticed a piece of apron on the floor of a common staircase leading to 108–119 Wentworth Dwellings. One corner was wet and later examination would reveal that it was smeared with blood and what appeared to be faecal matter. This smearing was very slight, insufficient even to penetrate the material.

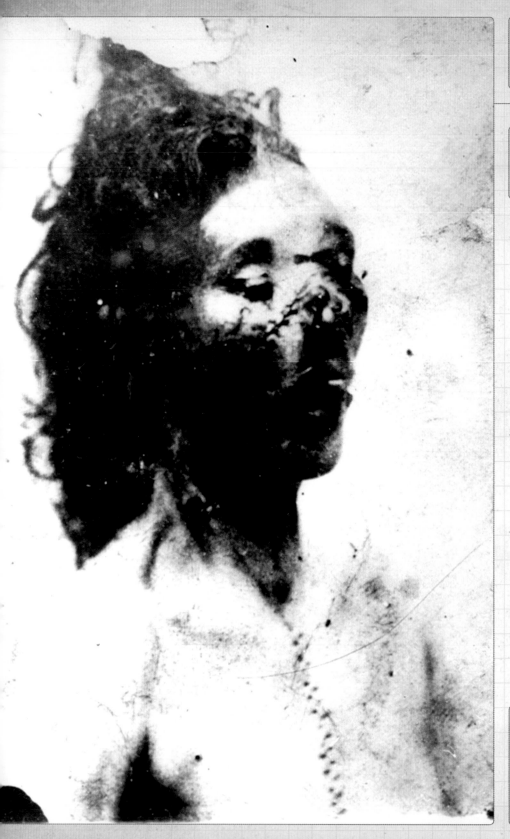

LEFT: Mortuary photograph of Catherine Eddowes, showing the facial injuries after post-mortem stitching had taken place.

OPPOSITE: Surveyor Frederick Foster's accurate plan of Mitre Square which was produced for the inquest of Eddowes.

OVERLEAF: Artist's reconstruction of the entrance to 108–119 Wentworth Dwellings which show the railings to the balcony recesses that would have existed in 1888. They were later covered to allow access to shops.

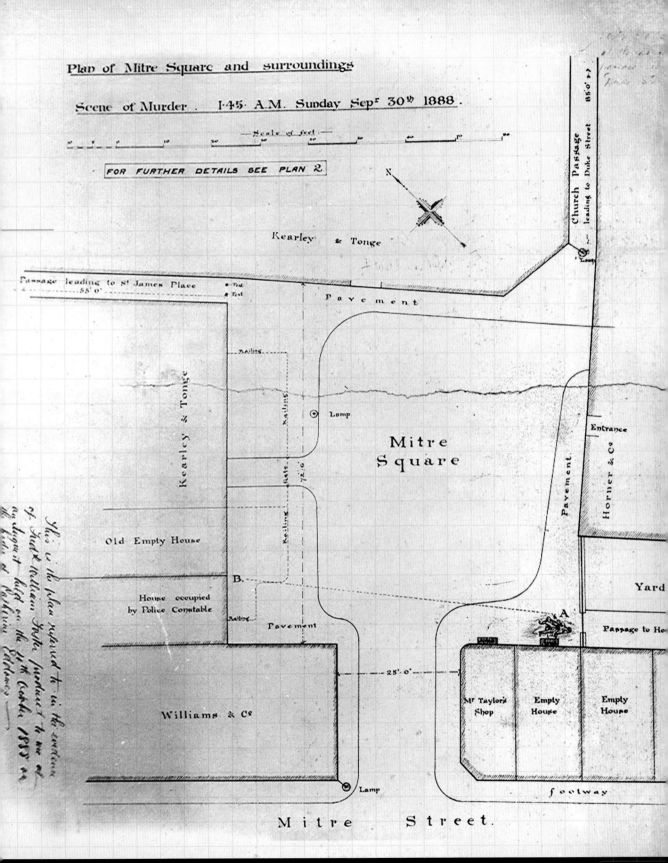

Plan of Mitre Square and surroundings

Scene of Murder. 1·45 A.M. Sunday Sept 30th 1888.

Scale of feet

FOR FURTHER DETAILS SEE PLAN 2

Church Passage leading to Duke Street

Kearley & Tonge

Passage leading to St James Place

55'0"

Pavement

Railings

Lamp

Kearley & Tonge

Railing

Gate

Railing

Mitre Square

Entrance

Horner & Co

Pavement

Old Empty House

B.

House occupied by Police Constable

Pavement

25'0"

Williams & Co

Yard

A

Passage to House

Mr Taylor's Shop

Empty House

Empty House

footway

Lamp

Mitre Street.

Wentworth Dwellings

Wentworth Dwellings were two blocks of model dwellings, both situated on corners of Goulston Street and Wentworth Street. They were constructed in 1886–1887 on land that had been cleared of slum properties following the Cross Act of 1875 (see chapter 1). They were five storeys high and contained 222 apartments in total. The block on the eastern side of Goulston Street had four street-level entrances, each giving access to communal stone staircases which led to Nos.90–107, 108–119, 120–131 and 132–143 respectively. At the time of the discovery of the Whitechapel Murders, Wentworth Dwellings was predominantly inhabited by Jews and certainly by 1900, the residents of the buildings were 95–100 per cent Jewish.

Rapidly deteriorating conditions in the tenements during the twentieth century provoked Tower Hamlets Council to promise swift demolition in September 1967, along with the Charlotte De Rothschild Dwellings in Thrawl Street. However, they were not demolished, and the buildings became homes for the newly-arrived Bengali immigrants. By the late 1970s, conditions were so bad that Wentworth Dwellings were bought under a compulsory purchase order; shocking reports on the unsanitary and outdated facilities in the flats appeared in the local press on a number of occasions.

Wentworth Dwellings were finally cleared of occupants in 1982 and as the entrances were bricked up, the threat of demolition loomed once more. However, in 1990, the buildings were refurbished, renamed Merchant House and once again used as apartments. Also at this time, the Happy Days restaurant (next to the former stairway to Nos.108–119) expanded and the doorway now forms part of the entrance to the restaurant.

ABOVE: The entrance to 108–119 Wentworth Dwellings, photographed in the mid 1970s.

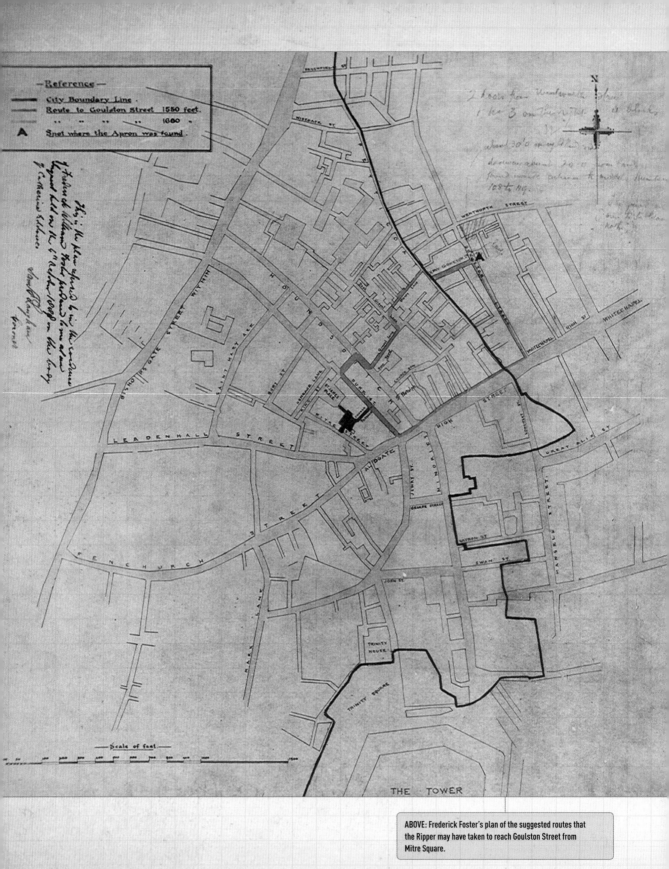

ABOVE: Frederick Foster's plan of the suggested routes that the Ripper may have taken to reach Goulston Street from Mitre Square.

ABOVE: Goulston Street in the 1900s looking north, with the overspill of neighbouring Petticoat Lane market in full swing. Wentworth Dwellings can be seen at the end of the street.

RIGHT: Mitre Square in 2010, looking towards "Ripper's corner", as the spot where Eddowes was murdered came to be known.

"Juwes" and the Masons

One of the most enduring stories about Jack the Ripper is that it involved the Freemasons, that "Juwes" was a Masonic word and that Sir Charles Warren, a devoted and high-ranking Mason, realized that the graffiti implicated the Freemasons and perhaps showed that Jack the Ripper was a Mason himself, and therefore had the writing erased.

It is claimed that Juwes was the collective name for Jubelo, Jubela and Jubelum, the murderers of Hiram Abiff, architect of Solomon's Temple. Hiram, known as "the widow's child", appears in the Bible, where he is called Huram-Abi, "a man full of skill, intelligence, and knowledge in working bronze" (1 Kings 7:13). He is the son of a widow belonging to the Naphtali, one of the Twelve Tribes of Israel who occupied lands which in time would become known as Galilee. In

Masonic ritual Jubelo, Jubela and Jubelum murder Hiram Abiff when he refuses to share the secrets known only to Master Masons. Their treachery is quickly uncovered, but days pass before Abiff's body is found, at which time Solomon raises him from the dead.

Unfortunately for this Jack the Ripper myth, in both the United Kingdom and the United States the collective name for this band of thugs is "Ruffians". Neither "Juwes" nor any words approximating to it, has appeared in Masonic ritual.

Also, washing the writing from the wall did not prevent the spelling of the word becoming known, and as far as we know there was never any attempt made to prevent it from becoming known. All the reasons given for Warren attempting to erase it on the basis of any Masonic connection therefore amount to nothing.

Following the murder of Annie Chapman (see chapter 5), a group of East End businessmen formed the Whitechapel Vigilance Committee, one of several such groups formed at that time with the purpose of adding to police and public resources to aid their attempts to apprehend the murderer. Its president was George Lusk, a painter and decorator of 1 Tollet Street, Alderney Road, Mile End. He was often in the local press and his address was frequently given, so it is no surprise to find that he was often on the receiving end of letters written by people claiming to be the Ripper. On the evening of 16 October, he received one such letter, this time containing half a kidney and a letter, which read:

> From hell
> Mr Lusk
> Sir, I send you half the Kidne I took from one woman and prasarved it for you tother piece I fried and ate it was very nise. I may send you the bloody knif that took it out if you only wate a whil longer
> signed Catch me when you can
> Mishter Lusk

The kidney was examined by several medical experts, among them Dr Thomas Openshaw of the London Hospital, who concluded that it was human. Others are believed to have observed that it was a "ginny" kidney, one that had been affected by alcohol, thereby generating conflicting viewpoints. Examinations of Catherine Eddowes's remaining kidney were said to show that it was in a similar condition, however Dr Gordon Brown believed it to be perfectly healthy. This conflict of medical judgement is made all the more frustrating because much of what we know today about these examinations comes from newspaper reports and police memoirs, unfortunately not always the most reliable sources, as official medical reports (assuming they were made and submitted to the police) have not survived.

The letter itself has been missing since the time it was photographed and the portion of kidney, of course, was long ago destroyed.

LEFT: George Lusk, recipient of the "From Hell" letter.

BELOW: The infamous "From Hell" letter which arrived at Lusk's house accompanied by a piece of human kidney. The original has been missing since 1888.

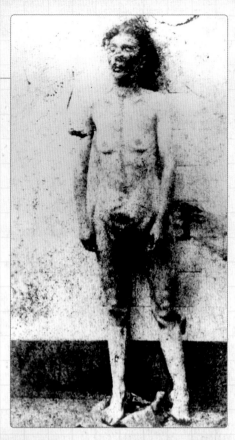

RIGHT: Mortuary photograph of Catherine Eddowes after post-mortem stitching.

BELOW: Catherine Eddowes's body lying in the mortuary shell at Golden Lane, prior to the post-mortem.

A few feet above the apron was some writing on the wall, written in white chalk on the black bricks. There were three lines of writing, described by Halse as being executed in a good schoolboy's round hand, the capital letters being about 2 cm (¾ in) in height and the others in proportion. There would later be some confusion over the order of the words, however; PC Long, who had noted the words down in his notebook, recalled them as saying:

> The Jews are the men that will not be blamed for nothing.

Detective Halse thought the wording was:

> The Juwes are not the men who will be blamed for nothing.

Long conceded that the spelling of the words "Jews" may have been "J-u-w-e-s" but the precise wording was never resolved and the meaning is ambiguous, although possibly a warning that the Jews would not take kindly to being blamed for something they hadn't done, this being a reaction to the anti-immigrant and anti-Semitic belief that the murderer was a foreigner.

PC Long summoned another policeman from an adjoining beat to make sure nobody entered or left the building, and perhaps with the murder of Martha Tabram (see chapter 3) in mind, examined the staircases and landings for a body or any trace of blood. He then went to the police station and reported his discoveries.

Various senior policemen visited both Mitre Square and Goulston Street, one of whom, Superintendent Thomas Arnold, the head of H Division, viewed the writing in Goulston Street with disquiet, worried that it could spark an anti-Jewish riot. He decided the best thing to do was to erase the writing, but waited for the authority of the Commissioner, Sir Charles Warren. It was not until 5:00 a.m. that Warren arrived at Leman Street Police Station and spoke with Inspector Thomas Arnold, immediately accepting that the writing should be erased. Taking personal responsibility for obliterating potential evidence, he went straight to Goulston Street, took a duplicate, and then ordered the writing to be washed away. Warren had long been the butt of press criticism, along with Home Secretary Henry Matthews, but on this occasion his decision won support even from the normally highly critical *The Star*, which wrote that Warren had "acted with blundering haste … but his motive seems to have been just a trifle more creditable than usual."

Behind the scenes of the crimes, public hostility towards the police and government had been growing, and one thing which fed the fires was the refusal to offer a reward for information leading to the arrest and conviction of the murderer. Various people had quickly offered rewards: the enormously wealthy Samuel Montagu, a businessman elected Member of Parliament for Whitechapel in 1885, had done so, and the Whitechapel Vigilance Committee had attempted to raise a subscription for one. Then, within hours of the discovery of Catherine Eddowes' body, the Commissioner of the City of London Police, Sir James Fraser, offered a reward of £500 (the equivalent of almost £3000 today), followed soon after by the Lord Mayor, who offered a £500 reward on behalf of the Corporation of London.

LEFT: The south eastern side of Dorset Street showing Commercial Street Chambers, a large doss-house owned by William Crossingham.

BUT NEITHER THE GOVERNMENT NOR THE Metropolitan Police had offered rewards, having abandoned the policy of doing so in 1884, and this brought them in for enormous criticism. The irony is that neither Home Secretary Henry Matthews nor the Commissioner Sir Charles Warren was altogether opposed to rewards, but they offered no explanation for not offering one and consequently appeared uncaring, especially when it was learned that Sir Charles, with very poor timing, had issued instructions to the police to maintain greater vigilance in order to identify publicans who served drunks. It all served to reinforce the opinion that the authorities were uncaring about the common man and woman, and it was widely voiced that "if the murders had happened in Mayfair we should have had rewards fast enough", as *The Star* put it. Such was the heat of public hostility that some newspapers feared revolution was in the air.

Henry Matthews, the Home Secretary, was see as a failure; *The Star* called him "a feeble mountebank". The *Daily Telegraph* said Matthews "knows nothing, has heard nothing, and does not intend to do anything…" and it suggested that he "should be promoted out of the way of some more competent man" (which eventually he was). This criticism mounted after the murder of Elizabeth Stride and Catherine Eddowes. A leader in the *Daily Telegraph* stated that Matthews was "a source of miserable weakness, a discredit" and "a fantastic failure", a man of "vacillation, ineptitude, crass ignorance".

In life, the poor women who became the victims of Jack the Ripper had been the flotsam of society, the unwanted and uncared about victims of their own vices and misfortunes. They could have vanished from the streets and few would have noticed and fewer would have cared. But in death they had achieved a staggering importance, revealing to the rest of the world the horrible underbelly of modern Victorian society, not the eighteenth-century-remnant world of Charles Dickens, but an age which was stepping into the twentieth century. In this frightening new world in which the working class were flexing their muscles, agitating, unionizing and overturning the old social order, these poor women suddenly had the capability to destroy honed political careers, even to bring down the Government.

Relations between the Home Secretary and the Metropolitan Police Commissioner had never been good and it was said that Matthews disliked dealing with police matters and left it to his civil servants, some of whom acted with less tact than might have been desired. On the question of whether or not to offer a reward, had Matthews had his finger firmly on the pulse of public feeling he would have realized that while a reward might not have achieved anything material, it would have done much to assuage public feeling. Warren, far more astute that Matthews, did realize this, but he also realized that if Matthews fell, as looked highly likely, he would claim to have acted in concert with Warren and thus taken Warren down with him. Consequently, Warren put on record that he had no opposition to a reward being offered. This move left Matthews floundering in a sad political wrangle that in the end boiled down to him upholding a policy he didn't really believe in because to do otherwise at this late stage meant he would lose face.

While the bickering went on behind the scenes, another woman was to fall prey to Jack the Ripper, the most elusive of all his victims, Mary Jane Kelly. She is elusive because her identity has not been established conclusively and possibly never will be. There was even confusion surrounding her name; she was known by the name Mary Jane Kelly, but also adopted the French-sounding name of Marie Jeannette Kelly. The police and press at first confused Jeannette with the more familiar name Janet. Official files on Kelly's murder, severely depleted as a result of culling for space, loss, pilfering, borrowing and possible misfiling, do not amount to more than a few documents. Researchers therefore have very little insight into the results of the police efforts to establish her identity and antecedents. This lack of firm information has enabled people to theorize and build solutions to the Ripper mystery around her past.

What is known is that Mary Kelly was about 25 years old, 1.7 m (5 ft 7 in) tall and stout. She had blue eyes, a fair complexion and her hair colour is variously given as blonde, ginger, light or dark. What appears to be agreed on is that she had an attractive face and managed to keep herself neat and clean, usually wearing a shabby black silk dress and black jacket. Walter Dew, the young policeman, who would become famous in later years when he arrested Dr Crippen after a tense trans-Atlantic chase, knew Kelly by sight. He said she invariably wore a clean white apron, but never a hat.

All we know about Mary Kelly is what she told her lover, Joseph Barnett. All of it, some of it, or none of it need be true. She said she had been born in Limerick, Ireland, but whether she meant County Limerick or the town of Limerick is not clear. She said her father was named John Kelly and that she had six or seven brothers and one sister. The family had moved to Wales when she was very young and her father worked as foreman in an ironworks in either Caernarvonshire or Carmarthenshire, probably the latter. She had married when only 16 years old, but her husband, a collier named

ABOVE: Mary Kelly's former lover Joseph Barnett, pictured in a press illustration made during the inquest.

The West End Bordello

Mary Kelly also told a story about working in a West End bordello and travelling to France. This sounds unlikely, but in the 1880s it was widely believed that a lot of young English women and girls were being lured, or sometimes even forcibly abducted, to Continental brothels. Although it is highly doubtful that involuntary prostitution was anything like as common as some people imagined, it is known that procurers were actively on the lookout for young and pretty prostitutes and would-be prostitutes to groom for foreign brothels. Such places were legalized and the girls had to register with the police, who had to be satisfied that the woman understood what she was agreeing to. The procurers promised money, a luxurious lifestyle and the prospect of marrying a wealthy man or aristocrat, and before going abroad the women were "groomed" in London, experiencing the good clothes and luxurious lifestyle which quickly vanished on going abroad, where they found themselves sold to a brothel and held as a virtual slaves.

RIGHT: Mary Kelly's room, 13 Miller's Court. The door can bee seen to the right with the passage leading from Dorset Street beyond.

OVERLEAF: Looking down Dorset Street from the junction with Commercial Street. The Britannia beer house, commonly known as "The Ringer's" stands on the northern corner.

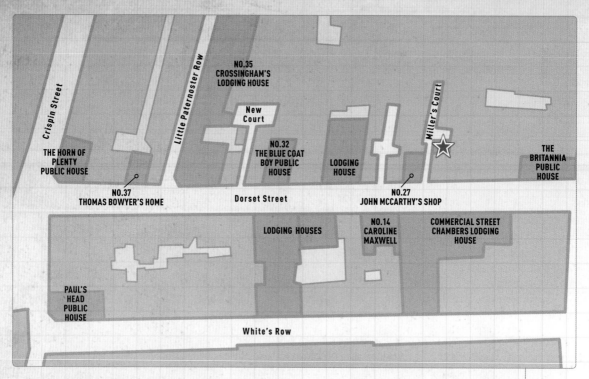

Map labels:

Crispin Street

Little Paternoster Row

NO.35 CROSSINGHAM'S LODGING HOUSE

New Court

Miller's Court

★

THE HORN OF PLENTY PUBLIC HOUSE

NO.32 THE BLUE COAT BOY PUBLIC HOUSE

LODGING HOUSE

THE BRITANNIA PUBLIC HOUSE

NO.37 THOMAS BOWYER'S HOME

Dorset Street

NO.27 JOHN MCCARTHY'S SHOP

LODGING HOUSES

NO.14 CAROLINE MAXWELL

COMMERCIAL STREET CHAMBERS LODGING HOUSE

PAUL'S HEAD PUBLIC HOUSE

White's Row

Davis or Davies, was killed in a mine explosion some two or three years later. Kelly had then lived with a cousin in Cardiff, and became a prostitute. There she apparently spent eight or nine months in Cardiff Infirmary.

It is possible that Kelly had troubles with her parents. Mrs Phoenix or Mrs Carthy, with whom she possibly later lived with in the East End, said that Kelly's family had discarded her. Joseph Barnett said that she had once hidden on learning that her father had come to London to look for her (it isn't clear whether this was while she was with Barnett or not). Five of her brothers lived in London, but Barnett only mentioned her being visited by one brother, Henry, who allegedly served with the 2nd battalion Scots Guards (but he cannot be identified in the Regimental records). Her sister, said Barnett, was very fond of her and was very respectable, travelling from marketplace to marketplace. Kelly had the aforementioned cousin in Cardiff and a friend named Lizzie Albrook said Kelly spoke of a relative who was on the stage in London.

Kelly apparently came from Cardiff to London; she told Barnett that she had worked for a French woman in a high-class bordello in the West End, possibly in or near Knightsbridge.

She claimed that she had been dressed well, had been driven about in a carriage and had gone across to France several times in the company of a gentleman. She hadn't liked it there, and had returned to London, where she had adopted the French spelling of her name: Marie Jeanette.

According to a newspaper interview with Mrs Elizabeth Phoenix, about three years before her death Kelly had been living in Mrs Phoenix's sister's house at Breezer's Hill, a road running

ABOVE: Map of Dorset Street in 1888 showing important locations.

★ Murder site

BELOW: Dorset Street circa 1900, looking east from the junction with Little Paternoster Row.

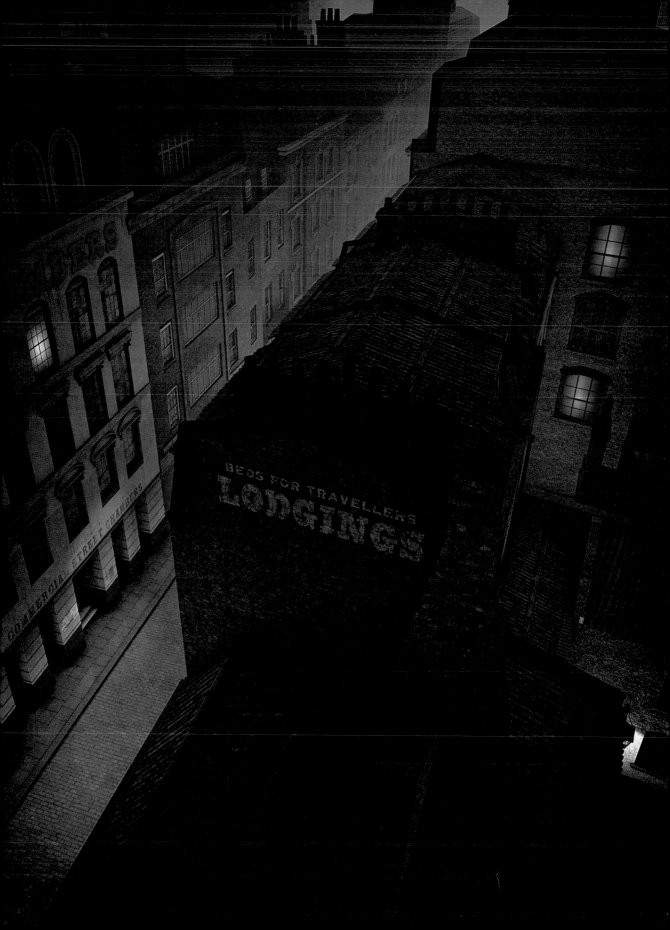

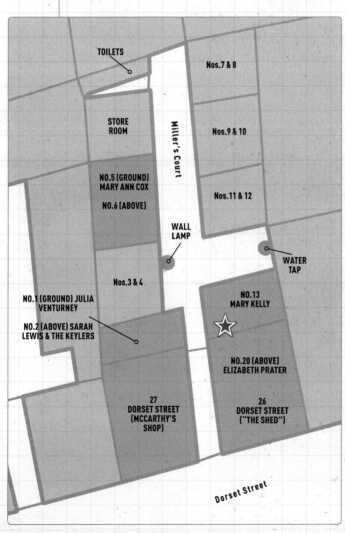

OPPOSITE: Aerial view of Dorset Street, with Miller's Court, lit by a solitary lamp, shown in the bottom right.

BELOW: Map of Miller's Court showing the location of individual rooms and the residences of the various witnesses in the Mary Kelly case.

⭐ Murder site

off Pennington Street near London docks. Mrs Phoenix's sister, Mrs Carthy, was interviewed and said that Kelly had left her house 18 months to two years earlier to live with a man who was in the building trade and he would have married Kelly. These ladies also said that on her return from France, Kelly had gone to live with a Mrs Buki who had accompanied her to the home of the French lady in Knightsbridge to claim a box of dresses that Kelly said were hers. It was during this time that Kelly began to drink excessively, and the alcohol turned her quarrelsome and abusive, and Mrs Buki was forced to ask her to leave.

The man in the building trade who would have married Mary Jane Kelly is probably Joseph Fleming, who Barnett said lived in Bethnal Green and of whom Kelly seemed very fond.

Barnett also said that Kelly had lived with a man named Morganstone somewhere near Stepney gasworks. Neither of these relationships lasted and by 1886 Mary Jane Kelly was living at Cooney's Lodging House, another of John Cooney's establishments, this one located at 16–17 Thrawl Street, next door to Wilmott's. It was on 8 April 1887 – Good Friday – that she first met Barnett, a porter at Billingsgate Market and sometime fruit hawker, in Commercial Street. They went for a drink, arranged to meet the following day and at that meeting decided to live together. Kelly moved out of Cooney's and with Barnett she took lodgings in George Street, then in Little Paternoster Row, Brick Lane, and finally a shabby room known as 13 Miller's Court, which was actually the back room of 26 Dorset Street, The weekly rent was 4s 6d (about £13 in today's money).

Dorset Street was notorious. It still exists, although today it is little more than an unnamed and unremarkable little road running at the rear of the former Spitalfields Fruit and Wool Exchange on one side (built 1928–1929) and a multi-storey car park on the other (built circa 1971). The eastern end almost directly faced the churchyard of Nicholas Hawksmoor's magnificent and imposing Christ Church on Commercial Street, and the other faced what was once the Providence Row Night Refuge and Convent in Crispin Street. Dorset Street had been built across the "Spital Field" in the middle of the 1600s and was originally called Datchet Street. It was then home to prosperous silk weavers and Thomas Wedgwood's first pottery outlet. But by 1888 the houses were decaying, the name had been corrupted to Dorset Street, and to some it was corrupted even further into "Dosset" or "Dosser's Street" because it was lined on either side by low-class common lodging houses. Although a very short street, it had three pubs. The Britannia, a large beer house in which Annie Chapman was drinking on the night she died (see chapter 5), was at the Commercial Street end. At the other was the Horn of Plenty, and in the middle a tiny pub called the Blue Coat Boy, one of the oldest recorded such establishments in the district. About a third of the way down from Commercial Street there was an arched passage between Nos.26 and 27 leading to what was little more than a yard containing some homes with one room on the ground floor and another on the floor above it. This was called Miller's Court.

On the poverty maps created by Charles Booth at the end of the nineteenth century (see chapter 1), Dorset Street was shaded black and classified as "vicious and semi-criminal". The policeman who guided Booth down Dorset Street described it as full of poverty, misery and vice, a cesspool into which the foulest and most degraded had sunk, full of "thieves, prostitutes, bullies", and he said that the women were dirty, unkempt, their skirts and clothing torn. Booth noted too that at one window there sat an obese woman who was too fat to get out of the door and who had remained in the room for years. Booth noted in his diary after a visit in 1898 that in the previous three months there had been three stabbings and one murder in the street. Canon Samuel A Barnett of St Jude's Vicarage called Dorset Street "the centre of evil" and referred to "the hells of Dorset Street".

The covered passage leading to Miller's Court was 8 m (26 ft 4 in) long and 0.9 m (2 ft 10 in) wide. This covered part finished just before

a door on the right-hand side was reached. The court beyond was tiny, just 15 m (50 ft) long and 2.4 m (7 ft 10 in) wide, narrowing to 1.7 m (5 ft 6 in). There were six small houses, with tiny rooms just 3.7 x 3.7 x 2.4 m (12 x 12 x 8 ft), but these were home to some 30 people according to the 1881 census. At one end of the court there were three public toilets, and at the other a public dustbin. There was also a solitary gas lamp and one water tap.

The door at the end of the passage was the rear door of 26 Dorset Street and opened into a room about 3.7 m (12 ft) square. A flimsy partition had been erected to cut it off from the rest of the house. It was very sparsely furnished. A bedside table was next to the door and next to it a bed, pushed up against the wall, with a table by the window and a chair. Underneath the bed was a tin bath. The only decoration was a cheap print called *The Fisherman's Widow* hanging over the fireplace. Two windows looked out into Miller's Court. The smaller of the two had two broken panes and a coat had been draped across it to keep out the draught. The door key had been lost recently and Kelly and Barnett used to reach through the window to push or

OPPOSITE: McCarthy's shop at 27 Dorset Street sat next to the narrow entrance to Miller's Court. It would have been an important supplier of provisions to the community.

BACKGROUND INTELLIGENCE **John McCarthy**

Nos.26 and 27 Dorset Street and all the houses in Miller's Court were owned by John McCarthy, who ran a chandler's shop (general grocer) at No.27. In one of Charles Booth's notebooks he described him as "the notorious John McCarthy of Dorset Street", but it isn't clear why he was regarded as "notorious" or if he should be regarded any differently to the other lodging house keepers in the area. As seen in chapter 7, Arthur Harding said McCarthy started out by selling old clothes and getting his money by "swindling the poor people out of small sums." Harding added, "McCarthy owned all the furnished rooms down there. He was an Irishman, a bully, a tough guy. Marie Lloyd used to see him, because there was a pub round the corner she used to go to. All his daughters were in show business on account of Marie Lloyd. They had plenty of money." Marie Lloyd was perhaps the most popular of all the music hall entertainers at the time.

It is possible that Harding meant the word "bully" to be taken in its conventional sense of

someone who intimidates and terrorizes those who are weaker than themselves, but the word also meant a pimp, and a brothel owner was known as a "bully boss". Charles Booth used "bully" in this context when he said that Dorset Street was full of "thieves, prostitutes, bullies".

On his death in 1935, however, the *East London Observer* recorded that John McCarthy was "held in the highest esteem by a large circle of East Londoners ... was a kind-hearted man and a generous subscriber to local charities. He was a life governor of several hospitals ... In fact he was always giving a helping hand to somebody."

Whether or not Hoxton-born Marie Lloyd assisted the stage careers of any of McCarthy's children, his son, John Joseph McCarthy, was a popular entertainer who used the stage name Steve McCarthy and married Marie Kendall, who was a major entertainer in her day. Steve McCarthy was the grandfather of the elegant actress Kay Kendall (1926–59) who played opposite Kenneth More in the 1954 movie *Genevieve*...

ABOVE: John McCarthy, from a contemporary illustration.

DARTNELL'S
ASK FOR
PRIZE MEDAL
GINGER BEER

STREET COURT

McCARTHY 27

HOME & COLONIAL TEA

HOVIS

PARAFFIN OIL 1⁴ Per Pint

BOVRIL

LYON'S COCOA

2⁶ 6⁶

PRICES
CANDLES

6⁶ 1¼

6d.
9d.
1s.
1s.
0d.
d.

WE CLOSE AT
TO DAY
HUDSONS

BATEY's
GINGER BEER

ASK
FOR
BRYANT
AND MAYS
MATCHES
SOLD
HERE

£100
REWARD

CAPTURE

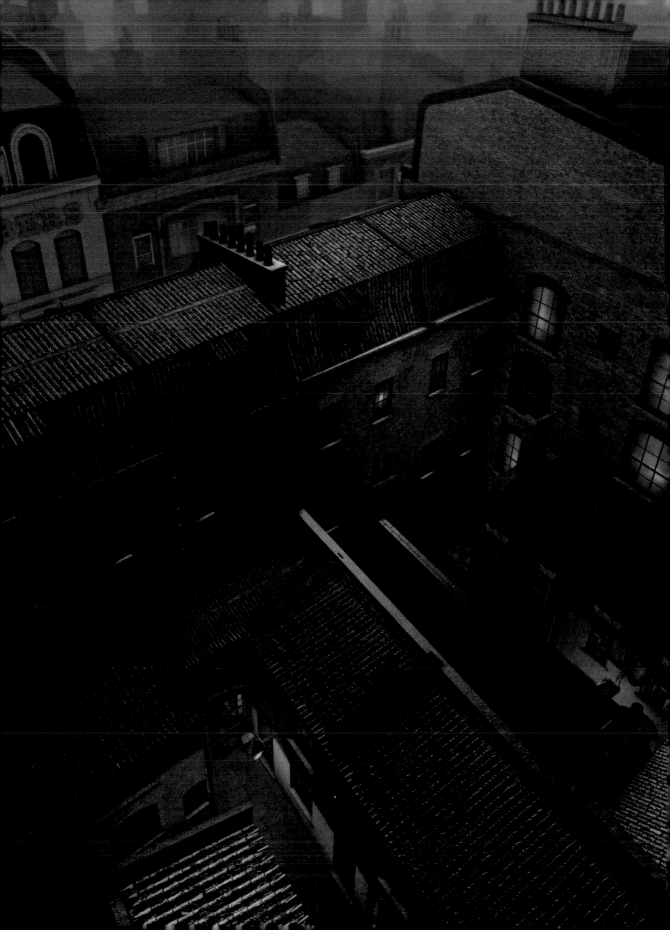

OPPOSITE: Aerial view of the backs of the properties on the south side of Dorset Street as they would have been in 1888. Miller's Court can be seen at the bottom of the picture.

draw the bolt that locked the room. The only illumination was from a candle Kelly had placed on top of a broken wine glass.

It was a sad and tawdry room, which afforded some privacy but otherwise didn't offer much in the way of better facilities than those in a common lodging house. In 1929 the journalist, MP and writer Leonard Matters, who was engaged in writing a book about Jack the Ripper, visited Dorset Street. It was by then known as Duval Street:

> At the time of my first visit to the neighbourhood most of the houses on the left-hand side of the street were unoccupied, and some were being demolished. The house in which Kelly was murdered was closed, save for one front room still occupied by a dreadful looking slattern who came out of Miller's Court into the sunlight and blinked at me.
>
> When she saw me focus my camera to get a picture of the front of the house, the old hag swore at me, and shuffled away down the passage.
>
> I took what is probably the last photograph of the house to be secured by anybody, for three days later Miller's Court and the dilapidated buildings on either side of it were nothing but a heap of bricks and mortar. The housebreakers had completely demolished the crumbling wreck of the slum dwelling in which "Jack the Ripper" committed his last crime!
>
> Miller's Court, when I saw it, was nothing but a stone-flagged passage between two houses, the upper stories of which united and so formed an arch over the entrance. Over this arch there was an iron plate bearing the legend, "Miller's Court." The passage was three feet wide and about twenty feet long, and at the end of it there was a small paved yard, about fifteen feet square. Abutting on this yard, or "court", was the small back room in which the woman Kelly was killed — a dirty, damp and dismal hovel, with boarded-up windows and a padlocked

BELOW: Illustration of Miller's Court from *Lloyds Weekly News*. Though accurate in most respects, the court has been "opened out" to allow for a view of room 13 and thus appears more spacious.

door as though the place had not been occupied since the crime was committed.

> But the strange thing was that nobody in the neighbourhood seemed to know the history of Miller's Court.
>
> I asked a very old man on the opposite side of the street how long he had been living there.
>
> "Over forty year," he answered.
>
> Then he told me that a murder had taken place when he was a young man. "That's the house," he said, pointing to one lower down the street. "They say it's 'aunted, but I never seen nobody comin' out of it at nights."

In July or August 1888 Joe Barnett lost his job and financial hardship began to put his relationship with Kelly under pressure. Kelly may have returned to prostitution, and Barnett certainly complained that she let prostitutes use their room. They argued, and during one altercation the window of their room was broken. In the early evening of 30 October 1888, Barnett walked out or was told to leave. He clearly cared about Kelly and evidently hoped that the separation would be temporary because he called in on her as often as he could and gave her money when he had some.

On Thursday, 8 November, Barnett visited Kelly at about 7:30 p.m. There was a young woman there, but she left soon after he arrived. He stayed for about half an hour. Nothing is known with any certainty about how Mary Kelly spent the next few hours. While there are several reported sightings during this time, none can be confirmed to be Kelly.

The first reliable report of Mary Kelly after 8 p.m. was by a prostitute, a widow named Mary Ann Cox, who lived in one of the houses in Miller's Court. At about 11:45 p.m. she turned from Commercial Street into Dorset Street and ahead of her Kelly was walking with a man. They turned into the passage leading to Miller's Court and as Mrs Cox turned down the passage herself she saw them going into Mary's room. Mrs Cox said, "Goodnight, Mary Jane", and Kelly slurred a reply, "I am going to have a song." The man then banged the door shut. Kelly, Cox realized, was very drunk and barely able to speak. Soon after, Kelly began singing. According to Mrs Cox, Mary's companion was about 36 years of age,

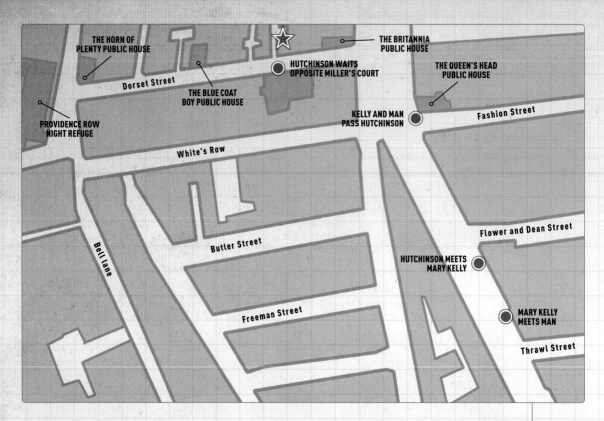

THE HORN OF
PLENTY PUBLIC HOUSE

THE BRITANNIA
PUBLIC HOUSE

HUTCHINSON WAITS
OPPOSITE MILLER'S COURT

THE QUEEN'S HEAD
PUBLIC HOUSE

Dorset Street

THE BLUE COAT
BOY PUBLIC HOUSE

KELLY AND MAN
PASS HUTCHINSON

Fashion Street

PROVIDENCE ROW
NIGHT REFUGE

White's Row

Flower and Dean Street

Bell Lane

Butler Street

HUTCHINSON MEETS
MARY KELLY

Freeman Street

MARY KELLY
MEETS MAN

Thrawl Street

ABOVE: Map of the area
traversed by Mary Kelly in
the last hours she was seen
alive, according to George
Hutchinson's testimony.

⭐ Murder Site
⬤ Key Location

stout and fair complexioned, but his face was marked by blotches. He had small side whiskers and a distinctive, thick carroty moustache. He was dressed in shabby dark clothes, a long dark overcoat and a black felt billycock hat. He was carrying a quart can of beer.

About half an hour later Mary was still singing the same song. And it was driving Catherine Pickett, a flower-seller who lived in Miller's Court, to distraction. She was going to complain, but her husband, David, stopped her: "If it hadn't been for my Dave – that's my old man you must know – I should have come out of my room and caught the white-livered villain! But Dave says to me, you just leave the woman alone so I stopped where I was. Worse luck for the poor dear soul! – and goes to bed . . ."

Elizabeth Prater, a prostitute living in an upstairs room in 26 Dorset Street had spent the evening drinking. Returning home about 1:00 a.m. on 9 November, she waited at the entrance to Miller's Court for about half-an-hour and had a chat in McCarthy's shop before going up to her room. She didn't bother to undress, but lay on her bed and immediately fell asleep. Nobody had entered or left the Court and there was no

sound from Kelly's room.

At approximately 2:00 a.m. George Hutchinson was walking along Commercial Street on his way back from Romford and met Mary Kelly near Thrawl Street. She asked if he could lend her some money, but Hutchinson said he was broke. Kelly, who seemed to be merry but not drunk walked to Thrawl Street and passed a man who was standing on the corner. Hutchinson had passed him earlier, but paid him little attention. As Kelly passed the man placed his hand on her shoulder and spoke to her. Kelly and the man laughed and Hutchinson heard Kelly say, "All right" and the man reply, "You will be all right for what I have told you." The man then put his arm around Kelly's shoulders and they walked towards Dorset Street. Hutchinson tried to get a look at the man's face as they passed him by the lamp of the Queen's Head pub, but the man "hid down his head with his hat over his eyes", as Hutchinson later explained to the police, and when Hutchinson stooped to try and see under the hat the man glared at him sternly. Hutchinson followed, keeping his distance, and watched as they stood at the entrance to Miller's

OVERLEAF: Nos 27 and
26 Dorset Street. No.26
was known as 'the shed'
and was generally used
for storage, although
it was said that it was
occasionally used as a
shelter for the homeless.
Catherine Eddowes is
rumoured to have been a
former resident.

Ten Bells and the Britannia

The Ten Bells in Commercial Street remains the East End pub most that is most associated with the Ripper murders, though there is very little actual testimony to warrant the title. This is essentially because it still stands, though contemporary drawings show that changes have been made since 1888. A pub of that name is believed to have stood there since the mid-eighteenth century, though the current building dates from 1845. Originally it was 33 Church Street, but the building of Commercial Street in the mid-nineteenth century brought it forward to the corner. Alterations appear to have been made in the early 1890s.

Newspaper reports had it that Annie Chapman was seen by the potman (a person who works at a pub serving customers and performing various chores) there at 5:00 a.m. on the morning of her death. Mary Kelly was also believed to be drinking in there with a friend named Elizabeth Foster on the night she died, leaving at about 7:00 p.m. Foster, however, appeared to change the venue of this meeting with almost every interview. Despite the lack of real evidence that the victims ever drank there, the pub has in the past traded on its history and was actually called the "Jack the Ripper" from 1975–1988. It may be fair to say that as the victims lived in close proximity to it, they most certainly would have been occasional, if not fairly regular visitors to this popular establishment.

The Britannia was officially a beer house situated at 87 Commercial Street, at its northern corner with Dorset Street. Unlike the claims of other pubs (such as the Ten Bells), the Britannia *was* actually able to lay claim to several connections with the victims of the Whitechapel Murders. It was known locally as "the Ringer's" after the landlord Walter Ringer, although it is commonly noted that his wife Matilda spent more time behind the bar than her husband. He is listed on the 1881 census, but research indicates that he died that year. It was apparently the scene of Annie Chapman's altercation with Eliza Cooper (see chapter 5) although some accounts claim that the fight took place in the kitchen of Crossingham's Lodging House at 35 Dorset Street.

Unconfirmed reports placed Mary Jane Kelly in The Britannia at 11 p.m. on 8 November 1888 in a drunken state. Elizabeth Foster also claimed to be drinking in there with her that evening, as opposed to in the Ten Bells as mentioned in a different account. Foster did not appear at the inquest. Witness Maurice Lewis claimed to have seen Kelly here at about 10 a.m. on 9 November, by which time she is supposed to have been dead. Another witness, Caroline Maxwell, also claimed to have seen and spoken to Kelly having stood outside the pub her earlier that morning.

The Britannia was demolished in 1928 along with the north side of Dorset Street to make way for extensions to Spitalfields Market.

ABOVE: The Ten Bells in 2010.

LEFT: A contemporary press illustration of the Britannia.

court for some minutes. He heard snatches of conversation: Kelly said "Alright my dear, come along. You will be comfortable," and they kissed. They went up the Court. Hutchinson waited for about 45 minutes, but saw neither Kelly nor the man, and he was certain nobody came down the street. Hutchinson finally wandered away at about 3:00 a.m.

Mary Ann Cox returned to Miller's Court around 3:00 a.m. It was raining hard, she said, and she called it a night, going to bed and sleeping. At the in inquest Sarah Lewis, who had possibly seen Hutchinson, said she woke at 3:30 a.m., upon hearing a clock chime, and shortly before 4:00 a.m. heard "a scream like that of a young woman, which seemed to be not far away. The voice screamed out 'murder'." In her room above Kelly's, Elizabeth Prater was awakened by her little black kitten Diddles walking across her neck. She, too, heard a cry of "Oh! Murder!" in a faint voice. Such cries were not uncommon, she said, and she took no notice, falling back to sleep. She woke at 5:00 a.m. and went to the Ten Bells for a glass of rum. The only people in the street were two or three men harnessing some horses. Mary Ann Cox heard a man's footsteps leaving Miller's Court at about 5:45 a.m.

OPPOSITE: Miller's Court was lit by a single gas lamp which was mounted to the wall opposite Kelly's room.

KEY EVIDENCE George Hutchinson

George Hutchinson was potentially one of the most important witnesses in the Ripper case. He was a groom who had taken to labouring but by November 1888 had been unemployed for several weeks. He said he had known Kelly for about three years, that he had been in her company several times and had sometimes given her money. Hutchinson described the man who went into Miller's Court with Kelly as of Jewish appearance, aged about 34 or 35, between 1.65 m (5 ft 5 in) and 1.7 m (5 ft 6 in) tall, pale-complexioned, with dark hair and eyes and a slight moustache curled up at each end.

He was wearing a dark felt hat turned down in the middle, and a long dark coat with the collar and cuffs trimmed with Astrakhan. It hung open and underneath Hutchinson could see a dark jacket and a light waistcoat, across which hung a very thick gold chain with a large seal and a red stone set into it. Beneath the waistcoat he was wearing a shirt with a white linen collar and a black tie to which a horseshoe pin was affixed. His trousers were dark and he had on button boots and gaiters with white buttons. He was holding a pair of kid gloves and a small parcel about 20 cm (8 in) long wrapped in a sturdy oilcloth known as American cloth with a strap round it.

Hutchinson did not come forward for three days, but when he did he was closely questioned by Inspector Abberline who thought Hutchinson's statement was true. Also, a young woman named Sarah Lewis walked down Dorset Street and turned into Miller's Court, where her parents lived, and said she had seen a man standing opposite, looking up the court as if

LEFT: George Hutchinson's sighting of Mary Kelly and a well-dressed man on Commercial Street in an llustration from *Famous Crimes Past and Present*, 1903.

he was waiting for someone. It is thought that Sarah Lewis saw Hutchinson and that her story corroborates his, at least insofar as he was there. Hutchinson, however, insisted that he had seen nobody in the street.

While it is odd that Hutchinson waited three days before coming forward, that his description of Kelly's companion is so extraordinarily detailed and that it is unclear why he waited in Dorset Street for so long, these points would no doubt have immediately occurred to Inspector Abberline, who would have satisfied himself as to Hutchinson's explanation. However, one United States newspaper, the *Wheeling Register*, reported on 19 November 1888 that Hutchinson had "invented" his detailed description of Kelly's companion and had got himself hired by the police at five times his usual salary to walk the streets to see if he could see the man again.

At 7:30 a.m. Catherine Picket knocked on Kelly's door to see if she could borrow a shawl as the morning was wet and chilly. There was no reply. Sometime before 10:30 a.m., John McCarthy sent his assistant, Thomas "Indian Harry" Bowyer to Room 13 to collect some rent. The door was locked, so Bowyer went to see if he could look inside through one of the windows facing Miller's Court. He reached through the broken window pane, and pulled back the covering on the window. He saw the unimaginably butchered corpse of Mary Kelly lying on the bed.

Bowyer fetched McCarthy, then both men ran to Commercial Street Police Station and spoke to Inspector Walter Beck, who returned to Miller's Court with young PC Walter Dew. Soon news of the murder had been telegraphed to police stations across London. The doctor was sent for and several constables were called down from Commercial Street Police Station (where they were being readied in case of Socialist disturbances in connection with the Lord Mayor's Show later that day) who were used to clear the Court and cordon off each end of Dorset Street.

Dr George Bagster Phillips looked into the room and, as it was obvious that Mary Kelly was utterly beyond need of his ministrations, he waited for the door to the room to be forced open. This was greatly delayed because it was believed that bloodhounds were being brought and that the room should not be entered before they appeared. It was not until 1:30 p.m. that Inspector Arnold arrived with instructions to enter the room, it turning out that dogs were not available after all. McCarthy used a pickaxe to force open the door.

The doctors began their examination of the body. It appears that Mary Kelly was in bed when the murder was committed and one of the examining medical men, Dr Thomas Bond, thought from a cut and blood-saturated sheet that it had been pulled over her face at the time. From this and other information it would seem that Kelly had taken off her clothes and laid them down as if preparing to sleep rather than for a romp with a customer. Her body had been close to the partition, which could mean either that she simply favoured that side of the bed or that she was sharing the bed.

The cause of death was severance of the right carotid artery. Mary was lying on the bed, her body was inclined to the left, her head resting on

ABOVE: Illustration from the *Illustrated Police News* of the man seen with Mary Kelly, according to the statement made by George Hutchinson.

ABOVE: Contemporary press illustration of Thomas Bowyer, who discovered Kelly's body.

the left cheek. The face was unrecognizable, the nose, cheeks, eyebrows and ears partly removed, even the lips were slashed in several places. Mary's neck had been severed down to the bone.

Mary's left forearm was stretched across her abdomen, her right arm rested on the mattress. Both arms had been mutilated. Her breasts had been cut off, and one breast was placed under her head, the other put by the right foot. According to Dr Bond's post-mortem report, Mary's heart was "absent", which almost certainly means it was taken away by the murderer.

The whole of the surface of the abdomen and thighs had been removed, the contents of the abdomen emptied and distributed around the body; the uterus and kidneys were placed under the head, her liver between the feet, intestines on her right side, the spleen by her left. Parts of the abdomen and thighs had been placed on the bedside table. The front of the right thigh was entirely stripped of skin, and the left thigh was stripped to the knee. Overall the body had been destroyed. It was as if the murderer's intention was to make it so that Mary Kelly did not exist.

Dr Bond believed that rigor mortis had begun between six and 12 hours after death, from which he calculated that death could have taken place

BACKGROUND INTELLIGENCE   Alive After Death?

One of the most curious features of Mary Kelly's murder is that several people claimed to have seen her alive long after the medical evidence showed that she was dead. This has given rise to a belief that the woman murdered in Miller's Court was not Mary Kelly, but one of the prostitutes whom Barnett had complained about Kelly allowing to use the room. The most "reliable" of the people who said they had seen her was Caroline Maxwell, whose husband was the night watchman at a lodging house opposite. She said she was going home after a night's work when she saw Kelly standing at the entrance to Miller's Court, and as it was unusual to see her that early she asked if anything was the matter. Kelly said she was hungover, and Mrs Maxwell suggested that she go to the Britannia and get a beer as a remedy for the hangover. Kelly said she had already done this and pointed at some vomit in the roadway to show that she had just brought

it back up again. Mrs Maxwell had left Kelly to run an errand and on returning to Dorset Street about half an hour later she saw Kelly outside the Britannia talking to a man. However, enquiries at the Britannia failed to confirm that Kelly had been drinking there that morning.

Mrs Maxwell was not a sensation-seeker, but a sensible woman with an excellent reputation, and she was unshakable in her conviction that she had seen Kelly that morning, and also explained to a journalist that she was certain of the day because she was doing things she only did on a Friday.

As credible a witness and as certain of her convictions as she was, and as comparable as Kelly's hungover sickness was with the drunken state in which she had been seen by Mrs Cox the previous night (although not with Hutchinson's description of her as "spreeish"), if Kelly was the murdered woman, Mrs Maxwell must have been mistaken.

Dr Thomas Bond was a very experienced surgeon used by the police and the report he produced after his examination of Mary Kelly is today recognized as containing an early example of offender profiling. It also shows that the authorities in 1888 were familiar with the modern phenomenon of serial killing.

Bond believed that the five murders from Nichols to Kelly were "no doubt" committed by the same person, but contrary to the other doctors he thought the murderer lacked anatomical knowledge – "In my opinion he does not even possess the technical knowledge of a butcher or horse slaughterer or any person accustomed to cut up dead animals." He also thought that the murderer's hands and arms would have been bloodied, as would his clothes, from which he assumed the murderer would have been wearing something such as an overcoat over the bloodstained clothes.

According to Bond, the murderer was physically strong, but quiet and inoffensive in appearance, probably middle-aged, and neatly and respectably dressed, although probably not in regular employment. He therefore had a small regular income or pension or lived with people of respectable character who likely entertained suspicions they self-evidently were not communicating to the police. The murderer was probably solitary and eccentric in his behaviour.

While not entirely discounting the possibility that the murderer killed in revenge for some real or imagined offence, or was inspired by a religious mania to kill prostitutes, Dr Bond thought it more likely that the murderer suffered from a "homicidal or erotic mania".

---

between 2:00 a.m. and 8:00 a.m. The remains of Mary's last meal – fish and potatoes – were in her stomach and intestines. Digestion ceases immediately on death and it typically takes two to four hours for food to pass out of the stomach into the intestines. Assuming that Kelly had eaten no later than between 10:00 and 11:00 p.m., time of death was narrowed down to between 1:00 a.m. and 2:00 a.m.

A tarpaulin-covered cart pulled by a single horse turned into Dorset Street at 3:50 p.m. and drew to a halt outside Miller's Court. A dirty and scratched coffin, obviously used many times, was taken into Kelly's room and the news that her body was about to be brought out attracted a crowd of people. The police cordon at the Commercial Street end of the street looked likely to break. After ten minutes the coffin was brought out and placed in the cart, and men removed their caps and women cried. Kelly's room was then closed up and the door padlocked. That night, thousands of people poured into the area. Dorset Street was patrolled by the police and nobody was allowed to loiter near Miller's Court.

On Saturday a murder pardon was issued. This was offerd to someone not actvely involved in the commission of the crime and read:

The Commissioner of Police
Metropolitan Police

Murder Pardon

Whereas on November the 8th or 9th in Millers Court Dorset Street Spitalfields, Mary Janet Kelly was murdered by some person or persons unknown, the Secretary of State will advise the grant of Her Majesty's Gracious pardon to any accomplice not being a person who contrived or actually committed the murder who shall give such information and evidence as shall lead to the discovery and conviction of the person or persons who committed the murder.

(Sd) Charles Warren
Commissioner of Police of the Metropolis
Metropolitan Police Office 4 Whitehall Place SW
10 November 1888

The offer of a pardon to an accomplice has naturally caused a lot of speculation, especially as it was restricted to the murder of Kelly and apparently based on information lacking in the previous murders, but Home Secretary Henry Matthews had considered back in October the possibility of offering a pardon, believing that it would be a palliative to public feeling yet less of a discreditable climb-down than offering a reward. It is therefore probable that the offer was without significance.

The new murder had quickly attracted the attention of Queen Victoria, who was at Balmoral in Scotland and sent a telegram to

OPPOSITE: An artist's impression (dated 1903) of the discovery by Thomas Bowyer of Kelly's body at about 10:45 a.m., 9 November 1888.

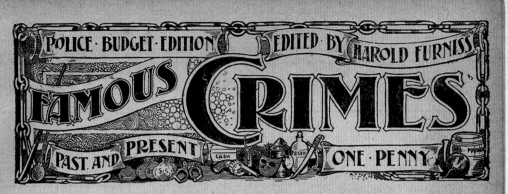

POLICE · BUDGET · EDITION
EDITED · BY · HAROLD · FURNISS
FAMOUS CRIMES
PAST · AND · PRESENT
ONE · PENNY

THE DISCOVERY OF THE SIXTH "RIPPER" MURDER.

Vol. II.—No. 18.

OPPOSITE: Mary Kelly's body as found in Miller's Court.

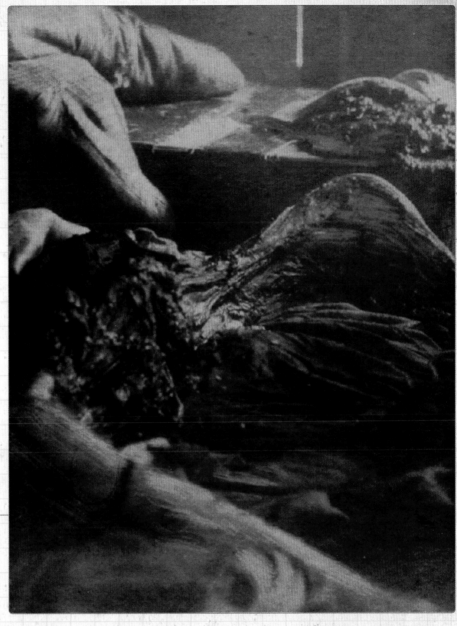

RIGHT: A second crime scene photograph of Mary Kelly, taken from behind the bed. The bedside table can be seen in the background.

Lord Salisbury:

This new most ghastly murder shows the absolute necessity for some very decided action. All these courts must be lit, & our detectives improved. They are not what they shld be. You promised, when the 1st murders took place to consult with your colleagues about it.

On Monday 12 November 1888, Dr Roderick Macdonald, the coroner for the north-eastern district of Middlesex, assisted by the deputy coroner, Mr Hodgkinson, opened the inquest into the death of Mary Kelly. In previous cases the inquest had been held by Wynne Baxter, who conscientiously inquired into every aspect of the murder, meticulously recording statements under oath in case an arrest should be made sometime in the future when the witnesses might be dead or untraceable. MacDonald, however, concluded the inquest within just one day, questioning sufficient witnesses to establish the circumstances of the death. The verdict was an unsurprising, "Wilful murder against some person or persons unknown."

LEFT: Poplar in the early 1900s. It was in this area in December 1888 that potential Ripper victim Catherine Mylett was found.

Briefing

It is accepted by many that the murder of Mary Kelly on 9 November 1888 was the last of Jack the Ripper's crimes, after which he seemed to disappear, leaving an exasperated world none the wiser as to his identity or his motives and forcing a plethora of armchair detectives, historians and true-crime authorities to try their hand at solving what could be considered the greatest true crime mystery of them all. Today, many believe in the "canonical five" Ripper murders of Nichols, Chapman, Stride, Eddowes and Kelly, yet at the time, such a delineation was not yet formed; Kelly's death was described by some newspapers as the seventh Whitechapel murder, the latest in a series that also included Emma Smith and Martha Tabram.

O F COURSE, AS THE WINTER OF 1888 DREW ON, there was not to be such closure. The awful affair in Miller's Court was seen as yet one more atrocity in an escalating series with no predictable end, unless the luck of the police should change and the perpetrator be brought to justice. Tensions were still running high in the East End.

A good example of the sensational release of such tensions came on 21 November, the day after the burial of Mary Kelly when, in the heart of the district of doss houses frequented by those unfortunate victims, a prostitute named Annie Farmer claimed to have been attacked by a man who she said was no less than Jack the Ripper.

Annie was the 40-year-old former wife of a City Road tradesman who, after the couple separated, had turned to a life of prostitution, going by a variety of aliases such as Laughing Liz, Flossie and Dark Sarah. At 7:30 a.m. on that morning of 21 November, Annie had picked up a potential client whom she described as "shabby genteel", and took him back to her lodging house at 19 George Street, the same doss house that had been home to Martha Tabram (see chapter 3) only months before. The man paid for both of them, but the liaison was not to prove successful, as two hours later a piercing scream was heard, after which the man was seen running from the house and turning into Thrawl Street. Passing two men standing in the street, he was heard to exclaim "what a ----- cow!" (the original expletive was never discovered and hence, the press reported it in this manner) before disappearing from view and, it seems, the story. Annie appeared obviously distraught, for her throat had been cut and she said she had been attacked by Jack the Ripper himself. In such a tightly packed neighbourhood, it was not long before word got out of another outrage and crowds began to assemble excitedly in front of No.19 and before long, panic seemed to overtake reason.

Fortunately, the police were more circumspect. The throat injury Annie sustained was rather superficial and it was subsequently discovered that she had been hiding coins in her mouth. This led the police to assume that she had attempted to rob the man, he had obviously remonstrated with her and, following her scream, made a run for it, a logical thing to do considering that such uproar may well have resulted in his being lynched by the mobs of George Street. Annie's wound may well have been self-inflicted. Despite this, she never recanted her story and the man never came forward to give an account of himself and thus the case was dropped.

Another Ripper scare erupted following the discovery of the body of Catherine (also known as Rose) Mylett in Clarke's Yard, Poplar High Street. The Mylett case was a peculiar one – at her inquest, four doctors, Drs Brownfield, Harris, Habbert and MacKellar all stated that the evidence pointed to death by strangulation, as there were signs that a cord had been used around her neck. Dr Thomas Bond, directed by Robert Anderson to make a late examination, changed his opinion from homicide to "natural causes". Anderson appeared to be wilfully pushing for a non-homicide verdict, as there were no signs of a struggle. Coroner Wynne Baxter also favoured death by natural causes, but in the face of weighty medical opinion, a verdict of "wilful murder against some person or persons unknown" was given. The evidence to suggest that Mylett was killed by Jack the Ripper was flimsy at best, but it is likely to be the timing of the homicide rather than the way it was done that put this crime in the category of the Whitechapel Murders.

These two attacks, although on women of the same class as previous victims, hardly stood up to

scrutiny as being the work of the Ripper. In July the following year, however, another unfortunate was killed in the heart of the Whitechapel district and this time the manner in which she was murdered gave observers every reason to assume that Jack the Ripper was alive and well and at work again.

Castle Alley was one of the more disreputable thoroughfares in the neighbourhood north of Whitechapel High Street. Its existence went back to the glory days of coaching inns and yards which served the main route out of London from Aldgate and it was originally known in the seventeenth century as Moses and Aaron Alley. Its southerly entrance was a tiny narrow passageway that, once it had passed the shops either side, opened out into a somewhat wider street. On the western side stood the tall warehouses of the Brooke Bond

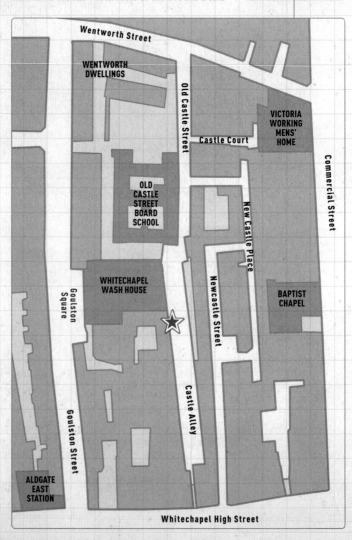

BELOW: Map of the Castle Alley / Old Castle Street area as it was in 1888 when Alice McKenzie was murdered.

★ Murder site

ABOVE: Gun Street, Spitalfields, photographed in 1912. McKenzie's lodging house, "Mr Tenpenny's" is on the left hand side.

widened following the demolition of some of the shops there in the 1890s. This was done specifically to improve access and to make the alley a safer place for those who passed through it, the decision to do so being influenced considerably by the cover that such a place offered the criminal fraternity and, perhaps as the final straw, by the discovery of another Whitechapel Murder in 1889.

By all accounts, the night of 16/17 July 1889 had been a quiet one in Castle Alley; at 12:25 a.m. PC Joseph Allen, 423H, one of two patrolling constables whose beats took them up the dark street, walked through the tiny entrance from the main road and perhaps noticing that all was quiet, decided that it was time for a light snack. He stood under a lamp near the back wall of the Wash House. He was close to two carts, a brewer's dray and a scavenger's wagon, which had been parked by the kerb and as he ate, he could see nobody around. After five minutes, he continued northwards up Old Castle Street and into Wentworth Street. As PC Allen was taking his light refreshment, the deputy of the Wash House, Sarah Smith, was in bed, her bedroom being on the other side of the wall to Castle Alley. She sat up reading until about 12:30 a.m. and heard nothing, not even the footsteps of the passing policeman. As Allen left it, PC Walter Andrews, 272H, entered Castle Alley; as he passed through the street, he saw nobody and continued his beat into Goulston Street, Whitechapel High Street, Middlesex Street and then into Wentworth Street, this time approaching Old Castle Street from the north. During this time it had begun to rain and as PC Andrews turned into Old Castle Street he met Sergeant Edward Badham, 31H, who was in the area checking on the constables' beats. They exchanged a brief acknowledgement that everything was fine before going their separate ways, Badham walking into Wentworth Street to check a neighbouring beat and Andrews walking down towards Castle Alley.

There, between the carts where PC Allen had had his supper, lay the body of Alice McKenzie. Her skirts had been pulled up exposing the abdomen, and a quantity of blood had pooled on the pavement beneath her head. Almost at once, Andrews heard footsteps and saw Isaac Jacobs passing along the street with a plate in his hand; apparently Jacobs, a boot-maker living in nearby

Tea Company, which then abutted the back of the Whitechapel Wash House. The Wash House, situated on Goulston Street and built between 1846 and 1851, was an important building in the district. It was the first of its kind in London, offering the local poor a place to clean themselves in a sanitary and often social environment. A brick wall stood opposite; it was effectively the rear of the yards of houses situated in adjacent Newcastle Street. At its northern end, Castle Alley became Old Castle Street, and a recently constructed Board School stood near the junction with Wentworth Street. Much of this area consisted of workshops and its proximity to Wentworth Street and the Petticoat Lane markets meant that at night the whole thoroughfare was often cluttered with costermongers' barrows and traders' wagons. Today, Castle Alley has been absorbed into Old Castle Street and the tiny entrance from Whitechapel High Street has been significantly

Mr Tenpenny's Lodging House

Mr Tenpenny's was situated at the southern end of Gun Street, Spitalfields, on the west side close to the junction with Artillery Street (now Artillery Lane). Variously described as being at No.52 or No.54, it was in fact a large establishment that consisted of four joined properties, Nos.50, 51, 52 and 53. No.50 was first registered in July 1854, No.51 in February 1879 and Nos.52 and 53 in April 1880. The collective houses were licensed for a total of 198 residents.

The owner was Thomas Tempany (his name has also been spelt Tenpany and Tampany), a Cambridgeshire-born lodging house keeper formerly of 6 Paternoster Row (part of today's Brushfield Street). In 1881 he was residing at 161 Bishopsgate, and ten years later he lived with his wife Sarah, eight children and a step-daughter at 6–8 Widegate Street. He took on the properties at Gun Street in 1877, gradually taking over the neighbouring houses.

He gave up ownership of the lodging houses in March 1894. Mr Tempany shared Alice McKenzie's funeral expenses with the proprietor of The Tower public house in Artillery Street (where the funeral procession started), having declined an offer from the London Evangelization Society and Common Lodging-house Mission to defray the cost of the funeral.

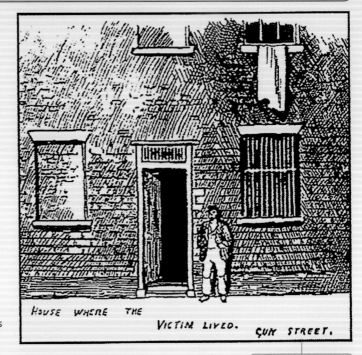

HOUSE WHERE THE VICTIM LIVED. GUN STREET.

The buildings were demolished sometime in the early 1970s.

ABOVE: A contemporary press sketch of Mr Tenpenny's lodging house in Gun Street.

New Castle Place, was on his way (coincidentally) to John McCarthy's shop in Dorset Street to get his supper. Andrews ordered him to stay put and blew his whistle.

Sergeant Badham was no more than 137 m (150 yards) from where he had previously met Andrews when he heard the signal, the sound of which sent him running back to Castle Alley.

Alice McKenzie, like Mary Kelly (see chapter 9) before her, had a mysterious past. It is believed she was born around 1849 and was brought up in Peterborough, moving to the East End sometime before 1874. She was known by many as "Clay Pipe Alice" on account of her regular habit of smoking a pipe. She had scars on her forehead and was missing part of a thumb, the result of an industrial accident some years previously. In about 1883, she had got together with a man named John McCormack, an Irish porter who had been doing casual work for Jewish traders in Hanbury

Street and they lodged together at various doss houses in the district over the years before settling at Mr Tenpenny's in Gun Street, near Spitalfields Market.

Between 3:00 and 4:00 p.m. on the afternoon of 16 July 1889, McCormack had returned to the lodging house after his morning's work. He had money, and finding Alice there, gave her 1s 8d (about £5 in today's money), the 8d (worth about £2 today) for the rent and the rest to do with as she pleased, before going to straight to bed. It was the last time he would see her and it later transpired that she left without paying the deputy Elizabeth Ryder the money. Another sighting of Alice McKenzie took place at 7:10 p.m., unusual in that according to a report made by Sergeant John McCarthy, the "sighting" was made by George Dixon, a blind boy. He claimed that Alice had taken him to a pub near the Cambridge Music Hall on Commercial Street:

He heard Mrs McKenzie ask someone if they would stand a drink and the reply was "yes". After remaining a few minutes Mrs McKenzie led him back to 52 Gun St. & left him there. The boy Dixon says he would be able to recognize the voice of the person who spoke to Mrs McKenzie in the public house.

The location of the pub was not clear, not unsurprising considering the boy's blindness, however enquiries were made at the Cambridge Theatre Tavern next door, where the proprietors had no recollection of Dixon and McKenzie, although they could not confirm that they were not there and that the incident did not happen. Other possible contenders could have been the Commercial Tavern at the corner of Commercial Street and Wheler Street (which still exists) or the White Hart on Little Pearl Street. Regardless of how many enquiries were made, however, the story could not be substantiated.

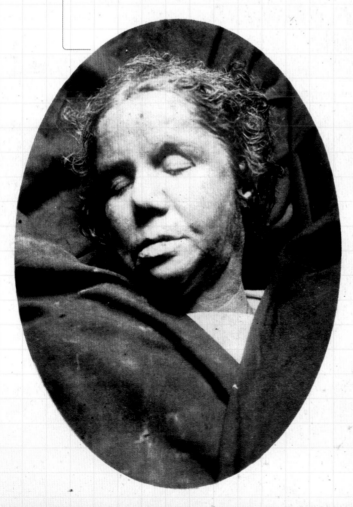

BELOW: The mortuary photograph of Alice McKenzie.

Elizabeth Ryder, the deputy of Mr Tenpenny's, saw Alice again between 8:00 and 9:00 p.m. at the lodging house. Alice was on her way out and it was noted that she had some money in her hand, and it was believed for a while that she had gone out with a fellow lodger named Margaret "Mog" Cheeks. According to Mrs Ryder, neither woman had returned to the house when she checked at 3:30 a.m. the following morning. No small concern was given to the welfare of Mrs Cheeks following the murder, but she eventually came forward and far from going out with Alice that night, she had been staying at her sister's. The final sighting of Alice McKenzie was made at 11:40 p.m. by a friend, Margaret Franklin, in Flower and Dean Street. Franklin was sitting on the steps of her lodging house at the eastern end of the street near Brick Lane with Catherine Hughes and Sarah Mahoney when Alice passed by, seemingly in a hurry, and when Franklin asked how Alice was, she merely replied "All right, can't stop now" before turning into Brick Lane and heading towards Whitechapel. A little over one hour later, PC Walter Andrews made his discovery.

With PC Andrews and Sergeant Badham at the scene, the process of reinforcements and enquiries got under way. Badham found PC Allen near Commercial Street and instructed him to go to Commercial Street Police Station to fetch other constables, who on arrival began making enquiries at the various properties nearby, and blocked both ends of the street. PC Joseph Allen was sent to fetch Dr George Bagster Phillips, who arrived at the scene at 1:10 a.m., moments after Inspector Edmund Reid. The wheels of investigation into another potential Ripper murder were already in motion.

Alice McKenzie's death was caused by the severance of the left carotid artery, which was common to the other victims, but the injury itself was slightly different. According to Dr Bond's report, there were two stabs in the left side of the neck "carried forward in the same skin wound", since the cuts were made left to right while McKenzie was lying on the ground. There was some bruising on the chest, five bruises or marks on the left side of the abdomen and a long 18 cm (7 in) "but not unduly deep" wound from the bottom of the left breast to the navel. Seven or eight scratches began at the navel and pointed toward the genitalia, and were accompanied by

RIGHT: The map of the Pinchin Street area produced for the inquest into the torso case in 1889.

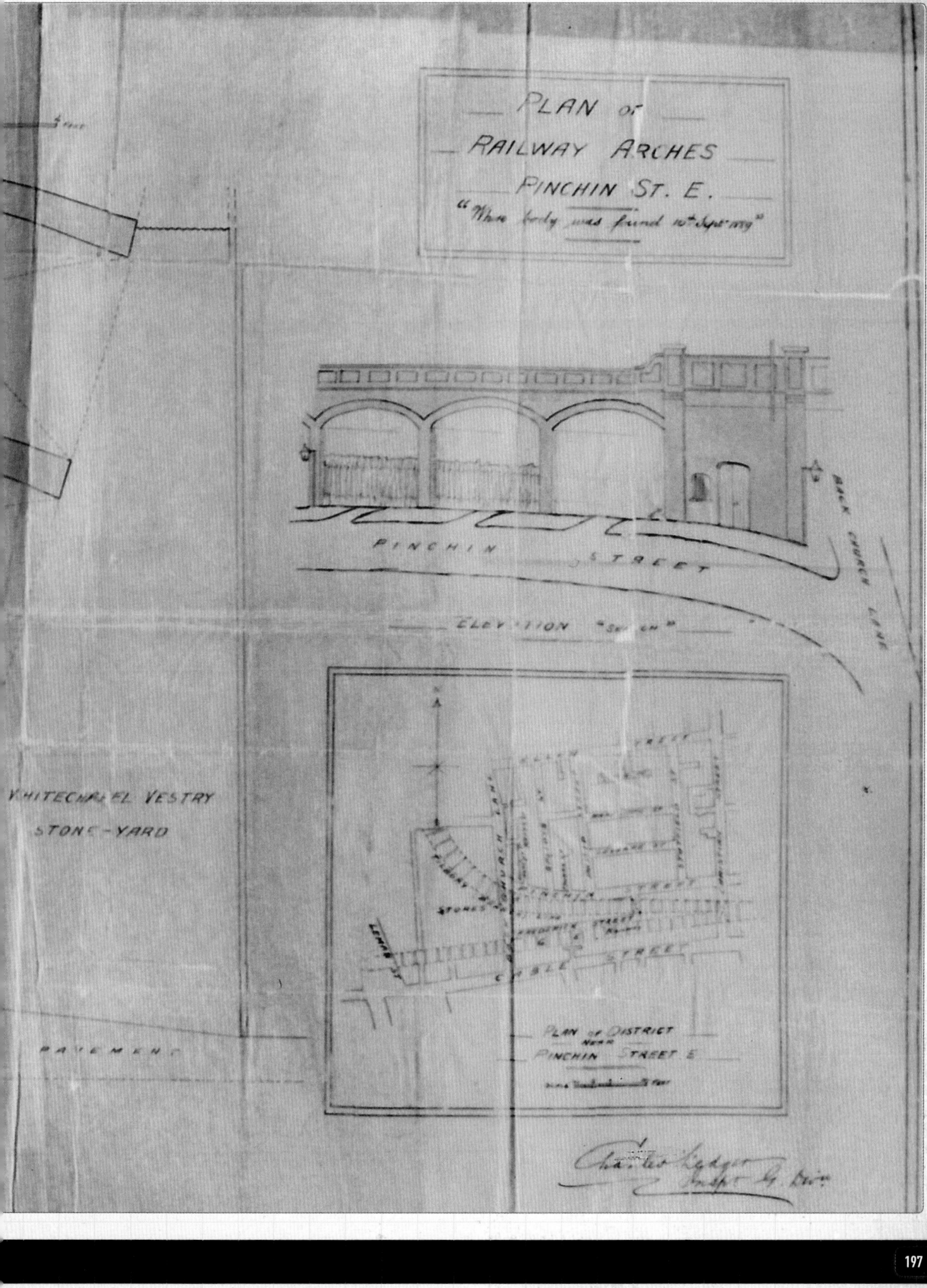

PLAN of
RAILWAY ARCHES
PINCHIN ST. E.
"Where body was found 10th Sept 1889"

PINCHIN STREET

ELEVATION "Sketch"

WHITECHAPEL VESTRY
STONE-YARD

PAVEMENT

PLAN of DISTRICT
NEAR
PINCHIN STREET E.

The candidacy of Alice McKenzie as a genuine Ripper murder has had its detractors and supporters over the years. Admittedly, the cutting of the genital area has shades of the Buck's Row murder (see chapter 4) and there is every possibility, what with the regularity of the passing constables, that the murderer may have been disturbed. However, Dr Phillips, the doctor who had been present at the post-mortems of nearly all the victims beforehand, was not convinced that the Ripper was culpable:

After careful and long deliberation, I cannot satisfy myself, on purely Anatomical and professional grounds that the perpetrator of all the "Wh Ch. murders" is our man. I am on the contrary impelled to a contrary conclusion in this noting the mode of procedure and the character of the mutilations and judging of motive in connection with the Latter. I do not here enter into the comparison of the cases neither do I take into account what I admit may be almost conclusive evidence in favour of the one man theory if all the surrounding circumstances and other evidence are considered, holding it as my duty to report on the P.M. (post-mortem) appearances and express an opinion only on Professional grounds, based upon my own observation.

Robert Anderson concurred. However, with unfortunate timing, he was on leave and it was up to James Monro, Chief Commissioner of the Metropolitan Police since Sir Charles Warren's resignation the previous year, to investigate the case. Monro felt that Jack the Ripper had struck again, as did Dr Thomas Bond who stated:

I see in this murder evidence of similar

ABOVE: Illustration from the *Penny Illustrated Paper* showing the discovery of Alice McKenzie's body by PC Andrews.

design to the former Whitechapel murders, viz. sudden onslaught on the prostrate woman, the throat skillfully and resolutely cut with subsequent mutilation, each mutilation indicating sexual thoughts and a desire to mutilate the abdomen and sexual organs. I am of opinion that the murder was performed by the same person who committed the former series of Whitechapel murders.

Although Dr Phillips had a weight of experience to bolster his belief, it is interesting to note that it was Dr Bond, after the murder of Mary Kelly, who produced a prototype "criminal profile" of the sort of character Jack the Ripper may have been (see chapter 9) and for him at least, the way Alice McKenzie was killed fitted that profile.

a small cut across the pubic bone. Dr Phillips put the time of death as 30 minutes before his arrival, in effect 12:40 a.m. The dry area beneath the body confirmed that it was there before it started raining at 12:45 a.m., therefore when the murder took place PCs Andrews and Allen were not too far away at the northern end of the street. Whoever killed Alice McKenzie had been taking a phenomenal risk.

This murder was perhaps more worthy of the press attention lavished upon it than the attack on Annie Farmer and as a Ripper crime it had more in its favour than did the death of Catherine Mylett. Again, newspapers and magazines

jumped on the incident featuring the usual accompaniment of garish illustrations, all in the style of what had been produced the previous year. Before 1889 was over, another mystery would perplex the people of the East End, and the question of whether the Ripper was still at large despite the police investigation came to the fore yet again.

On 10 September 1889, the headless and legless torso of a woman was found under a railway arch in Pinchin Street, a quiet, grim street in the parish of St George-in-the-East, only a few hundred yards to the south of Berner Street where Elizabeth Stride had met her death a year before (see

OPPOSITE: A contemporary newspaper sketch of the archway into Swallow Gardens. This view is from the south, from Royal Mint Street.

ABOVE: PC William Pennett, who found the Pinchin Street Torso.

chapter 7). Pinchin Street did not have the best reputation in the neighbourhood and it was one of those thoroughfares whose character had been altered for the worse by the construction of the railways almost half a century before. The *East London Observer* made this very clear on 14 September 1889:

In Pinchin-street, down in St George's East, is an ordinary railway arch, 14 ft or 15 ft [4 to 4.5 m] above the level of the ground, over which is laid the main line of the Great Eastern Railway from Fenchurch-street eastwards. Close by is a branch leading to the huge warehouses constructed by the London and Tilbury Company in Commercial-road, the erection of which necessitated the clearing a large extent of ground of the small and dilapidated buildings which formerly encumbered it. Like most parts of the district lying between Whitechapel and the notorious old Ratcliff Highway, Leman-street and neighbourhood are densely crowded, a large proportion of the inhabitants being Germans, Poles, and Russians, who follow the pursuits of tailoring and bootmaking, polish walking sticks, hawk pictures, and engage in various callings of a similar kind requiring no great physical exertion. The whole district is squalid. No one would be a bit the worse if, by some other great public works, half of it were cleared altogether.

Much of the north side of the street was heavily bombed during the Second World War, perhaps creating the opportunity for a long-deserved redevelopment. The arches today are used by shops and small businesses and the one where the torso was found, the last before Backchurch Lane, is bricked up with two small windows offering light to whatever concern resides within.

The grisly fragment of human remains was found by patrolling police officer PC William Pennett, 239H, at 5:25 a.m. as he was crossing from the north side of the street towards the arch, going in the direction of Backchurch Lane. As he approached the arch, the last before Backchurch Lane, he noticed a bundle lying among the stones inside. On approach he found that it was a portion of a human body, covered by two or three pieces of rag. What these were at the time was not certain, but with the exception of these the body was naked. He noticed that the head had been taken from the body, and that the legs were missing. The trunk was lying on its stomach, with the shoulders towards the west.

Without blowing his whistle, for fear of creating a scene and inviting a potentially excitable crowd, he waited for a few moments until a man passed along the street carrying a broom. Pennett stayed with the body, and instructed the man to fetch police officers from the adjoining beats. Constable 205H was the first to arrive, closely followed by constable 115H (sadly neither of these officers were named in the inquest report). Pennett instructed the former to fetch Inspector Charles Pinhorn, who upon his arrival told Pennett to start searching the neighbouring arches. Pennett found three men sleeping rough in the arches along Pinchin Street, two sailors, one named Richard Hawke and the other not named in any reports, and a shoe-black called Michael Keating. All three were taken into custody but later released.

Once the torso was taken to the St George-in-the-East mortuary, a post-mortem was carried out by Dr J Clarke, assistant to Dr Bagster Phillips. He observed that:

MIDLAND RAILWAY GOODS STATION WAY IN

R. CULLERSON STORES

45

I found the body appeared to be that of a woman of stoutish build, dark complexion, about 5 ft 3 [2.2 m] in in height, and between 30 and 40 years of age. I should think the body had been dead at least 24 hours. Besides the wounds caused by the severance of the head and legs, there was a wound 15ins [38 cm]. long through the external coat of the abdomen. The body was not bloodstained, except where the chemise had rested upon it. The body had not the appearance of having been recently washed. On the back there were four bruises, all caused before death. There was one over the spine, on a level with the lower part of the shoulder blade. It was about the size of a shilling. An inch lower down there was a similar bruise, about the middle of the back, also on the spine, and that was a bruise about the size of a half-a-crown. On the level of the top of the hip bone was a bruise 2 1/2ins [6 cm] in diameter. It was such a bruise as would be caused by a fall or a kick. None of the bruises were of old standing. Round the waist was a pale mark and indentation, such as would be caused by clothing during life. On the right arm there were eight distinct bruises and seven on the left, all of them caused before death and of recent date. The back of both forearms and hands were much bruised. On the outer side of the left forearm, about 3 in [7.6 cm] above the wrist, was a cut about 2 [5 cm] in in length, and half an inch [1.2 cm] lower down was another cut. These were caused after death. The bruises on the right arm were such as would be caused by the arms having been tightly grasped. The hands and nails were pallid. The hands did not exhibit any particular kind of work.

LEFT: Frances Coles, as depicted in a contemporary press illustration.

BELOW: The mortuary photograph of Frances Coles.

The woman's body was never truly identified, although an initial idea was that it was Lydia Hart, a prostitute who had been missing for some time, but without any official identification, she merely became yet another of the many women of her class who disappeared every year in the metropolis. It was perhaps the proximity to the East End of London and the apparent mutilation of the abdomen that sparked the initial fear that this may be related to the murders committed by Jack the Ripper. Many, however, believe that it fitted more readily into a series of unsolved outrages that had been discovered during previous years in different areas of London, later to become known as the

Also dubbed the "Thames Mysteries" or "Embankment Murders", this series was overshadowed by the Whitechapel Murders but was no less mysterious. In May 1887, workers pulled a bundle containing the torso of a female from the river at Rainham in Essex. Over the next few months, additional sections of the same body showed up in various parts of London, until an almost complete body, minus the head and upper chest, could be reconstructed. The verdict of "found dead" was given, as no evidence of a violent end could be ascertained.

On 11 September 1888, as the Ripper's "autumn of terror" was in full swing, an arm belonging to a female was discovered in the Thames off Pimlico. Another arm was found a few weeks later along the Lambeth Road and on 2 October, the torso of a woman, minus the head, was discovered. Later dubbed "The Whitehall Mystery", this discovery caused a sensation as it was made on the construction site for the new police headquarters at New Scotland Yard. After a long break, another part of a female torso was fished out of the Thames at Horselydown on 4 June 1889, and at about the same time a leg belonging to the body was found under Albert Bridge. Within a short period of time, different parts of the same body were recovered, either from the Thames itself or close by. These were eventually confirmed to be Elizabeth Jackson, a Soho prostitute of about 24 years of age.

Medical experts tended to agree that some degree of medical skill would have been required to commit these acts, however, the remaining bodies stayed unidentified and the perpetrator or perpetrators were never found. Other similar discoveries had been made in the Thames over the years, most notably in 1873–1874, and another case was recorded in central London (in the Tottenham Court Road) area in 1884.

"Thames Torso Murders", whereupon different parts of different women were found washed up or floating in various locations on and around the River Thames. In some cases, many of these parts were reassembled but only one firm identification resulted, that of Elizabeth Jackson in mid-1889.

After the excitement of 1889, 1890 provided a hiatus from any further suspected Whitechapel Murders. Things were still not going well in the police hierarchy as Sir Charles Warren's successor, James Monro found himself at loggerheads with Home Secretary Henry Matthews in much the same way as his predecessor had been. Inevitably, matters came to a head and Monro resigned his post in June, making him the shortest-serving Chief Commissioner of the Metropolitan Police on record. His replacement was Sir Edward Bradford who took up office in the recently completed police headquarters of New Scotland Yard, on the Thames Embankment. It was during his tenure, when 1891 was little more than six weeks old, that the final Whitechapel Murder occurred.

Swallow Gardens was a rather attractive name for what was essentially an unattractive railway arch that ran under the lines of the London Blackwall Railway. As its name wistfully suggests, Swallow Gardens were originally gardens or orchards laid out to the north of Rosemary Lane (now Royal Mint Street) and to the south of Chamber Street, a thoroughfare that still runs east-west between Leman Street and Mansell Street. By the mid-eighteenth century, small properties were beginning to encroach on the area, and major changes followed the coming of the railway (originally the Commercial Railway), which began construction in 1836 and was opened in 1840. The line ran from the Minories to Blackwall via Stepney, and was the same one that also ran alongside Pinchin Street, over the arch where the torso was discovered. Swallow Gardens has therefore changed drastically, and at this time it was merely an alleyway running to a length of about 12 m (40 ft) through a railway arch from Royal Mint Street to Chamber Street. This roadway was partially taken away and boarded up from the crown of the arch to the ground and the remaining space was only wide enough for one cart to pass at a time. There were two ordinary gas-lamps to light the passage, throwing light all the way along its length. The archway remains today, but like many such spaces is closed off for use by private businesses.

At about 2:15 a.m. on Friday 13 February 1891, PC Ernest Thompson, 240H, a constable making his first solo night patrol in the area, passed down Chamber Street, walking in the direction of the arch of Swallow Gardens. As he drew near, he heard the sound of walking footsteps, seemingly those of a man, emanating from the Mansell Street end of Chamber Street. PC Thompson could not see anybody and thought little of it until he turned down into the arch and promptly discovered a woman lying on the ground. She was bleeding from a wound in the throat, but was alive – Thompson believed he saw one of her eyelids move as he bent down to investigate. He blew his whistle three times, and was quickly joined by two other constables; PC Frederick Hyde, 161H, the first to arrive, was swiftly sent to Dr Frederick Oxley in nearby Dock Street and PC George Elliott, 275H, went to Leman Street Police Station. Within ten minutes, Dr Oxley arrived at the scene. At this point, the woman was still alive, but she died on the stretcher as she was ferried to the hospital. The victim was 32-year old Frances Coles.

Born in Bermondsey on 17 September 1859, Frances was the third child of bootmaker James Coles and Mary Ann Carney and she had two older sisters, Mary Ann and Selina, and a younger brother, James. There appears to be no evidence that Frances's parents ever married and Mary Ann senior was a somewhat enigmatic character, a Catholic supposedly born in Ireland, but for whom official documentation presents conflicting places of birth and ages. She was also the first member of the family to enter a workhouse, specifically St Olave Workhouse, in 1877. James senior also followed, first at Bermondsey Workhouse and then St Olave, which strongly suggests there was some sort of family breakup. Mary Ann Carney died sometime between the censuses of 1881 and 1891.

According to her sister Mary Ann, Frances, still living in Bermondsey, secured a job in a chemist's in the Minories. This was perhaps how Frances became acquainted with the East End and by 1883 she was living there as a prostitute, working the areas of Whitechapel, Shoreditch and Bow and residing at Wilmott's Lodging House at 18 Thrawl Street. The last time Mary Ann saw her younger sister was at Christmas 1890 and though it seems she believed that Frances was still holding down her job in the Minories, she noticed how her clothes looked dirty and that there was a

smell of alcohol on her breath. By this time, James Coles was a sick man and still a resident of the workhouse, and despite her lifestyle (which she appeared to keep a secret from her family), Frances visited him regularly and often attended church services with him.

Frances met a ship's fireman named James Thomas Sadler in 1889 in Whitechapel Road and as they obviously enjoyed each other's company, Sadler paid for them both to stay at her regular Thrawl Street lodging house, very likely Wilmott's. Sadler's job meant that he would soon return to sea, but the liaison was rekindled on 11 February 1891 when Sadler, recently discharged from the SS *Fez*, met Frances in the Princess Alice pub on

BELOW: A contemporary press illustration of James Sadler in the dock at Frances Coles' inquest.

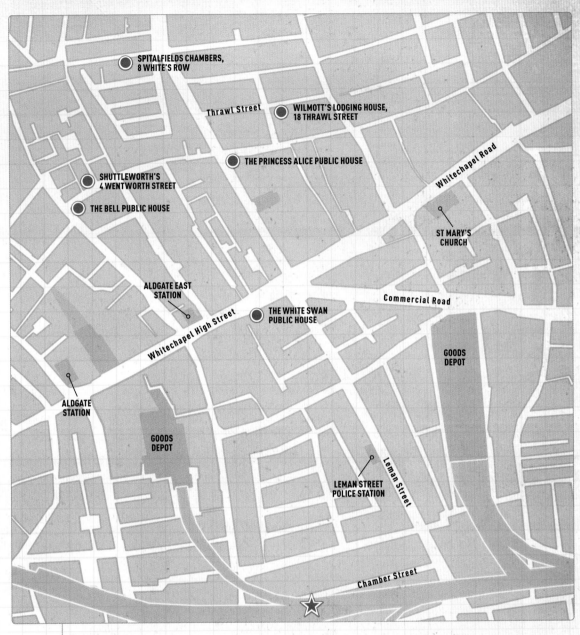

SPITALFIELDS CHAMBERS,
8 WHITE'S ROW

Thrawl Street

WILMOTT'S LODGING HOUSE,
18 THRAWL STREET

THE PRINCESS ALICE PUBLIC HOUSE

SHUTTLEWORTH'S
4 WENTWORTH STREET

THE BELL PUBLIC HOUSE

Whitechapel Road

ST MARY'S
CHURCH

ALDGATE EAST
STATION

Commercial Road

THE WHITE SWAN
PUBLIC HOUSE

Whitechapel High Street

GOODS
DEPOT

ALDGATE
STATION

GOODS
DEPOT

Leman Street

LEMAN STREET
POLICE STATION

Chamber Street

ABOVE: Map of Whitechapel
and Spitalfields showing
key locations in the Frances
Coles Case.

⭐ Murder Site
◉ Key Location

Commercial Street at about 9:00 p.m. Leaving
there, they visited a number of other pubs in the
area, including one on the corner of Dorset Street,
which would have been either the Britannia or the
Horn of Plenty. Sadler again paid for a double bed
for the couple, this time at Spitalfields Chambers,
the lodging house at 8 White's Row and with
them they took a half-bottle of whisky which
Sadler had bought from the White Swan pub on
Whitechapel High Street.

Leaving the lodging house the next day at
about 12 noon, they embarked on what can

only be described as a pub crawl, visiting various
establishments in the neighbourhood, one of
which was The Bell at the corner of Middlesex
Street and New Goulston Street. After a few hours
of talking and drinking they took the long walk
to Nottingham Street in Whitechapel (north of
Baker's Row and now part of today's Vallance
Road) to collect a hat that Frances had been
paying for, all the way stopping off at pubs. After
acquiring the hat and pinning her old one to her
dress, Frances walked back towards Brick Lane
where they stopped at the Marlborough Head

LEFT: Spitalfields Chambers, White's Row, as depicted by the contemporary press in 1891.

for more drinks. By now, the couple were getting noticeably drunk and the landlady there objected to them being on the premises. Soon, Sadler had to keep an appointment in Spitalfields and as he and Frances walked down Thrawl Street, Sadler was set upon and robbed by a woman and two male accomplices. From here on, the day became very messy.

Sadler remonstrated with Coles, feeling that she could have helped him when he was down and the couple parted in Thrawl Street under a black cloud. Frances, drunk and emotional, returned to Spitalfields Chambers and soon after, Sadler arrived, finding Frances sitting at a table crying. At about midnight, unable to secure a bed on credit, he left, leaving Frances to sleep but after only half an hour, she too departed, presumably because she did not have any money to pay for a bed herself. The next time she was seen was at 1:30 a.m. at Shuttleworth's eating house at 4 Wentworth Street. According to the shop assistant Joseph Haswell, she came into the shop and asked for 1d (approximately 25p today) worth of mutton and some bread. She was served, paying for it with a penny and two halfpennies, and sat down and ate it. Frances had been in the shop for about a quarter of an hour when Haswell asked her to leave as it was closing time. She told him to mind

his own business. With that, Haswell grabbed her by the arm and physically escorted her off the premises, watching her go off in the direction of Brick Lane.

Frances appears to have had money to spend on the food and it is likely she had been soliciting to earn it, for soon after 1:45 a.m. she met a friend named Ellen Callagher, also known as "Callana", by the Princess Alice. Ellen was promptly propositioned by a very short man with a dark moustache, shiny boots and blue trousers, but as she did not like the look of him, she refused and with that, duly offended, the man punched her in the face. Despite this obvious display of violence, Frances decided to go with the man, heedless of her friend's advice to stay well away. Ellen watched Frances and the man, who was described as looking like a sailor (but was not Sadler), walk up Commercial Street and turn into White's Row.

In the meantime, Sadler's night was going from bad to worse. Downhearted by the loss of his money, Sadler failed to keep his appointment and instead went to the London docks to get himself back on the SS *Fez*, but he was refused admission by a sergeant for being too drunk. At 1:50 a.m. a group of men left through the dock gates and one of them made a comment to Sadler. He returned the abuse, calling them "dock rats",

OPPOSITE: Now in use as a storage facility for a local business, this is the archway of Swallow Gardens today.

The Princess Alice

Sited at 40 Commercial Street on the corner with Wentworth Street, the original pub was built in 1850 following the construction of Commercial Street, though the current premises date from 1883–1884. It was designated as being at No.51 in 1871. Originally a four to five-storey building, the landlord in 1888 was Arthur Ferrar and it was a Truman's Brewery house.

The pub was allegedly frequented by Leather Apron. A reporter with *The Star* was directed to the Princess Alice by two women who claimed it was the most likely place to find him, adding that "it would be necessary to look into the shadows, as if he was there he would surely be out of sight".

Sometime in the 1940s the Princess Alice lost the two top floors, the result of wartime bombing. In 1986 it was renamed The City Darts and became a Thorley Tavern. It was refurbished and reverted to its original name in 2005.

LEFT: The Princess Alice at the corner of Commercial Street and Wentworth Street in 2010.

and with the dock sergeant turning a blind eye, the three men set about kicking and punching Sadler to the ground, before sloping off. Drunk, battered and bloody, he made another attempt to gain entry to a lodging house, this time in nearby East Smithfield, but naturally the deputy wanted nothing to do with him. Resigning himself to his lot, Sadler made his way slowly back to Spitalfields Chambers. Frances was not there and again, he was refused a bed by the deputy Sarah Fleming because he was so drunk and delirious he could barely stand, let alone speak. Sadler's disastrous night ended at 5:00 a.m. when he arrived at the London Hospital, where a kindly doctor treated his many wounds and allowed him sleep for a while. By this time, of course, Frances Coles had been dead for nearly three hours. A final possible sighting of her was made by William "Jumbo" Friday and two brothers named Knapton, who claimed that they saw a woman wearing a bonnet standing with a man who looked like a ship's fireman in Royal Mint Street, close to the southern entrance to Swallow Gardens. This was only minutes before Coles was found dead.

It appears that Frances was first thrown violently to the ground, a deduction made from the

RIGHT: Ann's Place, Wentworth Street in 2010. Annie Shuttleworth, owner of the eating house at 4 Wentworth Street which was visited by Frances Coles the night she died, lived here with her husband.

presence of wounds to the back of the head. Her throat was cut, most likely while she was lying down, but there were no abdominal mutilations. Dr Phillips believed the killer had held her head back by the chin with his left hand, and cut the throat with his right, the knife passing across the throat three times – first from left to right, then from right to left, and once more from left to right. The hat she had purchased the night before was lying beside her, her old hat pinned beneath her dress. Later, two shillings was found hidden behind a water pipe in the passageway, perhaps money she had earned from her final client.

James Sadler was arrested on suspicion of the murder of Frances Coles on 15 February 1889 and charged the following day. He seemed a likely suspect – he and Frances were in the same area at the time of her death, and the idea of his guilt was compounded when a man named Duncan Campbell later claimed that Sadler had sold him a knife on the morning of the murder. The sighting of the "ship's fireman" and a woman at the southern entrance to Swallow Gardens must have also reinforced any case against him. However, Sadler had fortune on his side. He was given sound legal representation by the Seaman's Union who had gathered some strong witnesses in his favour and he was released before the case could even hit the court. The knife he owned did not appear sharp enough to commit the injuries to Coles' throat and in any case, it was suggested that Sadler was so drunk at the time that he could not have coordinated such an attack effectively. Furthermore, any presumption that he could have killed Coles in his capacity as a potential Jack the Ripper were well and truly scotched when he gave the police a full account of his movements during 1888 – he was at sea when Mary Ann Nichols, Annie Chapman, Elizabeth Stride and Catherine Eddowes were murdered.

The death of Francis Coles was yet another case of "murder by person or persons unknown".

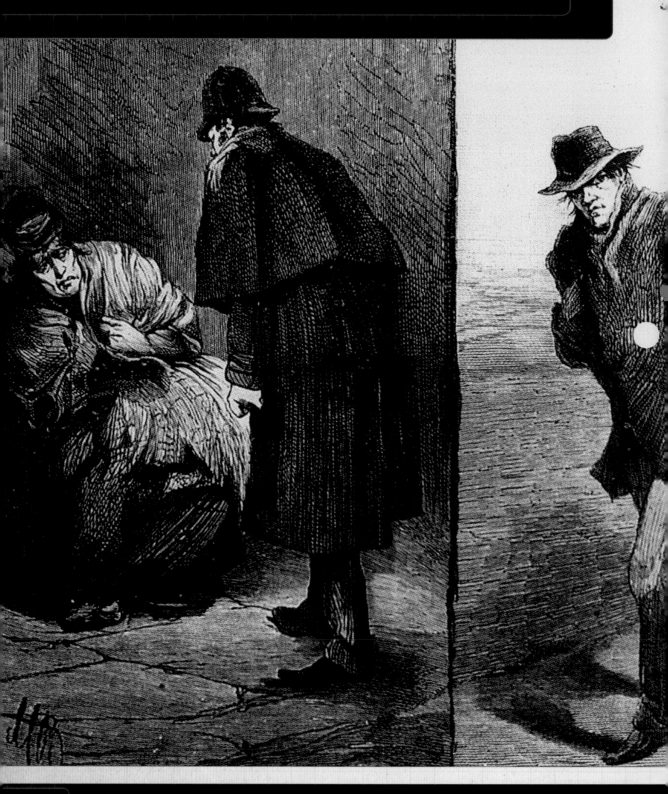

LEFT: Atmospheric press illustrations detailed the enquiries made by police during the Ripper scare, as well as the activities of the numerous "vigilance committees" which were set up at the time.

Briefing

In all likelihood, we may never know for certain the true identity of Jack the Ripper, not, at least, to everybody's satisfaction. As we know, in the years 1888–1891 the police investigation struggled against a wall of misinformation, blind alleys, red herrings and, perhaps more significantly, the apparent luck of an assassin who has since become the world's most infamous murderer. The uniqueness of these crimes took the investigating authorities and the civilians they served by surprise, for there was little or no precedent. The limitations of the investigative techniques available to the London police at that time made the task of finding the Ripper a lot harder than it would had those murders taken place in the twenty-first century.

TODAY, WE CAN CALL ON ALL THE TECHNOLOGY, science, psychology and experience acquired over the intervening 12 decades, and we should not judge the methods of those Victorian law-enforcers by our own standards. The men on the beat, armed with little more than handcuffs, a sturdy truncheon and a notebook, could only use nature's senses and a sound, calm reasoning to do their job. There was no airborne surveillance, CCTV cameras on every street corner, DNA testing, computer databases or two-way radio. Even fingerprinting, a technique which may well have offered interesting leads in the case, was several years away from being accepted as a crime-fighting tool. Those superiors at the top of the police hierarchy, far from being career policemen with years of experience behind them, were often men brought in from other walks of life on the strength of their man-management backgrounds, usually from the military, legal profession or high-level posts in the British colonies. It was all so different and, by today's standards, unsophisticated to the point of being alarmingly naive.

Criticism of the police investigation into the Jack the Ripper murders has always been a major theme in the overall story. Despite many authors' attempts to vindicate the investigation on the basis of what was available at the time, often producing well-researched and authoritative studies of the

PERFECTION.
COLOURS EXQUISITE.

SURFACE LIKE PORCELAIN
SOLD EVERYWHERE

ASPINALL'S ENAMEL.

A. MONARCH-KINO,
Art Tailor & Habit Maker.
Has Removed from CORNHILL, E.C. to
93 & 94, GRACECHURCH STREET, E.C.
His New and only West End Address is
NEW BOND ST., and CORNER OF BROOK ST.

LADIES' COSTUMES FROM £5 5s.

A. MONARCH-KINO,
Art Tailor & Habit Maker.
Has Removed from CORNHILL, E.C. to
93 & 94, GRACECHURCH STREET, E.C.
His New and only West End Address is
NEW BOND ST., and CORNER OF BROOK ST.

LADIES' COSTUMES FROM £5 5s.

No. 36. | New Series, No. 14. | LONDON: SATURDAY, SEPTEMBER 21st, 1889 | Price TWOPENCE.

Registered as a Newspaper at the G.P.O

JACK THE RIPPER

WHO IS HE? WHAT IS HE?
WHERE IS HE?

OPPOSITE: This 1889 front page from *Puck* succinctly illustrates, even at this early stage, that Jack the Ripper was becoming a uniquely compelling mystery.

men and their methods, the hackneyed opinion that police incompetence resulted in a killer getting away still raises its head with tiresome regularity. As can be seen from earlier chapters, this was not an opinion developed with hindsight. Even as the Whitechapel Murders were in full swing, the press in particular flexed their muscles in their condemnation of the authorities. With solutions seemingly out of reach for much of the time, many outside the ranks of the police felt it was their job to advise, instruct and offer solutions of their own. Thus began what even to this day remains a predominantly "civilian" obsession with solving the mystery once and for all.

There is a case to be made that theories as to the identity of Jack the Ripper and the thought processes that lead to those theories are often a reflection of the times in which those ideas came into being. There are certainly trends. In 1888, all the fears harboured about the East End and its diverse and fractious make-up became a sort of Pandora's Box and it was Jack the Ripper who was responsible for opening that box. Fear of poverty and the consciences it pricked, fear of the underclass, fear of the rising unemployed and fear of the foreign were all bubbling under, awaiting the catalyst that would allow those anxieties to hit the Victorian public – in the words of *The Star*'s T P O'Connor in 1889 – "right between the eyes".

For many, the Whitechapel Murderer was an alien, an outsider, with no community taking responsibility for those gross acts perpetrated on the poorest and most vulnerable examples of womankind. The Leather Apron scare of September 1888 (see chapter 6) was the most obvious manifestation of the alien theory, bringing into sharp focus the suspicions and resentment levelled at the thousands of poor Jews who had made the East End their home as it was claimed that no native Englishman would ever do something as terrible and horrifying as these murders. Bringing with them as they did their unfamiliar customs, their kosher slaughterhouses and their particular brand of "dangerous" politics such as Socialism and Anarchism, the Eastern European Jews took the first brunt of suspicion, a suspicion that was not just held by the people of the East End, but felt and then manifested in print for all to see by the sensationalist press.

It was not only outright anti-Semitism, however, since some believed that Jews working in the slaughterhouses would have the required deftness to slit the throat of a victim quickly without becoming drenched in blood. Others felt that the Jewish religion itself may hold the answer, as one writer communicated in a letter to the City police written on 15 October 1888:

I may state I have all along believed the murderer to be a Jew. As I know that a number of Jews, believe in the literal meaning of the law as laid down in their Bible, which says that a woman who is a prostitute shall be put to death. Now a Jew if a monomaniac would naturally reason that he was doing according to that law, if he was clearing the streets of these unfortunates, and he would find no difficulty in finding out that class, from other women, as all these poor victims, must have lain down before him for an immoral end, and they were then at his mercy.

The murder of Annie Chapman (see chapter 5), coming as it did at the early stages of the alien scare, also threw up another possibility, one which has stood the test of time and often contributes significantly in any theory as to the killer's identity. This is that the Ripper was a trained doctor or surgeon. It was Dr George Bagster Phillips' comments regarding the skill with which Chapman's organs had been removed that opened the investigation wider and highlighted a number of suspects who, despite having some form of medical training, were believed to be of unsound mind. Although these individuals were supposedly trained professionals in an outwardly respectable walk of life – medicine – their mental condition made them another example of the "outsider", the lunatic.

Foreigners would again be blamed for the murders in the form of sailors from other lands. With their vessels temporarily stationed at the London Docks, it was thought that they could come ashore for the limited time of their leave and wreak havoc in the slums, and then disappear again to the safety of a boat at sea. Queen Victoria herself appeared to be fond of this notion and made her thoughts clear in a telegram to the police authorities.

Lyttleton Stewart Forbes Winslow contributed to the growing collection of suspected "genre types" at this time. He was a medical man with a considerable (self-proclaimed) knowledge of the insane. He believed (and stated publicly) that not only was the murderer a lunatic and responsible for all the crimes, but also that he was "not of the class of which Leather Apron belongs, but is of the upper class of society." This theory began to find favour in other circles, particularly among the local criminals. Sergeant William Thick had received assurances from local law-breakers that they would be only too happy to hand the murderer over to the authorities, obviously in the belief that the latest atrocities were beyond the capabilities of even their dubious class. Sergeant Thick and his associates were reported as being convinced that the murders were "in no way traceable to any of the regular thieves or desperadoes at the East-end."

One other – and notably unusual – theory as to the identity of the killer made its debut on 18 September 1888, when Lord Sydney Godolphin Osborne wrote a lengthy letter to *The Times*, which began by criticizing the conditions of the East End and stated how they bred vice and crime. He then made a case that would probably have had his readers puffing with exasperation:

All strange, Sir, as it may appear to you and the generality of your readers, it is within the range of my belief that one or both these Whitechapel murders may have been committed by female hands. There are details in both cases which fit in well with language for ever used where two of these unfortunates are in violent strife; there is far more jealousy, as is well known, between such women in regard to those with whom they cohabit than is the case with married people where one may suspect the other of sin against the marriage vow.

There are, I have no doubt, plenty of women of this class known for their violent temper, with physical power to commit such a deed. As to the nature of their sex forbidding belief that they could so act, how many of them are altogether unsexed, have no one element in character with female feeling?

A woman of course would have been invisible to the police investigation, largely because everybody, barring Osborne it seems, was convinced that the killer had to be male. The descriptions of the men seen with victims such as Annie Chapman, Catherine Eddowes and Mary Kelly ensured that this assumption would stick. But if this was considered to be somewhat left-field, other suggestions by members of the public that the

Whitechapel Murderer was not even human stretched the bounds of rational thought. Escaped animals were blamed and one correspondent from the Isle of Wight wrote to the police to confidently assert that Jack the Ripper was an ape, one which would hide the murder weapon up the nearest tree after committing the deed, before loping back to the cage at the menagerie from which it had escaped.

Others named as Jack the Ripper suspects were Sergeant Thick, George Morris the Mitre Square watchman, Richard Mansfield the American actor, a young clergyman and Thomas Conway, Catherine Eddowes' former common-law husband, to name a few. Jack the Ripper escaped by dressing in women's clothes, using the sewers or hiding in the Jews' cemetery near Buck's Row. The desperation of the times fostered wide-ranging ideas but, of course, little or nothing came from them. Once the murders had apparently ceased nobody was any closer to discovering the identity of the killer than they were after the first murders had taken place. These opinions belonged to those who were perhaps not entirely conversant with the facts or procedure of the police investigation. But what about those who were? It wasn't long before the words of senior officials appearing in memoirs and interviews began to drop hints about a more definitive identification of the Ripper.

In 1898, a former Inspector of Prisons, Major Henry Smith, published *Mysteries of Police and Crime*, and in it he studied the Whitechapel Murders and came up with three potential culprits. The first was a Jewish lunatic who had been incarcerated in an asylum after being identified by "the one person who got a glimpse of him". The second was an insane Russian doctor who had been a convict in England and Siberia. Finally, Major Arthur Griffiths, a friend of both Anderson and Macnaghten spoke of a teacher on the borderline of insanity, whose own family had grave doubts about him and whose body was found floating in the Thames towards the end of 1888. These individuals appeared to exist, and they fitted some of the archetypes quite nicely – the lunatic, the foreigner, the toff, or a combination of any of the three. What was not made clear to the public at the time was that Griffiths had used notes made by Assistant Chief Constable of CID, Sir Melville Macnaghten in 1894. These notes were not in the public

POLICE NOTICE.

TO THE OCCUPIER.

On the mornings of Friday, 31st August, Saturday 8th, and Sunday, 30th September, 1888, Women were murdered in or near Whitechapel, supposed by some one residing in the immediate neighbourhood. Should you know of any person to whom suspicion is attached, you are earnestly requested to communicate at once with the nearest Police Station.

Metropolitan Police Office,
30th September, 1888.

Printed by M'Corquodale & Co. Limited, " The Armoury," Southwark.

ABOVE: Handbills like these were distributed in their tens of thousands to homes across the East End during the autumn of 1888.

the police officials who did choose to comment, did so with a certain amount of circumspection.

During their retirement years, some of the officers in post at the time of the murders made some strong claims, most notably former Inspector Frederick Abberline and Sir Robert Anderson. Abberline made comments in a press interview about Severin Klosowski, also known as George Chapman, a polish-born barber-surgeon present in the East End in 1888 and perhaps better known at the time of Abberline's interview as the Southwark Poisoner after he had killed three of his wives and been hanged for the crimes in 1903. Anderson's claims, originally made in 1907 and expanded in his memoirs in 1910, were unequivocal, stating that the identity of the Ripper was known to the police and that the suspect had appeared in an identification parade where he was picked out by a witness. However, as both witness and suspect were Jewish, the former refused to testify on the grounds that he would not send one of his own to the gallows.

It must be remembered that former policemen like Anderson, Macnaghten, Abberline and, later, John Littlechild – formerly of Special Branch – who named Dr Francis Tumblety as a "likely" suspect in a letter written in 1913, were men in a position to know things that perhaps we today are not, and may never be, party to. One can only assume that these high-ranking officers had very good reasons to name the individuals they did and it makes contemporary suspects like Druitt, Kosminski, Chapman and Tumblety important. Strangely, Michael Ostrog's inclusion is a bit of a mystery as he was known to be in prison in France at the time of the murders, but with a lack of solid documentation in the official files regarding *any* of these names, his place remains as much of a mystery as the others. The naming of Kosminski as Anderson's suspect in private notes made by Chief Inspector Donald Swanson in his copy of Anderson's memoirs has only served to muddy waters, which one would reasonably think should have been cleared by such a find since Anderson made claims that cannot be satisfactorily accounted for. Researchers over many decades have struggled to verify his claims.

The official files of Scotland Yard, the Home Office and the City Police, in those early years of the twentieth century, must have contained much that would enlighten and delight researchers

domain, but had been made in an attempt to exonerate a suspect called Thomas Cutbush from the accusations of *The Sun* newspaper in which it was claimed he was the Ripper. Macnaghten put forward the same three characters as better candidates and better still, named them: Kosminski, the insane Jew; Michael Ostrog the Russian doctor and convict; and Montague Druitt, the sexually insane and ultimately suicidal teacher. These names would not enter the public domain for another 65 years when Macnaghten's notes were discovered, but of all of these, the "doctor" who drowned himself in the Thames cropped up with surprising regularity in the observations of many who were party to inside information. Perhaps it is important to remember that when these claims were being made, the Ripper murders were fresh in people's memories, and there was every possibility that the killer was still alive. So

Assistant Chief Constable of CID, Sir Melville Macnaghten's "memoranda", which exists in two versions, aimed to set out the case for three suspects, Kosminski, Michael Ostrog and Montague Druitt (who Macnaghten erroneously identified as a doctor), whom he felt more likely to be the Ripper than one Thomas Cutbush who, in February 1894, had been suggested by *The Sun* newspaper as the Whitechapel killer. Some of the biographical details are now known to be wrong, but it remains an important document in the Ripper case:

(1) A Mr M. J. Druitt, said to be a doctor & of good family – who disappeared at the time of the Miller's Court murder, & whose body (which was said to have been upwards of a month in the water) was found in the Thames on 31st December 1888 –– or about 7 weeks after that murder. He was sexually insane and from private information I have little doubt but that his own family believed him to have been the murderer.

(2) Kosminski – a Polish Jew – resident in Whitechapel. This man became insane owing to many years indulgence in solitary vices. He had a great hatred of women, specially of the prostitute class, & had strong homicidal tendencies: he was removed to a lunatic asylum about March 1889. There were many circumstances connected with this man which made him a strong "suspect".

(3) Michael Ostrog, a Russian doctor, and a convict, who was subsequently detained in a lunatic asylum as a homicidal maniac. This man's antecedents were of the worst possible type, and his whereabouts at the time of the murders could never be ascertained."

today. But these files were closed to public view then, and thus the next wave of suspect theories could only rely on other esoteric and often elusive sources. The first important book-length treatment of the case, Leonard Matters' *The Mystery of Jack the Ripper* published in 1929, put forward a Dr Stanley as the likely murderer. The source was an anonymous article which appeared in a Buenos Aires newspaper and was written by an ex-student of the doctor who had been summoned to his death-bed, only to hear him confess to being Jack the Ripper. The story had it that Dr Stanley's son had contracted syphilis from Mary Jane Kelly (see chapter 9) on Boat Race night in 1886 and subsequently died of the disease. His enraged father, a brilliant London doctor, set about murdering Kelly and her friends as revenge before settling in South America in 1908. Again, the archetypal crazed doctor made for a comforting motif, yet the article that spawned this idea remained elusive to anybody other than Leonard Matters.

Similarly, the tale of Olga Tchkersoff, the Russian woman hell-bent on killing prostitutes after her sister died in a failed abortion attempt, became the theme of a book by Edwin T Woodhall in 1937, the source for this story again being a possible newspaper article reporting the tale told by Tchkersoff's confidantes, a Russian couple living in the USA. Unsurprisingly, this article has never been tracked down either. This, combined with

William Stewart's 1939 theory of the mad-midwife, set out in his book *Jack the Ripper: A New Theory*, the fairer sex certainly got some exposure in the early days of Ripper suspect theories. Stewart also noted similarities between the *modus operandi* of the Ripper and that of Mary Pearcey, who was hanged after stabbing her lover's wife and child to death and cutting their throats in October 1890. With Pearcey, the notion that a woman was incapable of the thought processes and physical strength to commit such atrocities was dashed, and even Sir Melville Macnaghten commented that he had "never seen a woman of stronger physique... her nerves were as ironcast as her body."

In 1959, Donald McCormick published *The Identity of Jack the Ripper*, a peculiar book for several reasons and one which could be seen as the final outing of the theorist scrabbling around with hitherto untraceable (or false) sources and strange foreign suspects who may or may not have actually existed. McCormick's suspect was Dr Alexander Pedachenko and his motive for the killings was said to be a Tsarist plot to discredit the Metropolitan Police, a wholly successful conspiracy which resulted in the resignation of Sir Charles Warren. The story was riddled with secret dossiers, aliases and claims of counter-espionage. The sources for this theory were numerous and relied heavily on Dr Thomas Dutton's *Chronicle of Crime*, an alleged collection of Dutton's notes which, conveniently enough, has never been found. McCormick is considered responsible for creating a number of Ripper myths.

In this early wave of Ripper theories put forward by writers outside of the police a new form of suspect was developing in the absence of a definitive word from those who were there at the time of the murders, most of whom had passed away. Mad doctors, midwives and abortionists were now implicated, the concept of a killer with medical know-how firmly rooted, regardless of gender. The obsessions of 1888 such as the crazed Jew, the mad butcher and the menacing transient foreign sailor were becoming a thing of the past.

What McCormick's theory did, however, was to place the Ripper, whoever he or she was, into a conspiracy, manipulated at the highest level.

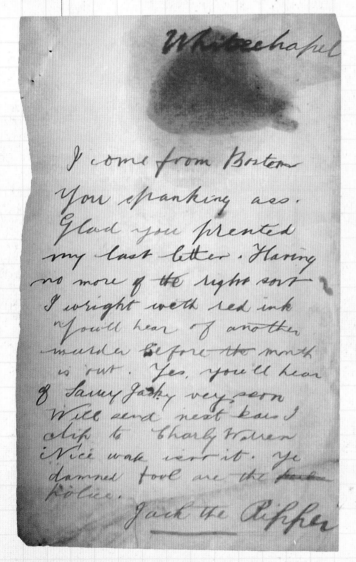

BELOW: Letters from the supposed killer came thick and fast throughout 1888 and beyond, many of them mocking and sinister in their tone. This one was sent to the City of London Police following the death of Catherine Eddowes.

Such ideas would bear fruit many years later, but in the meantime, the return of Macnaghten's favoured suspect, Montague Druitt, finally put forward in print by Tom Cullen in 1965, brought the idea of the well-heeled Ripper back into the mainstream. No longer was he – for now he was definitely male again – the dribbling lunatic from the slums, but he had become the sinister "toff". The movie industry, by now well enamoured with the melodramatic and horrific aspects of the Whitechapel Murders, helped to reinforce the visual image of the cloaked stalker in the fog, complete with gentlemen's top hat and the little Gladstone bag. Macnaghten's notes, discovered in 1959 by broadcaster Dan Farson, which claimed that the "Whitechapel Murderer had five victims and five victims only", created a canon that is still adhered to by many today.

Perhaps the most famous theory surrounding these unique murders came about in 1970 when Dr Thomas Stowell, in an article in *Criminologist* magazine, alluded that Jack the Ripper was Prince Albert Victor, grandson of Queen Victoria. Though Stowell always firmly denied that the Prince was his suspect, the story, emerging at a time when conspiracy theories and mysteries were becoming popular, soon developed a life of its own.

A BBC adaptation of the Ripper mystery in 1973 featured a lengthy statement by Joseph Gorman Sickert, supposedly the son of the artist Walter, in which he claimed that the murders were conducted by Sir William Gull, the Queen's physician, in a Government-backed attempt to silence five East End prostitutes who knew too much about a scandal involving Prince Albert Victor and a Catholic shopkeeper. This version was expanded by Stephen Knight in his best selling *Jack the Ripper: The Final Solution*, published in 1976. It was a terrific yarn, adding police complicity and Masonic overtones to the mix, but the story was wrong on too many levels and, although all those in the story really existed, there is no definitive evidence to suggest that they did the things that Stowell, Sickert or Knight claimed they did. Needless to say, the sensation and interest caused by this theory continues to the present day and remains the one that most people seem to know about.

The centenary of the Whitechapel Murders in 1988 offered the true-crime enthusiast a significant amount of Ripper-based material in the media and perhaps one outcome of that colossal wave of interest could be seen as a precursor to what was to become an important facet of "Ripperology" in the next two decades. At the request of Cosgrove-Meurer Productions, FBI Supervisory Special Agent John Douglas was requested to produce an analysis of the Ripper case to create a criminal profile of the type of person who, by the standards of 1988, could have been Jack the Ripper. By this time, the phenomenon of the serial-killer was much better understood than it was in 1888. The experience of the FBI in identifying the traits of these murderous personalities led to the belief that Jack the Ripper did not just stop killing and disappear into obscurity to lead a normal life. The way serial killers were understood by the late-twentieth century, however, suggested that he would not have *just stopped*. Many of the named suspects had a reason for stopping, such as suicide, incarceration or execution for other misdemeanours, even travel abroad had been considered enough to end the madness. These people are driven to kill, from any number of motives, but their innate compulsion to commit the acts they do means that in Jack the Ripper's case, there had to be a reason that he stopped.

By the centenary, the search for Jack the Ripper became less to do with archetypes and old prejudices and was more informed as the official documents, vital artefacts denied to researchers for so long, had come into the public domain. What was lacking were reports on suspects, the result

in the main of the many items missing from the files, documents that were either stolen, purloined as souvenirs or just destroyed by officials in the days before these files were deposited in the Public Record Office. Some, like the suspect's file itself, disappeared *after* the transfer. In spite of these missing documents, the reports that were available added much information, helping to dispel myths, clarify witness statements and generally give researchers on the case a firm grounding in a subject that needed to be nailed down with facts.

And still the suspects kept on coming.

One, Francis Tumblety, an American quack doctor, rose to prominence in the early 1990s following the discovery of the letter mentioned previously written by ex-chief Inspector John Littlechild. One of the negative marks against Tumblety's candidacy was as a result of the wealth of study put into the world of mass-murderers; namely, that Tumblety was a homosexual and it is generally accepted that homosexual killers only target other men. James Maybrick, the Liverpool cotton merchant supposedly poisoned by his young wife in 1889, became a well-known suspect following the discovery in 1991 of a journal, allegedly written by him in which he documented his execution of the Whitechapel murders. This "diary", as it is often referred to, was reminiscent of the theories of Matters, Woodhall and McCormick (see above), in that there is a written source, a confession with which to base a theory.

KEY EVIDENCE   Key Points from the 1988 FBI Profile on the Ripper

- Jack the Ripper was a male. He was of the white race in view of the fact that white was the predominant race at the crime-scene locations, and generally crimes such as these are intraracial (meaning that killings occur within racial groups).
- His age bracket was 28 to 36 years.
- He did not look out of the ordinary.
- He came from a family where he was raised by a domineering mother and a weak, passive and/or absent father. In all likelihood, his mother drank heavily and enjoyed the company of many men. As a result, he failed to receive consistent care and contact with stable adult role models.

- He was unmarried.
- His anger became internalized and in his younger years, he expressed his destructive, pent-up emotions by creating fires and torturing small animals.
- He sought employment where he could work alone and indulge his destructive fantasies. Jobs such as a butcher, mortician's helper, medical examiner's assistant, or hospital attendant.
- He would have had some type of physical abnormality. However, although not severe, he perceived this as being psychologically crippling.
- He would have been perceived as

being quiet, a loner, shy, slightly withdrawn, obedient and neat and orderly in appearance.
- He lived or worked in the Whitechapel area. The first homicide would have been in close proximity to either his home or workplace.
- Prior to each homicide, the subject was in a local pub drinking spirits, which had the effect of lowering his inhibitions. He would be observed walking all over the Whitechapel area during the early evening hours. He did not specifically seek a certain look in a woman; however, it was by no accident that he killed prostitutes.

Handwritten letter:

November 5/88
London.

Sir

From the shoe black at .11. o.clock this morning I saw A man go in to mr Barclay & son he had A bag in his hand and it snap open and I

METROPOLITAN POLICE / RECEIVED 6 NOV. 88 / CRIMINAL INVESTIGATION DEPT

CITY POLICE OFFICE / 7 NOV 1888 / LONDON

ABOVE: The general public were always more than happy to give their advice and help to the police in letters such as these. Undoubtedly many were of little help to the authorities, and some were just downright ridiculous.

Yet, this one was different. The earlier sources appeared untraceable, but this journal exists, has been handled by many and has been published and subjected to forensic testing. Unfortunately, those forensic tests on the ink and paper proved inconclusive, despite the advanced technology used. Thus the answer is still the same – nobody can be certain that it is genuine and therefore James Maybrick's candidacy as the Ripper remains as uncertain and eminently debatable as any other suspect.

Forensic testing also became a feature of author Patricia Cornwell's hands-on investigation into Walter Sickert, the impressionist painter. She used $6 million of her own money to finance tests on Sickert's personal documents and the Jack the Ripper letters housed in the National Archives. Others have used the FBI criminal profile as a springboard from which to put forward Joseph Barnett, Mary Kelly's former lover; Robert Mann, the Whitechapel Workhouse mortuary attendant; and wife-murderer William Henry Bury as potential Rippers. Offender profiling, much in use in today's murder cases, has been trotted out on numerous occasions, sometimes to dredge up and add meat to old suspects, but increasingly to bring new ones into the fold. Geographical profiling has also been used, creating models of where the Ripper may have lived in relation to the murder sites. Of course for this to work as intended, one needs to know exactly how many murders were committed and with so much debate surrounding the inclusion of victims like Martha Tabram (see chapter 3), Alice McKenzie (see chapter 10) and Frances Coles (see chapter 10), it would be fair to say that such technological advances can only be used to assist rather than to solve outright. With this, the very streets the victims and their killer walked take on a greater significance, with researchers looking at detailed maps of the locations to find any escape routes the killer may have taken or likely routes the victims may have chosen. This fascination for the geography of the East End often throws up new information that can be used by any potential cold case investigator to join the dots and flesh out the potential crime-scene information, a process that goes far beyond the mere "sightseeing" enjoyed by those curious onlookers of 1888 and beyond. As it so happens, the geographical profile model created for the Whitechapel Murders put the Ripper's likely bolt-hole in the Flower and Dean Street area, right on the doorstep of the poor unfortunates he mutilated so horrifically.

But is that the kind of person we are looking for? Jack the Ripper has been many things to many people, to the point where suspects have been drawn from the ranks of the rich and famous, one would assume to wring the last drop of sensationalism out of a mystery more than 120 years old: William Gladstone; Dr Barnado; William Booth; King Leopold II; Lewis Carroll; Joseph Merrick (the Elephant Man); Oscar Wilde; Lord Randolph Churchill; Frederick Abberline; Vincent Van Gogh, to give just a few examples. All these and more have had their moment in the spotlight, but the truth is probably a lot less

RIGHT: Gunthorpe Street, formerly George Yard, in 2009. Despite most of the buildings being post-1888, the site of Martha Tabram's murder still conjures up an atmosphere of the "autumn of terror" in the popular imagination.

sensational than many would wish it to be. It was Ted Bundy, the American serial killer, kidnapper and necrophile who, before his execution for 30 homicides in 1989, was quoted as saying "we serial killers are your sons, we are your husbands, we are everywhere..." The inference is obvious. We can dress Jack the Ripper up in any amount of melodrama and cod-glamour, make him any nationality we like or give him any face or personality that fits our idea of a mass murderer, but the probability is that the Whitechapel Murderer was cut from the same cloth as most other serial killers. We do not know what they're truly like until it is too late, until victims have fallen and the monster is caught. Then the true horrors come flooding out.

Maybe that is why Jack the Ripper was, and still is, so hard to find. Had he been caught, no doubt many would have gasped to see a person they felt they knew so well, who perhaps seemed to be a loner at times (but was also polite and quietly spoken), going to the gallows for committing a string of murders that shocked the world. He is likely to have been an unremarkable local man, a resident of the overcrowded slums who knew the people and knew the streets, who looked no different from, or any less inconspicuous than the thousands of down-at-heel citizens of the East End of London among whom he shared his precarious life.

Somewhere, probably in an unmarked pauper's grave, lies the body of the world's most infamous murderer. Around the world, there are people who, linked by the twisting branches of a family tree, unwittingly share his DNA or even some of his physical features. The latter is a potentially disquieting thought, but is by no means impossible. But will we ever find him? Many think so. Many feel they already have. However, as the years tick by, the chances grow progressively slim and even the discovery of a vital long-lost officially sanctioned police document naming him would generate as many claims of "fraud" as it would supporters.

Jack the Ripper got away without ever having to account for his crimes, and left behind a tangled mess of supposition, frustration, rumour, sensation and, eventually, folklore, for others to unravel.

As Major Henry Smith, acting Commissioner of the City Police in 1888, said in his memoirs, "the Ripper certainly had all the luck".

INDEX

FURTHER READING

Bibliography

The amount of published works on Jack the Ripper is so great that a complete bibliography in this context is impossible. However, for recommended writing on the case, several studies stand out and are therefore listed separately below. Some of the older books may contain dated errors, but are still considered important and are worth seeking out:

Autumn of Terror,
Tom Cullen (Bodley Head 1965; Fontana 1973)

Jack the Ripper In Fact and Fiction,
Robin Odell (Harrap 1965; revised Mandrake 2008)

The Complete History of Jack the Ripper,
Philip Sugden (Robinson 1994)

The Jack the Ripper A-Z,
Paul Begg, Martin Fido, Keith Skinner (Headline 1991, 1994, 1996; revised and updated as *The Complete Jack the Ripper A-Z*, John Blake 2010)

The Ultimate Jack the Ripper Sourcebook,
Stewart P Evans, Keith Skinner (Robinson 2000)

Jack the Ripper: Letters From Hell,
Stewart P Evans, Keith Skinner (Sutton 2001)

The Complete Jack the Ripper,
Donald Rumbelow (Penguin 2004)

Jack the Ripper: The Facts,
Paul Begg (Robson 2006)

Jack the Ripper: Scotland Yard Investigates,
Stewart P Evans, Donald Rumbelow (Sutton 2006)

The London of Jack the Ripper: Then and Now,
Robert Clack, Philip Hutchinson (Breedon 2007, revised 2009)

The Victims of Jack the Ripper,
Neal Stubbings Shelden (Inklings Press 2007)

Books on the East End

The Bitter Cry of Outcast London,
Andrew Mearns (1883)

The People of the Abyss
Jack London (MacMillan 1902, Diggory Press 2008)

The Streets of East London,
William J Fishman & Nicholas Breach (Duckworth 1979, Five Leaves 2006)

Rothschild Buildings: Life in an East End Tenement Block 1887–1920,
Jerry White (Routledge and Keegan Paul 1980)

East End 1888,
William J Fishman (Duckworth 1988, Five Leaves 2005)

East End Then and Now,
ed Winston G Ramsey (After the Battle 1997)

The Worst Street in London,
Fiona Rule (Ian Allen 2008)

Websites

Tower Hamlets History Online: www.thhol.org.uk

East London History Society: http://www.mernick.org.uk/elhs/ELHS.htm

Jewish East End Celebration Society: www.jeecs.org.uk

Survey of London Volume 27: www.british-history.ac.uk

Whitechapel Society 1888: www.whitechapelsociety.com

Casebook- Jack the Ripper: www.casebook.org

JTR Forums: www.jtrforums.com

Recommended Walking Tours:

www.discovery-walks.com

www.jack-the-ripper-tour.com

ACKNOWLEDGEMENTS

The authors would like to extend their deepest gratitude to their agent, Robert Smith for his sterling work in getting this project off the ground, to Jaakko Luukanen whose incomparable artworks form the backbone of this book, to our editor Jennifer Barr and picture manager Steven Behan at Carlton for their even-handed patience and to all those who contributed in any way, no matter how small, or unwittingly, to the visual and factual content of this book:

Debra Arif, Judy Begg, Sioban Begg , Neil Bell, Bishopsgate Instute Library, Trevor Bond, Howard Brown's *JTR Forums* and Stephen Ryder's *Casebook: Jack the Ripper*, Robert Clack, Stewart P. Evans, Andrew Firth, William Fishman, the late John Gordon Whitby, Hulton Picture Library / Getty Images, Rob House, Philip Hutchinson, Richard and Joanne Jones, Jeff Leahy, London Metropolitan Archives, The London Jewish Museum, Museum of London, Mirrorpix, Robin Odell, Laura Prieto, Mark Ripper, *Ripperologist* Magazine, Don Rumbelow, Dave Savory, Chris Scott, Neil and Jenni Shelden, Keith Skinner, Toynbee Hall Library and Archives, Tower Hamlets Library and Archives, M J Trow, Truman's Archives, Tom Wescott, Margaret Whitby-Green, The Whitechapel Society 1888.

The authors respectfully dedicate this book to David Savory for all his kindness and support in a variety of ways

Also To
Judy, Sioban and Cameron
And Laura

CREDITS

Photo Credits

The publishers would like to thank the following sources for their kind permission to reproduce the pictures in this book:

Author Collection: 8 (bottom), 9, 13, 15, 18 (bottom), 19, 26, 29 (bottom), 39, 40, 41 (bottom), 56-57, 71, 74-75, 84, 90, 95, 121, 135 (bottom), 150, 163 (centre), 179 (top), 179 (centre), 194, 204, 205 (top), 205 (bottom), 206-207, 208-209, 210, 213, 215, 217, 218-219

Casebook.org: 36

Robert Clack: 59

Evans Skinner Archive: 10, 18 (top), 20, 23, 25, 27, 28 (top), 32, 33 (top), 33 (bottom), 35, 42, 48, 49, 50, 51, 52-53, 62, 63 (top), 63 (bottom), 67, 73, 79, 83, 93, 96, 99, 100-101, 102, 103 (top), 103 (bottom), 104, 105 (top), 106, 107, 108, 109, 120, 122-123, 124, 128, 129, 132 (top), 132 (bottom), 133, 134 (top), 134 (bottom), 135 (top), 140, 141, 148, 149, 151, 155 (left), 155 (right), 157, 158, 159, 161, 162, 163 (top), 164 (top), 164 (bottom), 165 (top), 165 (bottom), 168, 169, 170 (bottom), 174, 177, 182, 184, 185, 187, 188, 189, 195, 196-197, 198, 199 (top), 199 (bottom), 202

Getty Images: Hulton Archive: 7 (bottom right), 8 (top), 105 (bottom), 138-139, 190-191; / London Stereoscopic Company: 16

Philip Hutchinson: 70, 87

Mary Evans Picture Library: 6-7

Mirrorpix: 144

Museum of London: 11, 12, 22-23

Neal Shelden: 81

Tower Hamlets Local History Library and Archives: 17, 28 (bottom), 58, 77, 193

Cover credits:
Topfoto.co.uk (Ripper figure)
CGI illustrations (c) Jaakko Luukanen 2012

Illustrations on cover and pages: 2, 24-25,30-31, 34-35, 37, 38, 44-45, 46, 54-55, 60, 64-65, 66-67, 76, 80-81, 82, 85, 86, 88-89, 94, 110-111, 112-113, 114, 117, 118-119, 126, 130-131, 137-137,146-147, 152-153, 156, 160, 166-167, 171, 172, 175, 176, 180-181, 183 and 224 © Jaakko Luukanen, Deep Pixel

Map artworks on pages 4, 13, 29, 39, 47, 61, 78, 83, 97, 125, 127, 142, 154, 170, 173, 178, 192 and 203 (c) John Bennett and Paul Begg 2012

Every effort has been made to acknowledge correctly and contact the source and/or copyright holder of each picture. Carlton Books Limited apologizes for any unintentional errors or omissions, which will be corrected in future editions of this book

Publishing Credits
Executive Editor: Jennifer Barr
Additional editorial work: Lesley Malkin, Barry Goodman, Ann Barrett
Design Manager: Russell Knowles
Design: Punch Bowl Design
Picture Manager: Steve Behan
Production Manager: Maria Petalidou

STAR
LARGEST CIRCULATION
EVENING PAPER

PRIZE MEDAL

GINGER BEER

27 McCARTHY 27

HOME & COLONIAL TEA

HOVIS

PARAFFIN OIL 1⁶ Per Gal

BOVRIL

LYONS COCOA

3   2⁶ 6

KEATING'S
POWDER

PRICES
CANDLES

6¹⁴

Ask
FOR
BRYANT
AND MAY'S
MATCHES
SOLD
HERE

THE PROPRIETOR

ILLUSTRATED
POLICE
NEWS

£100
REWARD

CAPTURE

MURDER

BAYLIS

STOVEPIPE

VARNISH